DON'T CRY

DON'T CRY

THE ENLHET HISTORY OF THE CHACO WAR

Edited by Hannes Kalisch
and Ernesto Unruh

*Spanish translation from the Enlhet and
commentary by Hannes Kalisch*

*Translation from Spanish into
English by Nicholas Regan*

McGill-Queen's University Press
Montreal & Kingston • London • Chicago

© McGill-Queen's University Press 2022

ISBN 978-0-2280-1083-8 (cloth)
ISBN 978-0-2280-1168-2 (paper)
ISBN 978-0-2280-1173-6 (ePDF)

Legal deposit first quarter 2022
Bibliothèque nationale du Québec

Printed in Canada on acid-free paper that is 100% ancient forest free
(100% post-consumer recycled), processed chlorine free

First published as ¡No llores! La historia enlhet de la guerra del Chaco, Relatos
recopilados por Hannes Kalisch y Ernesto Unruh. Traducción y comentarios de
Hannes Kalisch. Asunción, Paraguay: Centro de Artes Visuales/Museo del Barro –
Nengvaanemkeskama Nempayvaam Enlhet – ServiLibro
ISBN 978-99967-813-4-6

PLETT FOUNDATION

Publication of this translation was made possible in part by the generous financial
support of the Plett Foundation.

McGill-Queen's University Press is grateful for the financial contribution of the Embassy
of Canada to Argentina and Paraguay/Ambassade du Canada en Argentine et au
Paraguay towards the translation of this work.

Library and Archives Canada Cataloguing in Publication

Title: Don't cry! : the Enlhet history of the Chaco war / edited by Hannes Kalisch and
    Ernesto Unruh ; Spanish translation from the Enlhet and commentary by Hannes
    Kalisch ; translation from Spanish into English by Nicholas Regan.
Other titles: Do not cry!
Names: Kalisch, Hannes, editor, translator. | Unruh, Ernesto, editor.
Description: Includes bibliographical references and index.
Identifiers: Canadiana (print) 20210352744 | Canadiana (ebook) 20210352884 |
    ISBN 9780228010838 (cloth) | ISBN 9780228011682 (paper) | ISBN 9780228011736
    (ePDF)
Subjects: LCSH: Chaco War, 1932–1935—Personal narratives, Paraguayan. | LCSH: Chaco
    War, 1932–1935. | LCSH: Indians of South America—Paraguay—Colonization. |
    LCSH: Oral history—Paraguay.
Classification: LCC F2688.5 .D66 2022 | DDC 989.207/16—dc23

Set in 11.5/14 Sina Nova with Typold
Book design & typesetting by Garet Markvoort, zijn digital

CONTENTS

FIGURES AND MAPS

Figures

Maps

PREFACE
WHERE OUR VOICES COME FROM
HANNES KALISCH

One day a terrible thing happened: clouds gathered and covered the
people. They were very, very thick clouds, and the people sat below,
completely imprisoned; it was impossible to visit them. Their food
ran out; they had to eat deerskin. They ate their sandals, made from
the skin of the anteater, and several children died of hunger. From
outside people tried to open the clouds with an axe, but they were
as hard as stone and no axe was strong enough; after only a few
blows the blade split. There was one axe left, which had not been
used because it was soft and its blade would bend even more quickly
than the others. However, when they tried, because they had no
other choice, with this axe, the clouds lifted. The survivors came out,
but they were not the same as they had been before the disaster;
they were emaciated and their skin was yellow. The tragedy occurred
in the time of those who lived before us; my grandfather talked of
it, and when he spoke, he told the truth. There is a lot to say about
those who lived before us. We could start at nightfall and keep
talking until dawn.

Enlhet account[1]

The Gran Chaco of South America is a semi-arid plain divided among
Bolivia, Argentina, and Paraguay, which for a long time was not
in the sights of colonizers. Penetration from outside only began in
the second half of the nineteenth century, and the subjugation of the
Aboriginal Peoples to new political, territorial, economic, cultural,
religious, and intellectual regimes did not occur until the twentieth
century. While the borders between Argentina and its neighbours at
the beginning of the twentieth century were clear, the same was not
true of that between Paraguay and Bolivia. For this reason, as interest
in the Chaco grew, the dispute between the two countries over sovereignty in the region deepened until, in 1932, they declared war to resolve it by military means.

The region, known today as the Paraguayan Chaco, was inhabited,
at the beginning of the twentieth century, in the north by the Tomáráho and Yshir to the east, the Ayoreo in the centre – all peoples

of the Zamuco linguistic family – and the Ñandevá, of the Guaraní family, to the west. On the River Pilcomayo in the west lived (from north to south) the Manjui, the Nivaclé, and the Macá who make up the Mataco-Mataguayo linguistic family. The south of the region was occupied by Qom groups of the Guaicurú family. Finally, in the western zone were the territories of (from south to north) the Énxet, Angaité, Sanapaná, Toba-Enenlhet, and Guaná, who form, with the Enlhet, the Enlhet-Enenlhet linguistic family. The Enlhet people, to which the relators whose voices form the basis of this book belong, lived between these related peoples and the Nivaclé, occupying the centre of the Paraguayan Chaco. It is the largest of the peoples in its family, currently with over eight thousand members.

In the time when they lived independently, the Enlhet organized themselves into small local groups. With no fixed place of residence, they moved seasonally within specific regions, following the ripening of different forest fruits, the movement of animals, and the accessibility of water; in regions with large lakes, fishing was also common. Together with crop fields, herds of goats and sheep were important for the celebration of extended festivities where a considerable number of attendees needed to be fed.

Leadership relied on the personal authority of the leaders, based on their embodiment of certain important attitudes and their skillful handling of important abilities, such as the capacity to promote equilibrium between humans and the invisible world around them. As it was not formally legitimized, this leadership was not based on institutionalized loyalties that would permit the significant exercise of power. Consequently, within Enlhet society, there were no political units above the local groups. Instead, the Enlhet recreated internal coherency through constant relations among these local groups, relations that might extend also to neighbouring peoples.

The Enlhet, who called themselves the "people without things,"[2] emphasized equilibrium among social actors, a construction called *nengelaasekhammalhkoo*, "to practice mutual respect, to be well-disposed toward the other" (Kalisch 2011b). The accumulation of material goods and the creation of significant infrastructure within their territory, on the other hand, was not an objective for them. Coincidentally, the colonizers described the land in their territory as a desert.[3]

The colonization of the Paraguayan Chaco, which occurred from its eastern side, began with the establishment of factories for tannin extraction on the Paraguay River, beginning in 1887 (Dalla Corte 2009), and the activity of the Anglican mission among the Énxet, beginning in 1889.[4] The Enlhet were aware of these processes of foreign penetration into the Chaco and even made trips to the new economic centres. However, the first important contact with outsiders within their own territory occurred only in 1920 in the form of an expedition sent by Canadian Mennonites to prepare the ground for the mass immigration of Mennonite families, which started in 1927.[5] In the mid-1920s, military exploration of the region also intensified, resulting in the founding of several Paraguayan and Bolivian forts within Enlhet territory and thus setting out the line of the initial front (see map 1.1) for the so-called Chaco War (1932–35) by which the final subjugation of the Chaco region by a nation-state was defined. The experiences of the Enlhet people at that time are the subject of the accounts in this book.

In addition to military violence, the Enlhet experienced an outbreak of smallpox in 1932–33 that decimated the population within a few months. In the two decades after the war, the Enlhet found as well that the consolidation of the Mennonite colonies gradually limited their possibilities for movement within their lands, while their subsistence base was significantly reduced. In parallel to this process, the colonizers carried out energetic religious and cultural proselytism among them through which they legitimized and organized the subjugation of the native people under the new territorial, economic, political, and ideological regimes they had begun to establish. On the one hand, with pressure on them increasing constantly, the Enlhet saw closeness to the immigrants as ever more inevitable. On the other, with the wounds of the traumatic experiences of the war and the epidemic still open, this proselytism indicated to them that the mission, promoted intensively by the new masters of the territory, was the most promising place to reconstruct their life under the changed conditions (Kalisch 2021). Consequently, toward the end of the 1950s, not more than three decades after the arrival of the first settlers, nearly all the Enlhet submitted to Christian baptism in the Mennonite tradition within a few years (Regehr 1979, 274) and expressed the firm desire to be settled in a mission (Loewen 1965; 1966).

In the Enlhet view, baptism and reduction to the missions represented nothing less than a new era, characterized by the dominance of the word and logic of the immigrants.[6] Baptism and reduction manifest themselves, thus, as symbols of a capitulation whose effect goes far beyond a definition of how they would cohabit with the victors, the settlers, from then on. With this capitulation, the very way in which the Enlhet looked at their own being and future changed radically: at this moment there began a clear orientation to external protagonism and a corresponding rejection of all that had applied under the terms of their own tradition.

Reduction to the missions – today called Indigenous communities (*comunidades*) – meant an extensive contiguous territory was replaced with extremely limited spaces split apart from one another.[7] While the original territory of the Enlhet extended over approximately 20,000 square kilometres, today they live in five neighbourhoods in the Mennonite towns and six rural communities with a combined extent of 440 square kilometres. The rest of their traditional lands are occupied in the main part by three Mennonite colonies and, to a markedly lesser extent, communities of other Indigenous Peoples of the Chaco and Paraguayan settlers (see map 1.2). As arable and livestock farmers, the new masters of these lands have deforested them almost completely (see map 1.3). The forest around the communities has disappeared; even within them, it has become scarce. With the constant expansion of agriculture and livestock farming, the new owners have also increasingly restricted access by the Enlhet to their former territory. Consequently, it has become almost impossible for them to carry out traditional practices for their subsistence; these practices are no longer in any way sufficient to sustain a family. Neither does small-scale agriculture, which the settlers have introduced to the Indigenous communities as an alternative to their traditional economic model, guarantee the necessary sustenance in the arid Chaco region (Regehr 1979). In the end, to have an income, the majority of Enlhet must leave their community regularly and live outside it, which often leads to the prolonged separation of nuclear families. Whether in fixed employment or as day labourers, they are obliged to live in a relationship of labour dependency with Mennonite employers.

As modern units of a colonized and fragmented society, the Enlhet communities are no longer called missions. Nevertheless, their internal organization continues to be based on the terms of the new masters of the territory. On the one hand, each community is managed by a so-called *asesor* or "advisor," a Mennonite who lives within the community as the delegate of the Mennonite Association of Services for Indigenous Cooperation,[8] an institution run by the three Mennonite colonies. On the other hand, the mission church, in the Mennonite tradition, though today formally independent of the settlers, is understood by the Enlhet as a fundamental tool with which to frame their relationship with the Mennonites. For this reason, it constitutes a space that is very susceptible to external interference. Despite being tied to Mennonite thinking, it plays an important role in defining what is seen within Enlhet society itself as a life and shared living to aspire to.

In short, the Enlhet accept, at both the practical and ideological levels, the incursion of the new masters of the territory deep into their society, even though they base themselves in objectives, values, ideas, and actions that find no correspondence within native Enlhet tradition or history. Worse still, these external proposals frequently run contrary to the daily practices of the Enlhet, which, like a prism, refract a complex transfiguration of numerous traditional guidelines for action, perception, reasoning, valuing, and defining motivations. Framed within such enormous contradiction – the lasting effect of the capitulation of six decades ago ingrained under specific constellations of power – Enlhet society has neglected and even suppressed its internal communication regarding the world of its own historical trajectory. Multiple silences have been created within the society, which make it impossible to work on the traumas of the past. These silences also hamper reflection on the deep-rooted practices of their daily life. They impede the evolution of concepts that continue to mark their present-day life and define prevailing potentialities (Kalisch, forthcoming).

■■■

Don't Cry presents a small sample of the accounts that make up the memory of the Enlhet people of the time of the Chaco War. Originally written in Spanish, it is not a book *for* the Enlhet, but neither is it intended to be a book *about* them. Its function is to provide access to some of the voices circulating in Enlhet society and to make the reader a participant in the communication between the relators and their people. As elements in concrete communication, the reader may find a parallel in these voices that serves as an incentive to express in new words some of their own reflections, observations, and experiences made before reading the accounts: this book is intended as a space of encounter.

Who are the actors in this encounter? The original Spanish-language version of *Don't Cry* was addressed, in the first place, to members of Paraguayan society. The narrative of the Chaco War constitutes a fundamental element in the image this society has of itself. It is a narrative of great suffering that led to a glorious victory over the enemy and served to deliver the nation from the threat of extermination. To this day, public speech in Paraguay about the war centres on triumph, makes absolute the winner's perspective, and is guided by highly euphoric and nationalist rhetoric.[9] It is true that in Paraguayan society there are views on the war other than those of the winner. However, these views do not break from an entrenched fear of themes that habitually go unbroached: similarly to the Enlhet narrative, the Paraguayan narrative of the war with Bolivia is constructed on silences that continue to cry out within the protagonists of the conflict. These silences oblige them, in their fluctuating condition as both winners and victims, to understand their continued suffering – which did not end with the cessation of military hostilities – as a betrayal of their country. They have been forced to suppress it, not only for those around them but also for themselves. It did not seem to correspond to reality.

This is seen, for example, in the way in which a Paraguayan neighbour of the editors remembers her grandfather. He participated in the bloody battle for Fort Boquerón in 1932, near the editors' homes, and died in 1991 not far from the fort.[10] Toward the end of his life he would tell his grandchildren about the war, but he did not do so when they asked him to. He spoke when he felt the desire – or perhaps the need – to speak, and often, according to his granddaughter, he would begin to cry as he spoke. He mentioned the trenches at Boquerón, dug by Enlhet Indigenous men.[11] He described the cruel combat. He highlighted the frequent rape of Paraguayan nurses by soldiers on the same side who did not even care that their husbands were with them on the battlefield. When they were girls, his granddaughter goes on to say, and they mentioned these things in school, the teacher would insist that what they said was untrue. She reproached them for spreading lies and made them promise not to speak like that. For her, the reality was different.

That veteran and the Enlhet relators in this book speak from a different position than the commonly-held narrative, known to all in Paraguay and received as true. They also share the silences that have descended over their experiences like a cloud that veils them and, even more than that, renders them unreal. That is why, if they succeed in making their voices heard, they will challenge what society believes it knows and what is commonly held as reality. These voices can produce frictions with habitual narratives and demand explanations for the silences on which those narratives were constructed. They can shake acquired convictions and thus invite a readjustment of what it is admissible to think. They invite an end to the permanent recreation, by what is not expressed, of the wall between the correct and incorrect, between the good and the bad, between us and them; that wall that serves as a weapon in maintaining silences and perpetuating the impositions those silences serve to support. This is why the giving of space to these silenced voices has huge potential for liberation. For this reason, Enlhet voices, which have never been heard outside their native society, are of importance both for the veteran soldier's society and beyond. They can demand explanations of all societies built on the colonization of Aboriginal Peoples and the disarticulation of their territories. For all of these colonial societies stand on the pillars of the immense silences around the fact of having colonized and of being colonized.

There is no doubt that the modern nations of the Americas, with their high degree of internal complexity, are very different from one another. Their histories of relations – or confrontation – with Indigenous Peoples differ considerably. The present of the Indigenous Peoples within these nations varies greatly from country to country and is always subject to contradictory dynamics. In general terms, however, recognition and restoration of native rights by the State remain weak; they are often non-existent, even denied. Indeed, in many regions of the continent, physical occupation of Indigenous territories is increasing and the ideological colonization of native societies continues unabated (Kalisch 2018). In parallel to this, the daily existence of these societies is characterized by a multiplicity of discriminatory actions and attitudes against them, even on the part of the States themselves. The recovery of territories, autonomy, and possibilities for real agency, in turn, remain a difficult struggle, marked by many obstacles and little support. Although the elder Enlhet men and women in this book speak from the Paraguayan context, their voices invite work on a dark chapter in the history of the Americas that remains unfinished.

Several of the elder men and women whose company we have shared over the last two decades – almost all of them are now dead – asked that their voices be made accessible to the society of the country of which they now form part without having been asked whether they wished to or not. They knew that, to redress their condition as dispossessed and excluded, it is crucial to build bridges across the silences and seek ways for their voices to be heard outside their own, native, society. Through their accounts, they reach out their hands to people who appear stronger than them.

To make one's voice heard from an unknown point of view, and in opposition to its being actively silenced, is a form of action. Further, it creates the possibility of interaction. Through their hereto unheard voices, the Enlhet relators cast new light on what their readers know, observe, or feel; a light that reformulates the play of light and shade those readers are used to and reveals new contours in it to them. It is a light that makes them reconsider, for example, ideas of who are the actors within the colonial process, thus promoting an awareness that the connection between the colonizing society and displaced peoples cannot be reduced to a relationship between the fortunate and the marginalized – between victor and vanquished, colonizer and colonized, subjugator and subjugated, aggressor and victim, employer and employee. In this way, an experience of communication between the relators and the reader is created through which the relators invite the reader to explore a shared path. For this reason, the present book is more than a compendium about history. It is a political act.

The elder Enlhet men and women reach out their hands to those who are stronger than them not to ask something of them, but to invite them. Indeed, they have something to offer them: to work together with them on the silences and wounds of a past filled with injustices, impositions, and dispossessions. To do this is vital to all those who dream that a dignified life in their country is possible, not only the displaced but also the settlers. For one's dignity does not exist as long as one denies the other a dignified life. The relators make their voices heard in the hope that there are interlocutors who understand that the necessity for a shared path is a necessity for all.

Our wish as editors is that the act of reading the present collection of Enlhet accounts might become the beginning of a meeting between people and groups who see themselves reflected, in some way, in the history of the Enlhet with the Paraguayans; that it might become an act of communication between native peoples and the societies that have occupied their territories; that it might support the imagination of a future that is neither subject to the exclusions and injustices of the past, nor continues to perpetuate them.

▪▪▪

Don't Cry is divided into four parts. The first, "An Opening of Paths," summarizes the specific context from which the Enlhet relators gave their testimonies and the significance of the presentation of their voices. An outline is given of Enlhet memory, with an explanation of how it relates to the time of the Chaco War, and the historical constellations characterizing the life of the Enlhet people in the years before the war are summarized.

The second part, "The Accounts," contains the testimonies of the Enlhet. This book was written so that their voices should be heard. For this reason, it is the editors' wish that no reader should put down this book without having read these accounts.

In the third part, "In Dialogue with the Enlhet Accounts," notes are provided on the accounts, expanded occasionally with information from external sources. These notes do not seek to offer a thoroughgoing presentation of the theme of the Enlhet and the Chaco War.

Rather, they focus on the theme of relations between the original masters of the territories and the people who invaded them. They reflect the intention to offer ways into the issues and identify questions that invite the reader to a new communication – an unprecedented interaction – with the Enlhet or, in different contexts, with other Aboriginal Peoples. This communication will include the voices, experiences, and views of those peoples as fundamental. These two sections, "The Accounts" and "In Dialogue with the Enlhet Accounts," are structured in parallel so that the reader can read the authentic Enlhet voice without interruption from external reflections and will at the same time find it easy to locate the corresponding notes should they wish to study them alongside.

The final part of the book explores existing and possible connections between "The Enlhet Accounts and Paraguay" as a paradigmatic example of relations between the native worlds and modern societies of the Americas. This section is an invitation to travel through a landscape as fascinating as it is concerning: one of reflection on Indigenous protagonism, its essential conditions, and its indisputable potentialities. On the journey through this landscape, I discuss silences and what they do to people. I discuss the existence of radically different views of the world and of what this implies for shared living among distinct societies within the same country. I explore the modus operandi of Enlhet memory, the necessary conditions for it to function as a tool for the Enlhet, and the potentialities it holds. The discussion deals with the question of what a past that has been silenced is and the potential that a society's past has when that society assumes it again to set out a future that derives from this past without returning to it. It examines requirements and possibilities for redressing the patterns of exclusion and subjugation that dominate the current world, for arriving at communication between national society and Indigenous societies that takes seriously the other and their world. The proposition of balanced articulation between the societies inhabiting a single country necessitates a reflection on who represents whom; on who defines what the options are and who manages them. In this regard, I highlight potentialities in Indigenous societies that favour the construction within a country of a society that is not only more just for the Indigenous but for the great majority of its inhabitants.

■■■

In the first place, *Don't Cry* is a book of accounts whose authors were elder Enlhet men and women concerned with "where they are from" and at the same time with the communication that is necessary among people living together in the same country. They understood the importance of continued dialogue with the other to constantly reconstruct equilibrium during relations with them. The accounts presented here represent only a small part of those which Ernesto Unruh, co-editor of this book, and myself have collected and edited over the last twenty years in the Enlhet language. The book belongs to all those who have shared their accounts, whether they are included in these pages or not.

Don't Cry would not exist without the people of the Enlhet communities who, over the last two decades, have profoundly influenced my reflections by inviting me, and obliging me, to extensive processes of learning. Neither could it have come about without *Nengvaanemkeskama Nempayvaam Enlhet*, the institute where Ernesto Unruh and myself have been working for the last twenty-five years to put into circulation what constitutes the Enlhet universe and to highlight its potentialities.[12] Finally, *Don't Cry* cannot be understood without another, complementary, collection of Enlhet accounts, *Qué hermosa es tu voz*, (How Beautiful Is Your Voice), which traces Enlhet history through the last century (Kalisch and Unruh 2014; 2020). Both books are born from the conviction that to approach native realities it is crucial to listen to the voices of the original masters of their respective regions.

The idea of presenting the accounts of the war in the form of this book was the fruit of my discussions with Nicolás Richard over a decade ago. To him, I owe, in addition, several important sources on the conflict that reflect the views of the warring sides. With Luis María de la Cruz, I have spoken at length about territorialities in the Chaco. As a historian, Ignacio Telesca posed questions to me that convinced me of the need to write the final part on "The Enlhet Accounts and Paraguay." I have exchanged ideas with Marisa González de Oleaga for some years on the theme of memory; her acute observations on a previous version of the final section have been crucial. She has also made available to me several important bibliographic resources. Of the people outside the Enlhet world, Lea Schvartzman has left the greatest mark on this work. The perseverance with which she entered into dialogue with the text is admirable, and I would not wish to be without her critical questioning, be it in relation to the detail or to the structure of the book itself. Nicholas Regan has translated the book into English; our close communication during this process has re-energized a friendship of many years.

H.K., Pa'lhama-Amyep (near the former Fort Boquerón),
29 September 2020

DON'T CRY

PART ONE
AN OPENING OF PATHS
HANNES KALISCH

Dreadful crimes are daily enacted
in this hidden land of the Chaco,
atrocities which are seldom brought to the knowledge
of those who are near neighbours.

. . .

[Y]ou see on one bank
primitive man as he was centuries ago,
and on the other
the highly cultivated European,
both equally ignorant of the life of the other.

W. Barbrooke Grubb (1911, 18)

An unknown people in an unknown land. It was under this title that the Anglican who began the first missionary work among the Lengua people described his time with them (Grubb 1911). What has changed since W. Barbrooke Grubb wrote more than one hundred years ago of unknown lands and unknown people? Grubb speaks from and toward an external perspective. To this distant perspective, the most striking change has been in the name of the people, the "Lengua." Although the denomination Lengua is still commonly used in popular speech in Paraguay, since the National Census of 2002 the group has been designated, at the official level, by the term it uses to name itself (compare Melià 1997 with DGEEC 2003). This revision is not merely a detail; it implies more than a simple change of name. The designation *Lengua* referred to the *Énxet* and the *Enlhet* peoples at the same time,[1] even though they, from their perspective – the view from inside – have always insisted that the two are different groups with different languages (Unruh and Kalisch 2003).

This new distinction requires differentiation of what is said, uncritically, from the outside, about the Lengua. The great majority of texts, including Grubb's, concern the Énxet, or Lengua Sur. By contrast, references to the Enlhet, or Lengua Norte – who speak in this book – are relatively few, for reasons that are not discussed here.[2] In parallel to this, the term *Énxet* is relatively well known at the national level, whereas the name *Enlhet* continues to be *unknown*. Even if a few do recognize the name, the group itself nevertheless remains unknown, not only in the eastern region of the country but also among their immediate neighbours in the Chaco, both Mennonite and Paraguayan.[3] A demonstration of the degree to which the Enlhet have been forgotten is visible in the fact that the Museum of Indigenous Art[4] at the Centre for the Visual Arts/Museo del Barro, in the nation's capital of Asunción, counts only a very few Enlhet pieces among its collection (Escobar and Colombino 2008).

The Enlhet continue to be unknown, but this does not mean that they and their lands have remained the same as they were a hundred years ago. Those unknown lands, which were theirs and were intimately familiar to them, were taken from them and used for agriculture and livestock farming, which has destroyed them. The new occupants, before even coming to know the lands properly, deforested them, homogenized them, and carved them into grids; what was within was mutilated. In parallel to the resulting elimination of diversity in the landscape and the vast environmental destruction, in only a few decades the Enlhet were dispossessed completely of the space in which they had constituted their society and their way of recreating themselves: today they hold title to approximately 2.8 per cent of the area they occupied before the start of the Chaco War (Kalisch and Unruh 2014, 571; 2020, 583); they have access to the rest only if it is part of a public road (Kalisch 2021). This terrible dispossession, perpetrated without a perceived need to know the Enlhet beyond what was needed for labour relations and conversion (Kalisch and Unruh 2014; 2020), was accompanied by an unimaginable loss of lives: during the early years of the 1930s, a smallpox epidemic wiped out more than a half of the Enlhet population. To this day, they have not recovered from the catastrophe: we estimate that in 1930 there were approximately 10,000 Enlhet (Kalisch and Unruh 2014, 513–14; 2020, 517), while the National Census of 2012 records some 8,200 individuals (DGEEC 2014, 78).

The radical dismembering of Enlhet society and the loss of the political, social, cultural, and economic construction within the lands we call their territory has had a profound impact on the Enlhet. However,

Figure 1.1 ■ "Immeasurable dispossession led to a grave disarticulation of their society." A home in an Enlhet neighbourhood in the outskirts of one of the largest Mennonite towns.

the destruction of their territoriality is not the same as the destruction of the people, whose members continue to be subjects and actors. Rather, that immeasurable dispossession, which caused a rapid reduction of all possible spaces for action, led to a grave *disarticulation* of their society including, among other aspects, the political, cultural, spiritual, and economic. To this day, the Enlhet continue to fight with great dedication and energy against the effect of this disarticulation to survive as a people and to avoid their definitive destruction.

■■■

This book gathers accounts by elder men and women who describe the experiences of the Enlhet at a crucial moment in their recent history, the Chaco War (1932–35). During that period, they suffered great in-justices that are neither known of nor acknowledged. For besides ig-norance of what the Enlhet were, the dominant society is unaware of what they have gone through and is uninterested in what they are today. On the contrary, the dynamics of dispossession – reaching far beyond the geographical question to affect possibilities for pro-tagonism – remain in force, while the State and the society it repre-sents orient toward a model of development that obliges Indigenous Peoples to situate themselves in a world constructed and managed by interests and objectives that are not their own. This forced situating – this imposition – is called "inclusion," but makes any initiative from within protagonism on Enlhet terms difficult and even impossible; it is, in reality, sequestration within spaces assigned and managed by others. It is an imprisonment that maintains the practice of violation of the historical rights of Aboriginal Peoples. It is into this context of submission that the present collection of authentically Enlhet voices is directed.

Bearing in mind these adverse conditions, by presenting native voices my intention is not that readers should acquire more informa-tion about the Enlhet. My aspiration is that they see that the Enlhet were, and continue to be, actors, political subjects. For they are not freed from their condition as unknown, dispossessed, and excluded simply because others hold information about them. Their condi-tion of marginalization will be redressed only when they cease to be understood as objects to be observed; when they are understood as actors with whom one interacts; when they are assumed as peers.

When, from outside, the Enlhet are assumed as actors, there is no change in what they are, for they have always been actors. There is a change in the way they are perceived. The accounts collected here can play a part in this change of perception. For the relators do not speak only of themselves and their people. They speak at the same time of the people who entered their territory and took it from them, and of their descendants. Unavoidably, therefore, their accounts serve as a mirror with the potential to bring the intruders and their descendants – whether Paraguayans or Mennonites – to understand something of themselves through the eyes of the Enlhet. To the extent that this occurs, they will find themselves obliged to take a stance in relation to these unknown and ignored people. In this way, through their voices, the relators interact with the other, the reader in this case.[5] In addition to presenting their people as actors, they become protagonists in an act of communication with the reader. They extend an invitation to build new channels of communication – a communication that includes the Enlhet voice as fundamental; they invite the reader to enter into a process of articulation.

■■■

The present book is not a book about Enlhet history and culture. Rather, it evokes images of an encounter, a collision, between specific actors: the Enlhet and the *valay* – the Paraguayans. Although the Enlhet did not perceive it at the time, the valay collective masks a complex constellation. It includes the Paraguayan State, which comes out in defence, in its own words, of its sovereignty. It includes the representatives of this State, the military, in the form of an army that behaves very much according to its own dynamics. Finally, it includes civil society, although civil society was rendered invisible when civilians were called upon, with varying degrees of coercion, to lend military service in an army that did not correspond to civilian dimensions. In synthesis, with varying intensity, in each soldier – whether a permanent member of the armed forces or a civilian recruited to serve – representation of the State and all things related to Paraguayan society intersect.

In the accounts, references to the valay collective – the Paraguayans – do not differentiate between civil society, the military, and the State. Rather, Paraguayans are perceived solely through their condition as military. The very meaning of the word *valay* demonstrates this. In its original sense, the sense used in the accounts, the word denotes both a Paraguayan and a generic soldier – the Guaraní word *volái*, from which valay comes, means "man in uniform." This dual reading, Paraguayan and soldier, shows that Paraguayans are characterized – that is, are *always* seen – as soldiers.[6]

Today, the Enlhet understand that valay society is more complex than it appeared at the time of the war and in current usage valay no longer means soldier. Nevertheless, they perceive a clear continuity between the wartime valay – Paraguayans-soldiers – and the national society of today;[7] the original view that identified Paraguayans as soldiers has never really been modified. Indeed, the disdain, mistrust, and prejudices commonly experienced by the Enlhet to this day in their relations with the valay – the Paraguayans – allow them no insight into the complex heterogeneity within Paraguayan society, founded on Guaraní- and/or Spanish-speaking tradition. The generalized discrimination that the Enlhet suffer at the hands of Paraguayan society hides from them the fact that within that society there are marked inequalities of power and linguistic accessibility, and that it contains barely compatible cultural dimensions; in sum, that it is very diversified and, as a result, extremely complex.

The Enlhet do not have a detailed understanding of the internal functioning of Paraguayan society and neither do they distinguish clearly between civil society and the State and its representatives. On the one hand, until the end of the dictatorship in 1989, they had met few members of national society that were not military.[8] On the other, they see that national society identifies with the State and that the two share fundamental logics, for example, the logic that justifies the exclusion of the Indigenous.[9] For instance, although the State allows violation of the rights of Indigenous communities, the same State does not allow that of landowners, businesses, or residential neighbourhoods. The message is clear: it defends its own people.

While the Enlhet perspective suggests ambiguity between civil society and the State and its representatives, the view from Paraguayan society itself is dominated by the perception of a dichotomy. There is a shared perception that the State does not represent the whole of society, but only a very few within it and, at the same time, that it exercises hegemony over society and even oppresses it. Although this situation is hidden behind a discourse of democracy, there is a clear understanding that, in practice, democracy does not exist beyond the formal, and does not function. However much the State claims to represent it, national society finds the task of changing the structures of exclusion on the basis of which the State is run extremely challenging.

Given the disparity between Enlhet perception and Paraguayan self-perception, the mirror provided by the Enlhet accounts may provoke contradictory feelings in the reader. On the one hand, the reader forms part of the collective that has violated Indigenous rights and subjugated and excluded Aboriginal Peoples and continues to do so. On the other, readers may identify themselves with the Indigenous, finding their own liberty restricted by the hegemony exercised by the State based on the interests and privileges of the few. The mirror provided by the Enlhet accounts invites the reader on a journey through these contradictions as it demonstrates the need, and sets out the possibility, for new forms of communication and new encounters with Indigenous Peoples. It invites us to work on another dark chapter in the history of Paraguay, a chapter not yet concluded.

■■■

The conditions for the beginnings of communication between the Enlhet and the Mennonites are different from those for the Paraguayans, although they are in no way less difficult. In the present book, however, the sphere of collision between the Mennonites and the Enlhet is mentioned only in passing, as it is extensively described in other work, to which I would direct the interested reader (Kalisch and Unruh 2014; 2020).

Enlhet Memory and the Chaco War

As I have pointed out, outside Indigenous societies themselves, very little is known of what they experienced – what they protagonized and suffered – during the Chaco War. In military sources, mention of the Indigenous population of the Chaco, the original population, is minimal (Capdevila et al. 2008). At the same time, the war is described as a war between two nations, obscuring the other war within it. This "war within a war" (Richard 2007) had a very specific effect: the military colonization of the Chaco. It is abundantly clear that the Chaco War originated in the territories of sovereign peoples, but ended with territories controlled by the Paraguayan state.[10]

Looking beyond the military sphere, the internal dynamics of the different Indigenous Peoples before, during, and after the Chaco War have been understood only superficially. That is, the societies enveloping autochthonous societies[11] are unaware of the perspective of the original peoples as well as of the complexity of the impacts of the war on them, impacts that crystallized in the superposing of multiple and often contradictory processes. In their view as winners, then, these enveloping societies have produced static hypotheses on colonial history that do not combine the capacity for action of the Indigenous Peoples – the capacity to be actors and subjects – with their condition of having been subjected to powerful and violent actions of others that rapidly reduced their spaces for action. In other words, these hypotheses do not include the tension between the exercise of an Indigenous protagonism sustained by a particular logic and the limiting of possibilities for protagonism on native terms during violent processes of pressure fed by a different logic. It was under this tension that the superposing of heterogeneous dynamics occurred and the course was set for contradictory processes through which the Indigenous Peoples subscribed and were subscribed to a new society as it established and consolidated itself in the decades following the Chaco War. It was a society that absorbed, overwrote, and excluded many of the ways that Indigenous societies traditionally articulated within and among themselves.

Static hypotheses do not recognize that native societies have the role of actors and simultaneously fail to account for the existence of *processes*. These hypotheses thus lead to an understanding of the *results* of processes of dispossession and annihilation, which culminated in a marked reduction in possibilities for Indigenous protagonism, as the natural and essential condition of native peoples.[12] They lead to the seeing of native peoples as malnourished, poor, and sick; impoverished mentally and spiritually; as beings dispossessed of their symbolic universe;[13] as lacking any perspective, or, at least, a valid perspective; as objects to whom nothing remains but to react in an almost automatic way to external initiatives and stimuli. This is the view that originated, for example, the firmly entrenched myth in the Mennonite conscious that the native peoples approached the colonies because they were attracted by the supposed benefits they might find there.[14]

■■■

Extensive accounts of the time of the Chaco War are maintained within the different Indigenous societies themselves. These accounts were based on concrete experiences and are synthesized in each group's narrative. These group narratives, which might be called a group's "own history" – an Enlhet history, a Nivaclé history, an Ayoreo history, etc. – are configured and managed through an oral dynamic. This makes necessary a brief examination of the concept of orality.

Through the oral dynamic, words are not invariably stored up as is possible on paper, in writing. Rather, orality implies constant work on that which is expressed and transmitted, through the interplay of hiding and highlighting, synthesis and projection on transformed conditions. During these processes of transmission, accounts of the past are constantly updated in relation to the present: the accounts are elements in a communication within the ethnic group that is named memory and serves, among other things, to maintain a connection with the group's past. In other words, through memory, bridges are built from the present to the past (Hassoun 1996); to a past that has consequences for the present.

■ ■ ■

In their accounts of the Chaco War, the Enlhet relators offer an immense quantity of information that is unknown outside their world. Through this information, they illustrate the dynamics and processes of Enlhet society during the war, as well as the consequences of the war for the Enlhet. However, the accounts are more than a simple record of (information about) the war and its effects. They suggest and reveal views of the past; they offer personal readings of experience in such a way that those readings serve to explain the present. It is crucial to note that the views and readings manifested in the accounts evolved through constant oral sharing,[15] as is pointed out by, for example, Sa'kok-Nay' (in account 1) and Maangvayaam'ay' (in account 31). It is this continuous insertion of the accounts into social reformulation that renders them part of the memory of the people.

To summarize: the communication within the people that is called memory is synthesized in its own narrative – Enlhet history. Stated in the inverse, memory is this narrative placed into circulation; it is the social conscience of the narrative. The accounts, in turn, constitute the visible manifestation of the narrative; that is, the narrative (and memory itself) is managed through these multiple accounts. Thus, it does not constitute a monophonic synthesis; it is a polyphonic communication.

▪▪▪

Having said this, during the colonial processes that began at the time of the Chaco War for the Enlhet, and in the radical changes these caused, the oral dynamic within Enlhet society has been gravely damaged. Society has ceased to share and constantly repeat the accounts. For this reason, today, its narrative is not managed by the whole group but, basically, by the few people old enough to have participated actively in social communication when orality was still current. Consequently, in our day, this narrative circulates in a fragmented form, woven through incomplete accounts subject to momentary forgetfulness. The reduction of the management of the narrative to the Elders of the people runs parallel to the substantial lessening of its wider discussion through a social process during which it would constantly be reaffirmed and made into memory: the memory of the people has become obscured. This obscuring means more than that definitive loss of knowledge of the past (which is circulated exclusively at the oral level). It results, above all, in a growing difficulty in understanding the present from the Enlhet's own historical trajectory and the concrete consequences of this. It thus destroys important possibilities for protagonism.

In the last section of this book – "A Further Reflection: The Enlhet Accounts and Paraguay" – I discuss at length the characteristics of oral processes in the ruinous context of today that situates the accounts on the thin line between what is memory and what is recollection, between the communication of constitutive information for individuals and their society and the simple representation of past events. Here, I will simply highlight the importance in this desolate context of the relators who speak in this book: they belong to the group of the last individuals to work actively on the shared fund of information maintained by the Enlhet people. They are indispensable to the task of undertaking a reconnection with its hidden memory.

■■■

Before entering into the accounts, it is necessary to summarize the historical constellations around the Chaco War in Enlhet territory. In that place, at that time, diverse unprecedented events combined to change the life of the people abruptly and radically.

Historical Constellations Around the War

Looking from outside, there are many references to the "fierce natives" of the remote Chaco who lived in a constant state of warfare among themselves.[16] P.P. Klassen supposes that "life was a battle of everyone against everyone else" (1983, 135; 1999, 135) and Stahl goes so far as to speak of an "Indigenous world war" (1982, 10). Statements such as these have also been made with reference to the Enlhet themselves;[17] however, they are always generic in nature and are never based on conflicts whose historical existence is borne out by personal testimony. Indeed, the concrete descriptions of traditional life provided in the accounts indicate the relative absence of armed conflict among neighbours. Thus, the theme of the present book – the war brought to Enlhet territory by national armies – warrants a brief look at the role of war in Enlhet tradition. This purpose necessitates a distinction between different geographical contexts.

On its eastern side, Enlhet territory bordered that of the Énxet, the Sanapaná, and the Toba-Enenlhet. Although some detailed accounts of an armed confrontation between the Enlhet and the Sanapaná exist (though not of conflicts with the Toba-Enenlhet or the Énxet), it is not possible to place it in a precise historical moment. That is not the case with relation to the western side of the territory. According to some Enlhet relators, violent conflicts with the Nivaclé took place when the Nivaclé invaded the region inhabited by the Enlhet in the interior of what is today the Paraguayan Chaco. Although Enlhet references to these conflicts are scarce and lack detail, they are reflected in sources external to the Indigenous world. Hunt (1915, 258) mentions that the Nivaclé occupied an area around the River Bermejo, but due to conflicts with the Argentinian military they abandoned that region "and joined their compatriots on the other side of the River Pilcomayo." De la Cruz (1991, 102) estimates that this move occurred before 1900. Although the Pilcomayo was part of the Nivaclé territory of the time, this movement would have meant an increase in the population of the Pilcomayo area and subsequent Nivaclé pressure on Enlhet territory to the east of the Pilcomayo. However, the Enlhet state that the resulting tensions between them and the Nivaclé in the area did not last long, and soon a wide zone of shared territorial space was formed or reaffirmed (Kalisch 2021). This zone encompassed all of the western side of the Enlhet territory, from Mariscal Estigarribia to Nanawa (*Nanaava'a*). In 1916, when the Anglican mission was founded in Nanawa (Hunt 1932: 301), this sharing of territorial space was already established and both Enlhet and Nivaclé approached the mission without any interethnic conflict being recorded. Indeed, a reconstruction of known family relationships between the Enlhet and Nivaclé demonstrates that by the 1920s at the latest, extensive bilingual Enlhet-Nivaclé groups had become established.

In the southwestern part of the Enlhet territory (in the same region as Nanawa), the situation was even more complex, as it included the Macá. The people of that region were often trilingual and frequently had relatives in all three groups. This tripartite relationship is clearly remembered among the Enlhet and family relations are still maintained with both the Nivaclé and the Macá.

As participants in tri-ethnic processes, some Enlhet were included in traditional Nivaclé skirmishes against the Pilagá – the *aa'ey* – on the Argentinian side of the Pilcomayo. Thus, although the Enlhet as a people did not participate in this warring dynamic, accounts circulate about it in which they appear. From an external perspective, it should be noted that this dynamic did not include ambitions of expansion. Rather, it was based on cyclical conflicts between equally balanced forces underpinned by a complex symbolic construction (Barbosa and Richard 2010). Through armed conflict, a mode of relating was established that maintained clear separation between the groups at the same time as it fomented the inclusion of the other – the members and habits of the other group (Sterpin 1993) – with the capture, for example, of members of the opposing group or the acquisition of scalps that gave access to the power of the original owner of the hair.

In the north, Enlhet territory bordered that of the Ayoreo and the Tomáráho; here the situation was different. Traditionally, the Enlhet occupied the region around *Namaalhek*, a place two days' travel northeast of *Nahapong* – descriptions in the accounts lead us to suppose that *Nahapong* was Faro Moro. That is, *Namaalhek* would have been, or would have bordered, the famous Pitiantuta lagoon. Coincidentally, Belaieff (1941, 19) mentions that the Enlhet "previously reached the area beyond Pitiantuta."[18] However, we do not know the precise northern limit of the Enlhet territory, as this northern region had already been abandoned before the Chaco War. The last Enlhet Elders from *Namaalhek*, Pitiantuta, died in the first years of the new millennium; according to their testimony, their parents had to abandon those northern lands when they, the Elders, were children because they were unable to resist pressure from the Zamuco on the area.[19] The Enlhet retreated entirely from Pitiantuta, and to Belaieff, as he carried out his explorations for the Paraguayan army from 1931, this lagoon seemed to mark the limit between the Ayoreo and the Chamacoco (or Tomáráho; Belaieff 1941, 19; Richard 2008).[20] Meanwhile, *Nahapong*, Faro Moro, another important Enlhet place in the north, was still regularly visited by *Yamasma'ay'* (who died in 2010) and his group after the Chaco War, although by that time the Enlhet no longer lived there permanently because the Ayoreo had claimed it from them (*Yamasma'ay'*, in unpublished accounts). As an indication of this recent process of displacement, the Enlhet accounts speak of deadly fights with the Ayoreo; they highlight the warlike attitude and bravery of the Enlhet in their resistance against them. The armed conflict between the two groups is also reflected in the accounts of the Ayoreo; like the Enlhet, the Ayoreo report that Tamacode – Faro Moro in the Ayoreo language – was an important place for the Enlhet (Fischermann 2003). As Fischermann points out, Ayoreo displacement toward the south during the 1920s was motivated by pressure from the colonial front from Bolivia and the founding of forts in Ayoreo territory.

Conflicts with the Ayoreo ceased during the Chaco War. It was only in the second half of the 1940s that the Ayoreo once again attempted to advance southward: for example, in 1948, a Mennonite family fell victim to an Ayoreo attack in the north of Filadelfia; in 1952, a mixed group of Enlhet and Nivaclé suffered an attack on the outskirts of the

Mennonite village of Wüstenfelde, named *Vayna'* by the Enlhet.[21] At this stage of events, however, the Enlhet ceased to put up resistance to the Ayoreo and instead abandoned all of the northern region that remained to them. They remember this as a time of great tension and emphasize that fear of the Ayoreo was an important reason for their moving toward the new Mennonite colonies.

▪▪▪

According to the information provided by the Enlhet accounts, the territory of the group in the years before the outbreak of the Chaco War can be sketched as follows in a counter-clockwise direction (see map 1.1): Faro Moro/*Nahapong,* southeast of Mariscal Estigarribia; Laguna Negra/*Meyva-Saang*; the open country around Fort Corrales called *Toopak*; Platanillo/*Ya'kal'a*; Pozo Brillante/*Tengkat*; Ávalos Sánchez/*Na'tee-Ptelhla-Maaset*; Nanawa/*Nanaava'a*; Misión'i/*Manyeheme-Antamay'*; Sombrero Pirí/*Tahanmaklha-Paana'*; Anaconda/*Lhengva'alhva*; east of Campo Esperanza/*Pongkat-Napoolheng*; Kilómetro 180/*Hovaypo*; Faro Moro/*Nahapong*.

From this, it is clear that the initial front in the war between Paraguay and Bolivia was drawn across Enlhet territory (see map 1.3). This is also where the principal battles took place, for example those of Boquerón/*Yelhvayvoo-Pyettek* (September 1932)[22]; Arce/Gaspar Rodríguez de Francia/*Yaatektama-Yelhem* (October 1932); Toledo/*Havko'* (February/March 1933); Nanawa/*Nanaava'a* (January and July/September 1933); Gondra (October/December 1933); Alihuatá/Zenteno/*Loom-Popyet* (December 1933); Saavedra/Ávalos Sánchez/*Na'tee-Ptelhla-Maaset* (December 1933) and others (according to Joy 1992).

▪▪▪

We thus come to the Chaco War, which began under a particular set of historical constellations. In 1920, Fred Engen made his first exploratory trip into the northeast of the Enlhet territory, a trip that paved the way for Mennonite immigration a few years later.[23] At the time, the Enlhet in the region had little contact with the white world that was about to encircle them, although they did know of it. Creole pelt hunters came into their territory, and they made journeys to the River Paraguay, at first by preference to Puerto Pinasco, *Lheete-hepya'mehe'*, but soon also to Puerto Casado, *Maklha-Nempeena*, and Puerto Sastre, *Maklheyaat*. However, 1927 saw an important change. On the most visible level, it was marked by the beginning of the mass immigration of different groups of Mennonites. Over the following five years, the Mennonites would occupy a large area of Enlhet territory extending from east to west along the line of latitude of what is known today as Loma Plata and Filadelfia. In parallel to this, and less visibly, the Paraguayan and Bolivian army explorers who founded the forts in the area of the future front began to enter the region.[24]

In the south of Enlhet territory, the colonizing front advanced earlier. In 1889, the Anglican mission of *Maklhavay* was founded in the lands of the neighbouring Énxet people.[25] Encouraged by the advancing missionary work, different foreign ranchers settled in the Lower Chaco (Bajo Chaco). The Pozo Colorado ranch, *Vasee-Yaamelket*, founded by US citizen George Lohman (*Yoyi Looma*) in the decade after 1910 was not far from the eastern edge of Enlhet territory and the Enlhet of the region of Paratodo were already in contact with the ranch before the Chaco War, exchanging wild animal skins for articles from the white world.[26] At the same time Argentinian creoles were gradually entering from the area of the Pilcomayo river and, in 1916, Anglican missionaries founded the Nanawa mission in *Nanaava'a*[27] to the southwest of Paratodo in a region shared by the Enlhet, Macá, and Nivaclé peoples.[28] Military exploration began earlier in the southern region of the Enlhet territory than in the north, in the middle of the 1920s.[29] Both in the south and the north, these first military movements fixed what would a few years later be the initial front, drawn in Enlhet territory.

Military exploration constituted the first phase of the war. It was followed by a second that was characterized by the consolidation of the military in the recently founded forts. A third phase was initiated with the outbreak of war in 1932 and the arrival of huge numbers of soldiers, bringing ferocious violence. The war also coincided with the establishment and consolidation of the colonies of Menno and Fernheim by Mennonite immigrants in the northern region of the

Enlhet territory. As if this was not enough, the summer (December–February) of the years 1932–33 (M. Friesen 1997: 306; 2016, 250) saw a cruel smallpox epidemic that claimed the lives of at least half of the Enlhet population (Kalisch and Unruh 2014, 513–14; 2020, 517). The movement away from the area of the military front toward the end of 1933 marks a fourth phase of the war, which left the Enlhet behind the lines.[30] For the classification of contexts relevant to the description of the Enlhet people's experiences during the war, these phases should also be differentiated according to the different regions of the Enlhet territory. This book does not set out to make such a fine-grained analysis. Instead, the accounts offer an overview of the experiences, decisions, and reactions of the Enlhet based on the people's own voices to illustrate the Enlhet narrative of the Chaco War.

Maps

Maps 1.1a and 1.1b show the places mentioned in the accounts in this book, with their Enlhet name and, in some cases, its equivalent in Spanish and in the language of the Mennonites. Also shown are the approximate limits of Enlhet territory before and after the Ayoreo displaced the Enlhet from their northern region in the 1920s.

So that the Enlhet places can be compared with the current geographical situation, maps 1.1a and 1.1b additionally show principal new towns and some modern roads. The railway from the Casado S.A. tannin factory began at Puerto Casado and reached Haalhama-Teves (Kilómetro 145 or Puntarriel) around 1929, continuing as far as Kilómetro 160 during the Chaco War (1932–35). The Trans-Chaco highway was built between 1956 and 1961 and was paved at the end of the 1980s as far as the area occupied by the Mennonite colonies.

The Central Chaco, the region of the Mennonite colonies, is the territory of the Enlhet. They were its original inhabitants, practising their own forms of interaction with its different landscapes and having their own system for naming places of importance to them. Immigrants to the region founded new settlements in or near to places already named by the Enlhet without, in the majority of cases, being aware of their importance to the native inhabitants. The new localities were selected following criteria different from those applied by the Enlhet in establishing their own; they fulfilled other functions and had other names. That is, they created a new geographical regime unconnected with the geographical traditions of the Enlhet. The same applies to places occupied by the Paraguayan military and civilian populations. Today, there are three geographical regimes and three systems for naming places and localities in Enlhet lands. It is also why in many cases there is a German equivalent for an Enlhet toponym but none in Spanish or Guaraní.

It should be added that detailed maps exist of two areas of Enlhet territory, the regions around Comunidad Enlhet Ya'alve-Saanga and Comunidad Enlhet Campo Largo, respectively. These maps are accessible online (Kalisch and Unruh 2019; 2020).

Map 1.2 shows the extent of land owned by the three Mennonite cooperatives, Menno, Farnheim, and Neuland, in 2010. The map does not include land owned by the settlers but to which the deeds are not held by the Colony as a formal entity. Additionally, the current Indigenous communities (*comunidades*) in Enlhet territory are indicated with the respective ethnic group(s) living there (after Sawatzky 2011).

Map 1.4, a satellite image, shows the extent of deforestation in Enlhet territory in early 2020; the light-coloured sections of the map are deforested areas (NASA Earthdata, MODIS satellite, Terra sensor, March 2014).

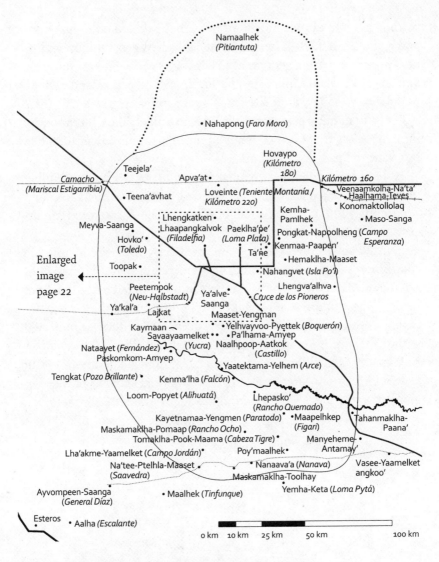

Namaalhek
(Pitiantuta)

Nahapong *(Faro Moro)*

Hovaypo
(Kilómetro 180)

Kilómetro 160

Teejela'

Apva'at

Camacho
(Mariscal Estigarribia)

Teena'avhat

Loveinte *(Teniente Montanía / Kilómetro 220)*

Veenaamkolha-Na'ta'
Haalhama-Teves
Konomaktollolaq

Kemha-Pamlhek

Maso-Sanga

Meyva-Saanga

Lhengkatken
Lhaapangkalvok
(Filadelfia)

Paeklha'pe'
(Loma Plata)

Pongkat-Napoolheng *(Campo Esperanza)*

Kenmaa-Paapen'

Hovko'
(Toledo)

Ta'me

Enlarged
image
page 22

Toopak

Hemaklha-Maaset

Nahangvet *(Isla Po'l)*

Peetempok
(Neu-Halbstadt)

Ya'alve-Saanga

Lhengva'alhva

Cruce de los Pioneros

Ya'kal'a

Lajkat

Maaset-Yengman

Kaymaan

Yelhvayvoo-Pyettek *(Boquerón)*

Savaayaamelket
(Yucra)

Pa'lhama-Amyep

Nataayet *(Fernández)*

Naalhpoop-Aatkok
(Castillo)

Paskomkom-Amyep

Yaatektama-Yelhem *(Arce)*

Tengkat *(Pozo Brillante)*

Kenma'lha *(Falcón)*

Loom-Popyet *(Alihuatá)*

Lhepasko'
(Rancho Quemado)

Kayetnamaa-Yengmen *(Paratodo)*

Maapelhkep
(Figari)

Tahanmaklha-Paana'

Maskamaklha-Pomaap *(Rancho Ocho)*

Tomaklha-Pook-Maama *(Cabeza Tigre)*

Manyeheme-Antamay'

Lha'akme-Yaamelket *(Campo Jordán)*

Poy'maalhek

Na'tee-Ptelhla-Maaset
(Saavedra)

Nanaava'a *(Nanava)*

Vasee-Yaamelket
angkoo'

Maskamaklha-Toolhay

Ayvompeen-Saanga
(General Díaz)

Maalhek *(Tinfunque)*

Yemha-Keta *(Loma Pytá)*

Esteros

Aalha *(Escalante)*

0 km   10 km   25 km   50 km   100 km

Map 1.1a *(above, facing)* ▪ Enlhet places mentioned in the accounts.

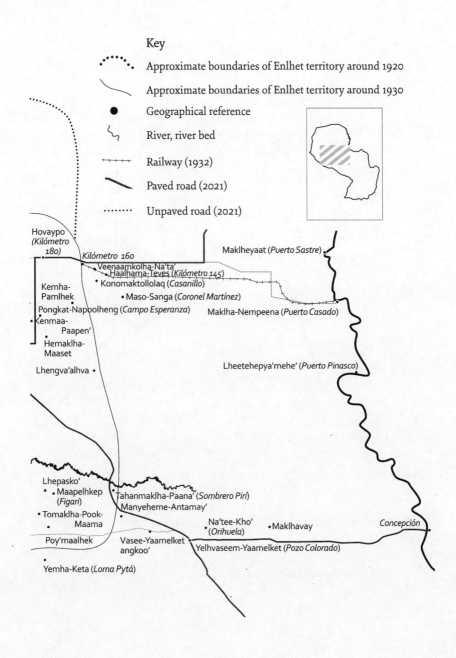

Key

.... Approximate boundaries of Enlhet territory around 1920

⌒ Approximate boundaries of Enlhet territory around 1930

● Geographical reference

River, river bed

Railway (1932)

Paved road (2021)

.... Unpaved road (2021)

Hovaypo
(*Kilómetro
180*)

Kilómetro 160

Maklheyaat (*Puerto Sastre*) ●

Veenaamkolha-Na'ta'
Haalhama-Teves (*Kilómetro 145*)
● Konomaktollolaq (*Casanillo*)

Kemha-
Pamlhek

● Maso-Sanga (*Coronel Martínez*)

Pongkat-Nappolheng (*Campo Esperanza*)

Maklha-Nempeena (*Puerto Casado*)

● Kenmaa-
Paapen'

Hemaklha-
Maaset

Lhengva'alhva ●

Lheetehepya'mehe' (*Puerto Pinasco*)

Lhepasko'
● Maapelhkep
(*Figari*)

● Tahanmaklha-Paana' (*Sombrero Piri*)
Manyeheme-Antamay'

● Tomaklha-Pook-
Maama

Na'tee-Kho'
(*Orihuela*)

● Maklhavay

Concepción

Poy'maalhek

Vasee-Yaamelket
angkoo'

Yelhvaseem-Yaamelket (*Pozo Colorado*)

●
Yemha-Keta (*Loma Pytá*)

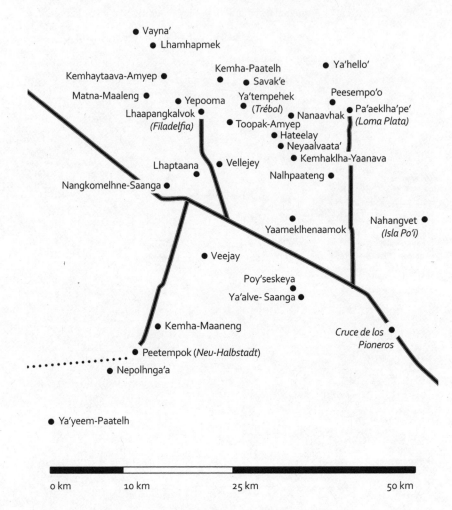

● Lhengkatken

● Vayna'
　● Lhamhapmek

Kemha-Paatelh　　　● Ya'hello'
Kemhaytaava-Amyep ●　　● 　● Savak'e
Matna-Maaleng ●　　　　　Peesempo'o
　　　● Yepooma　Ya'tempehek　●
Lhaapangkalvok ●　　(Trébol)　● Nanaavhak　● Pa'aeklha'pe'
(Filadelfia)　　● Toopak-Amyep　　　(Loma Plata)
　　　　　　● Hateelay
　　　　　　● Neyaalvaata'
Lhaptaana　● Vellejey　● Kemhaklha-Yaanava
Nangkomelhne-Saanga ●　　Nalhpaateng ●

　　　　　　　　　　Nahangvet ●
Yaameklhenaamok ●　　(Isla Po'i)

● Veejay

Poy'seskeya
Ya'alve- Saanga ●　●

　　　　　　Cruce de los
● Kemha-Maaneng　　Pioneros ●

● Peetempok (Neu-Halbstadt)
● Nepolhnga'a

● Ya'yeem-Paatelh

0 km　　10 km　　　25 km　　　　50 km

Map 1.1b ▪ Enlhet places mentioned in the accounts (enlarged).

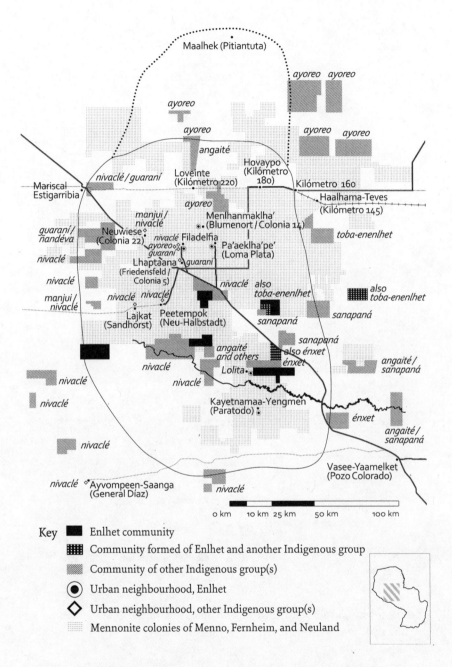

Maalhek (Pitiantuta)

ayoreo   *ayoreo*

ayoreo

ayoreo

ayoreo   *ayoreo*

angaité

Hovaypo
(Kilómetro
180)

Loveinte
(Kilómetro 220)

nivaclé / guaraní

Mariscal
Estigarribia

Kilómetro 160

Haalhama-Teves
(Kilómetro 145)

ayoreo

*manjui /
nivaclé*

Menlhanmaklha'
(Blumenort / Colonia 14)

toba-enenlhet

*guaraní /
ñandéva*

Neuwiese
(Colonia 22)

nivaclé Filadelfia

ayoreo
guaraní

Pa'aeklha'pe'
(Loma Plata)

nivaclé

Lhaptaana
(Friedensfeld /
Colonia 5)

guaraní

nivaclé   also
toba-enenlhet

also
toba-enenlhet

*manjui /
nivaclé*

nivaclé   *nivaclé*

Lajkat
(Sandhorst)

Peetempok
(Neu-Halbstadt)

sanapaná

sanapaná

sanapaná
also *énxet*

*angaité
and others*

Lolita

énxet

*angaité /
sanapaná*

nivaclé

nivaclé

nivaclé

Kayetnamaa-Yengmen
(Paratodo)

énxet

*angaité /
sanapaná*

nivaclé

Vasee-Yaamelket
(Pozo Colorado)

nivaclé

Ayvompeen-Saanga
(General Díaz)

nivaclé

0 km   10 km 25 km   50 km   100 km

Key
◼ Enlhet community

▦ Community formed of Enlhet and another Indigenous group

▨ Community of other Indigenous group(s)

⊙ Urban neighbourhood, Enlhet

◇ Urban neighbourhood, other Indigenous group(s)

Mennonite colonies of Menno, Fernheim, and Neuland

Map 1.2 ▪ Land holdings by Mennonites and Indigenous communities, 2012.

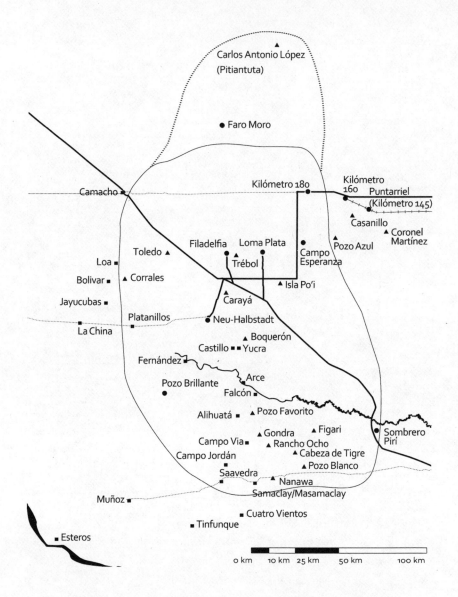

Map 1.3 (*above, facing*) ▪ Paraguayan and Bolivian army positions at the beginning of 1932.

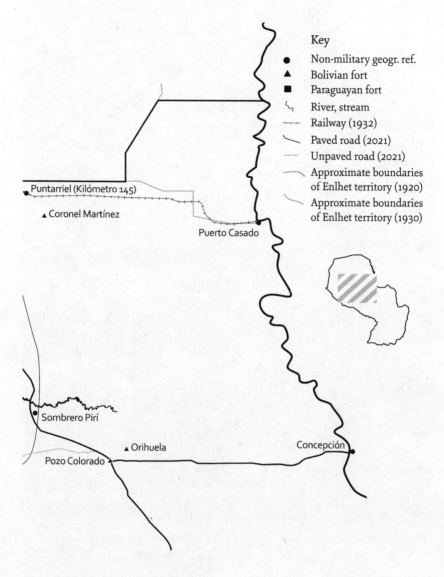

Key

- ● Non-military geogr. ref.
- ▲ Bolivian fort
- ■ Paraguayan fort
- ⌇ River, stream
- ┈ Railway (1932)
- ⌒ Paved road (2021)
- ⋯ Unpaved road (2021)
- ⌇ Approximate boundaries of Enlhet territory (1920)
- ⌒ Approximate boundaries of Enlhet territory (1930)

Puntarriel (Kilómetro 145)

▲ Coronel Martínez

Puerto Casado

Sombrero Pirí

▲ Orihuela

Pozo Colorado

Concepción

(See appendix for Enlhet names of the forts.)

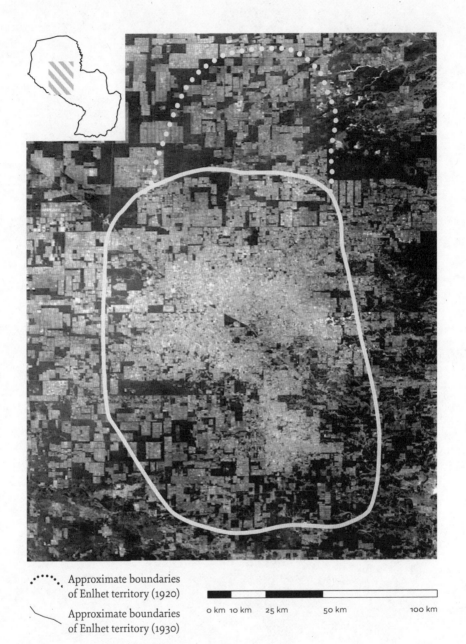

Map 1.4 ▪ Deforestation in Enlhet territory, March 2020.

PART TWO
THE ACCOUNTS

HANNES KALISCH

This book presents a small selection of the large archive of accounts by elderly Enlhet men and women collected by Ernesto Unruh and myself over the last fifteen years within the framework of *Nengvaanemkeskama Nempayvaam Enlhet*.[1] I have organized the accounts, which represent only a tiny part of those that constitute the Enlhet narrative of the Chaco War,[2] according to certain aspects of the relationship between the Enlhet and the military. These are defined by particular contexts and dynamics; although they represent different perspectives, they are not necessarily mutually exclusive and can, for example, overlap in terms of chronology.

As well as the five historical moments presented here, many other viewpoints could be used as a basis from which to consider the Enlhet narrative of the Chaco War. Some of these – which are reflected with varying intensity through the accounts presented – include the military and smallpox; prostitution; battles; Enlhet guides, mediators, and combatants; Enlhet resistance; internal processes within the groups; the dynamics of flight; the reconfiguration of the group behind the front; approaching the Mennonites as a response to violence, and the reconfiguration of territory by region after the war.[3] The present selection of Enlhet voices, then, offers only an initial – and very incomplete – overview of the narrative held by the Enlhet around the Chaco War. They are voices hitherto unheard outside their society.

■ ■ ■

In the section following "The Accounts," entitled "In Dialogue with the Enlhet Accounts," I set out comments that provide a framework within which Enlhet voices can be read and heard regarding processes in the construction of the relationship with the intruders at a specific historical moment, a moment characterized by marked violence that altered the life of the Enlhet people completely and permanently. The logic that this initial relationship followed remains in place today; it is the logic of racism and contempt. My notes, therefore, highlight the current need for the reconstruction of this relationship.

"The Accounts" and "In Dialogue with the Enlhet Accounts" are set out in parallel across the aforementioned historical moments in the relationship between the Enlhet and the military. The reader can thus access the authentic Enlhet voice without the interruption of external opinions but can also, should he or she wish, easily refer to the corresponding notes and study them in parallel.

SECTION 1
EXPLORERS

This Constitution recognizes the existence of Indigenous peoples, defined as cultural groups pre-dating the formation and organization of the Paraguayan State.

National Constitution of Paraguay, Article 62

In Enlhet accounts of the Chaco War, a clear first phase emerges, namely the military exploration of the Enlhet territory and the building of military forts. The following accounts describe this period.[4]

Account 1: A Meeting Between Leaders
Sa'kok-Nay' [5]

In Pa'aeklha'pe', that is, Loma Plata, there didn't use to be the large number of people there are now.[6] The Mennonites didn't live there; neither did most of the Enlhet – they came because the Ayoreo pushed them there from the north. But my father lived there, and my mother, my elder brother, and my uncle Sixto. My father hunted and collected honey; we always had enough to eat. My mother gathered *kentem'* – the edible type of the karaguata plant. That was before the *lengko* came, the Mennonites. We ate the seedpods of the *teves* tree, too. The seedpods were kept on a shelf covered over with grass, the same way they made their houses. That way they had food in times when food was short.

In those days before the Mennonites, we didn't stay permanently in the place where we had our grass houses, in Yaanmaan-Tengma, where Loma Plata is now, right where the Mennonites built their supermarket later. We moved all the time; me with my mother, always. I went with her to get *kentem'*; when she gathered firewood and put the *kentem'* on the fire. I would go out with my mother because nobody was left at home. My father was out collecting honey or hunting. If I stayed alone I might meet valay, Paraguayans. Their road ran south of Yaanmaan-Tengma.

At first, a small group of valay came. One of them was an *apveske'*, a person with authority, just like my own father was an apveske'. I don't

Figure 2.1 ▪ Sa'kok-Nay'.

remember any of the details, I was still very young, but my father told me about it. This apveske' came before the Mennonites, from the east.[7] He was a Paraguayan, not a Bolivian. Yaanmaan-Tengma, where we lived, was surrounded by forest, but the Paraguayan had a machine that he looked through to scan all around and he found our village. It was one of those machines they put on top of a pole to scan the area.[8] When he came toward our houses we kept quiet. We didn't run away, I do remember that. I haven't forgotten these things, these experiences, because my father told me them all the time.

The Paraguayan, the apveske', came to our village with four soldiers. I vaguely remember him coming. But the war I remember well. He came before the war and before the Mennonites arrived. It was only later that the Paraguayans came in large numbers. This Paraguayan made my father an apveske' – an authority figure. My father was an apveske' for the Paraguayans. It wasn't the Mennonites that made him an apveske', it was the Paraguayans. As an authority named by the Paraguayans, he had access to food; he got a lot of food from them. I remember him getting it. He brought *seppo* [mandioca] flour, wheat flour, dried maize, all kinds of things. He got sugar, soap, shoes. They gave him everything, blankets, mosquito nets, things that the Paraguayan had brought. The Paraguayan, the apveske', had made him an apveske' just like him, you see. People still talk about Cacique Vaaso. That was my father. He wasn't an apveske' for the Mennonites, an authority designated by them. He was an apveske' for the Paraguayans; he was named by the Paraguayans.

The valay, the Paraguayan, wanted to open up a road and my father acted as his guide. They took metal poles with two points on them and used them to mark out the route. They went beyond what's now the road from Haalhama-Teves, Puntarriel, to Mariscal Estigarribia and set one of these poles to the north of Loveinte, Teniente Montanía. They went further on and placed other poles, I don't really know where. One was near Vellejey, Wiesenfeld [near Filadelfia]. Another was in Toopak-Amyep, Gnadenheim, and there was another in Yav'aa-Na-Pma'aok, near the southern edge of Loma Plata. My father went to all of these places guiding the Paraguayan apveske'. Much later I saw the pole to the north of Teniente Montanía. A Mennonite took us to find the old road.

We stayed, the women that is, in our village in Yaanmaan-Tengma, where the Mennonite supermarket is today, but that was before the Mennonites came. The Paraguayan left his vehicle in Yaanmaan-Tengma. He hid his little truck there, the one he brought the supplies in. From Yaanmaan-Tengma they continued on foot. The Paraguayan apveske' had two Enlhet apveske' with him: my father and Kalape'e, who lived in Toopak-Amyep. They were both apveske' like the Paraguayan. With my father were his brothers Lospata and Sixto. They took turns to carry the metal poles and the Paraguayan apveske' scanned in front of them with his machine to find the way. They travelled alone, the men, the chiefs, because they were on foot and working, putting up the metal poles in places a long way away. We women would have got very tired if we'd gone with them.

It was during that time when they were marking out the road that my father received things; he got blankets and mosquito nets. It was a good while before the Mennonites came. You didn't see any Mennonites at that time, only these Paraguayans. Later, when the war started suddenly, other Paraguayans came who wanted to kill us. It's no coincidence I get frightened seeing them putting stones on the main avenue in Loma Plata, paving it.

"That's what the Paraguayans did when they were getting ready for the war," I always say. "They dug up the earth."

Even now I don't go near Paraguayans, even if they have food. I'm still afraid of them.

Account 2: The Bolivians Arrive in Alihuatá
Malhkee·tko-Ngkoyoy' [9]

We lived in Loom-Popyet, Fort Alihuatá, when the preparations for war started. It was where my mother was from; she and my father lived there. One day, a long time before the war, some *yaamvalay*, Bolivians, arrived and set up camp there and in Yaatektama-Yelhem [Fort Arce, which the Paraguayans called Gaspar Rodríguez de Francia]. Around that time, my mother stopped visiting Kenma'lha, Fort Falcón, another place that was important for the Enlhet in the area, because the valay, the Paraguayans, had a fort there.[10]

My grandmother lived in Loom-Popyet, Fort Alihuatá. It was one of the places where they used to build their grass houses, and one day the Bolivians came. I don't remember it because I was born later. I don't know much about when they arrived, and I don't know how the people that lived there reacted either. But I learned some things listening to my mother and father talk about it. The Bolivians explored the area. They found our homes because they used some Enlhet apveske', leaders, as guides who could show them the way. At first, the soldiers

Figure 2.2 • "Loom-Popyet was one of the places where they used to build their grass houses." Grass houses used by the Enlhet when staying for an extended period in one place.

stayed in Na'tee-Ptelhla-Maaset, Fort Saavedra [what the Paraguayans call Ávalos Sánchez]. Later they came to Loom-Popyet, Alihuatá. They opened up the road that the soldiers would use later. The Enlhet worked on it. The road left Na'tee-Ptelhla-Maaset, Fort Saavedra, passed through Loom-Popyet, went to Yaatektama-Yelhem, Fort Arce, and arrived in the place where I lived today. There they stopped in the place the Enlhet call Savaayaamelket, Fort Yucra, near Fort Boquerón.

When my father got married he went to live in Loom-Popyet, which was my mother's home. But they used to go and visit the place my father was from, further south, and then come back to where the Bolivians were. On one of those visits, I was born in Yemha-Keta, Loma Pytá. I was still in my mother's belly when the Bolivians came to Loom-Popyet. That's what I was told. The Bolivians weren't angry; they even brought their wives to live with them there.[11] One of the Bolivian women almost adopted me, my mother told me. She picked me up when I was still very small but my father wouldn't let her take me and went to fetch me back. Even though I was very small I remember it a little. The memory of it is like in a dream, but I often heard my father talk about what happened.

The Bolivians established a military position in Loom-Popyet. I used to listen to my father talk about working for the Bolivians, cutting down trees and hauling the trunks out. They planted corn, a lot of corn, to use as fodder for their horses. In fact, the Enlhet thought the explorers had been sent to find land, that the Bolivians were looking for land to grow crops like the Mennonites did later. That's what my father said; these aren't things I saw myself. But the Paraguayans didn't let them because they claimed the land for themselves. The Enlhet assumed that the Bolivians wanted to live with the Paraguayans, but the Paraguayans weren't interested in that. They had no intention of sharing the land.

Account 3: We've Got Indians With Us[12]
Savhongvay' [13]

I know how the war started. One day some valay, Paraguayans, came to Kemha-Maaneng, the place the Mennonites later called Lichtenau, in the area that's Colonia Neuland today. It was when the Paraguayans had only just started coming into Enlhet territory. They were already near when somebody saw them.

"Look! There are valay coming on horses," one of the Enlhet said.

People started running to hide but one of the Paraguayans spoke to us in our language.

"Don't be afraid! Don't run! We're Enlhet. We're exploring the country," he said.

He made a sign with his hands.

"We're not dangerous."

"They're Enlhet!"

So it was an Enlhet who explored these lands first, Kapetaan Loope, Captain López, the father of Loope'e who died in Ya'alve-Saanga. Loope had the rank of captain. He accompanied the military explorers who were led by a Paraguayan captain with a fat belly. This was before the war.

"We're surveying the Enlhet territory. Paraguayans are going to live here," said Loope.

That was why they were so interested in the land. They were look-ing for a place to live.

Loope told us: "We're not soldiers. We're not going to kill any Enlhet. We're inspecting the region," he said. "Don't be afraid of the Paraguayans. They're not dangerous. You're going to live together with them. The soldiers are looking for land. The Paraguayans are going to be your neighbours. Paraguayans are going to live here."

That's what the Enlhet told us.

"*Heey'*, good."

The Enlhet agreed. But in reality the Paraguayans were already pre-paring for the fight against the Bolivians.

"Alright."

They shared what they'd brought with them and we had some of it: meat, dry biscuits, *yerba*, rice, tobacco. The Enlhet threw the *yerba* into the undergrowth, though.

"That might poison us. It's not edible," they said.

Later they learned that *yerba* is good. This was when we didn't know what it was.

"Alright," they said. "Okay."

The Enlhet agreed. My grandfather agreed when he heard what they said. Because they couldn't imagine what was going to happen, that actually these people were going to start a war. Who could have foreseen that? And in fact, the Bolivians were already approaching from the other side.

■■■

Loope was from the east. He could speak Guaraní because he'd spent time with the Paraguayans. His son Loope'e had been made a sergeant and when the soldiers set out to find the Enlhet he guided them on their reconnaissance trips too.[14] One time Loope'e came to a Bolivian camp accompanied by some Paraguayans. The Enlhet went into the camp first, then after him the corporals and finally the lieutenant. The Bolivians greeted them.

"*Akva'ak ko'o*, I've arrived."[15]

"*Heey'*, good. What news?" they asked.

"None, all's well."

"Good."

They'd come from Nahangvet, Isla Po'i. The Bolivian camp was at Boquerón, where there was a battle later where a lot of people died. We call the place Kelyelhvayvoo-Pyettek.

The lieutenant came into the Bolivian fort last and greeted them. "I've arrived too."

"Good," answered his Bolivian counterpart. What news do you have?"

"Nothing, all quiet. Only good news. We're surveying the land."

"Good. So are we," replied the *yaamvalay*, the Bolivian. "We're exploring the land as well. We're going to live here."

"We're going to settle here too," replied the *valay*, the Paraguayan. "Look at this man. Do you recognize him? He's a genuine Indian. These lands belong to the Indians," he said to the Bolivian.

The Bolivian stared at the Enlhet, at Loope'e. He didn't take his eyes off him. Loope'e started to feel afraid and was getting ready to run, but the Bolivian just said:

"Now you look. We've got Indians with us too, two of them. There they are sitting over there."

The Paraguayan looked at the Bolivians that were Indians.

"We've got Indians with us as well. And they're not mixed, they're pure Indian," the Bolivian said, to emphasize his point.

The conversation ended and the Paraguayans came away. Loope'e was very scared as they left the camp. He glanced discreetly over his shoulder because he was expecting them to shoot him. But nothing happened.

▪▪▪

I know why they became furious with each other. It all started here in Enlhet territory, in the area we live in. The Paraguayans and the Bolivians were fighting over this land. Both sides claimed it for themselves. They were fighting to decide who was going to live with us, the Enlhet. This is Enlhet land. The Paraguayans were in Nahangvet, Isla Po'i, and the Bolivians had occupied the west. The Bolivians gave names to places in Ayoreo territory, in the north, too. They went as far as Macá territory, as far as Nanaava'a, Nanawa. When they finished building their forts, when they finished digging their trenches, the Bolivian military leaders talked among themselves, and that's when the war started.

Account 4: We're Friends[16]
Ramón Ortiz [17]

Before the war, people already used to travel to visit places along the [Paraguay] river. Some Enlhet went to Lheetehepya'mehe', Puerto Pinasco; others went to Maklha-Nempeena, Puerto Casado. They would stay about two months and when they came back they would bring clothes, axes, and knives. They would also bring small pieces of metal that they used to make tips for their arrows. They called arrows with a metal tip *sooya'angka* [iron arrow]. They used them to kill deer and the different kinds of pigs to eat.

We lived in Lhengkatken, to the north of Filadelfia. We also lived in the area of Apva'at to the north of Teniente Montanía. But we left those places. It was in Veenaamkolha-Na'ta', Kilómetro 152, that I first entered the world of the white man. The reason we approached the valay, the Paraguayans, was that some of them had come to the places where we lived deep in the forest, some soldiers.

"There's going to be trouble!" people said when they saw them.

But one of them shouted: "*Vaaaa*, don't run! We're friends." They shouted like that in our language as they approached the group.

"What's this?"

The Enlhet picked up their bows and their arrows, and grabbed their clubs. "It's us," said the one who had shouted.

And then they recognized him. It was Pa'ayvaeklha'ay', the father of Yohoon Alhaaye', who died a few years ago in Ya'alve-Saanga. He was an apveske', a leader for the Paraguayans designated by them. There were other apveske' with him, Cacique Mita'i and Cacique Mitapuku. They came to our homes with eight soldiers. In those days we didn't wear clothes; we didn't have clothes.

"It's us. These men have brought *apaava*, clothes, fabric. We've been looking for you," said the chiefs.

No one answered him because the Enlhet were afraid. They were about to become violent.

Then the soldiers took out the *apaava*, the clothes. They weren't pants, they were what we called *pangyeelo*, pieces of cloth. They gave them to the women. They wrapped them around their hips and fastened them with belts. The Enlhet liked that: at that time we didn't have cloth. The women were happy. They put a piece of cloth around my hips too; it made a very handsome loincloth. Then we went with the Paraguayans. We took our animals with us, our goats, our sheep.

"There's work there," they said. And it was true. We worked there and they cooked for us in big pots. The men cut down trees; they cleared what was to be the train line. They were building the railway that came out of Puerto Casado and was slowly extending toward Kilómetro 152. The women dug out the stumps of the trees their husbands cut down. Even the children worked; they swept the cutting as it was cleared. That's how the construction of the railway line advanced until it reached Kilómetro 160; that's where it ended. But when we came out of forest it was at Kilómetro 152. We'd been deceived by accepting *apaava*, clothing, and we were deceived by having accepted food.

"It all seems true," people said when they arrived.

We found that the Paraguayans had a lot of food, biscuits, and other things. The Paraguayans didn't reject us and we hadn't refused them.

Account 5: Play the Woman!
Seepe-Pyoy' [18]

My father used to tell us how he acted as a guide for the Paraguayans when they were exploring the region. He told us how they advanced a long way to the south of Nanaava'a, Nanawa, my father on foot and the soldiers on horseback, about twenty soldiers. With them was a sergeant named Teniente López, Lieutenant López. He was the *apveske'*, the chief. My father told of one night when they were in a place a long way away. Beyond the place they stopped for the night they'd found burnt grass, just like after someone burns a field. My father knew what it meant. No Paraguayans lived in the area; only *aa'ey*, Pilagá, came to that region. So he explained to the Paraguayans what the ashes meant.

"Our enemies did this," he said. "They're called the *aa'ey*, the Pilagá. They come to our homes to attack us. But we're not afraid of them."

They spent the night there while some of the soldiers kept watch over the camp in case anybody came near. That's what soldiers do; they watch over their camp during the night.

That night something disgusting happened. Lieutenant López tried to take my father up the backside. It's actually normal for Paraguayans to have no control of themselves.

"Play the woman! I'm going to put it in you," the Paraguayan ordered him.

But my father wasn't interested and he answered the Paraguayan in his language, in Guaraní: "I'm not a woman. I'm a man. And I'm your comrade besides."

The way my father told it, the Paraguayan listened to him and changed his mind, decided not to take him up the backside. "You're right."

My father was able to stand up to him because he could speak the Paraguayans' language. It's obviously not a very difficult language because the Enlhet who spent time with them learned it quickly. The Enlhet soon got used to the Paraguayans' language, and that often saved them.

Account 6: The Beginning of the Conflict
Kenteem [19]

The conflict started in the region of Alkeete', around Fort Toledo. It all began there, and soon the valay, the Paraguayans, started fighting with the *yaamvalay*, the Bolivians. In Alkeete' the Paraguayans snatched a woman and took her to Hovko', to Fort Toledo. She was the mother of Haakok Yenmongaam [who died a few years ago in Campo Largo]. Her people refused to abandon her and they divided among themselves the task of getting her back.

"You take hold of the Paraguayan," one was told. "You're very strong." The men caught up with the soldiers; the one of them they'd designated grabbed the Paraguayan who'd kidnapped the woman and was carrying her with him.

He grabbed the soldier, but he touched his rifle while he had hold of him and the rifle went off. The bullet hit Haakok Yenmongaam's father in the stomach and he fell dead. That's where Haakok

Yenmongaam's name comes from, "Orphaned of his father by a rifle."
A rifle killed his father while he was trying to take his wife back; he
died in the attempt. That was the beginning of the conflict between
the Paraguayans and the Bolivians. Immediately an Enlhet Elder
named Soopkaatek went to Fort Camacho [Mariscal Estigarribia][20] to
tell the Bolivians what had happened. They went straight to Alkeete'
and Fort Toledo – Camacho is not far away. And then the fighting
started; the Bolivians defended the Enlhet.

That was the beginning of the war: the Paraguayans were taking
women. I sometimes hear other reasons for the start of the war, but
they're not right. That's what the Paraguayans were like. When they
saw a woman they raped her. If they didn't want to kill her afterwards,
they took her to where they lived; they stole her. They did the same
thing in Neyalvaata', Chortitz, and in Yepooma, Friedensruh. That's
how they are. They steal women.

SECTION 2
INSIDE THE FORTS

. . . where unity and equality reign.

Paraguayan national anthem

The forts were built in strategic locations, specifically those with a more or less constant supply of water. Because of the scarcity of such places in the Central Chaco (and the serious drought during the years of the war reported by the Enlhet, for which see also P. P. Klassen 1996, 91–2), for many Enlhet groups risking contact with the military was unavoidable at certain times of the year. The following accounts report experiences around the forts.

Account 7: Fort Isla Po'i
Haakok Maaset [21]

The Paraguayans' war didn't reach Ya'alve-Saanga, where we lived. There was a Bolivian fort at Veejay to the west that they called by its Enlhet name, Huihay. The Paraguayans called it Carayá. The Paraguayans were in the east and the south at Nahangvet, Fort Isla Po'i, and Yelhvayvoo-Pyettek, Fort Boquerón. The Bolivians had light brown uniforms; the Paraguayans' uniforms were green. My grandfather used to visit the Bolivians at Fort Veejay. They weren't aggressive. He also visited the Paraguayans at Fort Isla Po'i – the Enlhet didn't usually go to Fort Boquerón – to take them sweet potatoes. The encampment was big, and everything was the same Paraguayan green colour. Whenever the Enlhet arrived, a soldier would come out of the fort to meet them. Then he went back inside to let his superior know and the superior would come with meat, dried meat. He'd bring a lot of dried meat in exchange for the sweet potatoes; he'd also bring *seppo* [mandioca] flour. The Enlhet didn't go right inside Fort Isla Po'i; they stayed some distance away. I wonder what would have happened if they had gone inside. I imagine they would have killed them. The soldiers asked them to bring more sweet potatoes and fresh *seppo*, but soon war broke out and the Enlhet were afraid to go near the fort again.

Account 8: My Mother
Malhkee·tko-Ngkoyoy' [22]

In Loom-Popyet, the Bolivian fort of Alihuatá, there was a hospital. The doctor's house was next to the dry riverbed. Someone else lived a little further away; I suppose it was an *elle*, an Englishman. He lived right on the riverbank on a spot higher up. I remember him. He wasn't a doctor; the doctor lived nearer the camp. But the *elle* had his own house and lived away from the *sengelpelhteetamoo*, from the soldiers. Our grass houses were near his house, which would have been about a hundred metres from the hospital, about the same distance as from here to David's house. The Englishman lived between us and the soldiers. He lived with his wife and two small children. One was a girl. We used to see them around their house.

He was the only *elle* who lived in Loom-Popyet. He was from the same place as the Bolivians; he'd come with them. He lived in the fort but we never saw him working. I think his job was to look after the soldiers. Like the *elle* at the Anglican mission in Maklhavay, he had special knowledge that he knew how to use. He probably taught the Bolivians too; they were probably his disciples.

■■■

We lived in Loom-Popyet, Fort Alihuatá. My mother lived there and so did my grandmother. The place is called Loom-Popyet but the Bolivians called it Alvaata', Alihuatá, [literally, "water course" in Enlhet]. It's to the south of Yaatektama-Yelhem, Fort Arce. My mother often went to the Bolivians' houses to earn food washing their clothes. The food I ate was from what she got for her work. We ate it with venison. My father worked for the *elle*, the Englishman; he cleaned his house. He also worked for the Bolivians in Loom-Popyet, feeding dried maize to the horses and things like that. They paid him in food and gave him clothes and a little money too. In Loom-Popyet there was a small store where we could buy supplies. Or sometimes my father took his money to Na'tee-Ptelhla-Maaset, to Fort Saavedra, where there was a big store. In those days the Enlhet lived and moved around mostly without serious problems; the war hadn't broken out yet.

Figure 2.3 ▪ Malhkee-tko-Ngkoyoy'.

My father also went out hunting and would bring back things like deer. The Bolivians liked venison and they even ate ostrich meat. When they got meat they shared their own food in exchange. The chief's wife would bring some of what she cooked. That's how we lived; they behaved like the Enlhet when they treat their neighbour well. My father also collected honey in the area around Loom-Popyet; the Bolivians didn't stop you going onto their fields like the Mennonites do.

My grandmother gathered *kentem'* and we ate it even though we lived with the Bolivians and their food. It was only later when we lived in Na'tee-Ptelhla-Maaset that we stopped eating *kentem'*.

There were some Enlhet groups who lived a long way from the military camp. They didn't mix with the Bolivians. They occasionally came to exchange food with them, but they lived at a distance. My mother often went to where they lived. For example, when a girl had her first period, the Enlhet held *yaanmaan*, the initiation celebration for a young woman. On those occasions they invited everybody in the area.

"There's going to be a *yaanmaan*."

"When is it going to start?" they would ask.

"When the moon is bright enough to light the gathering."

Whenever an invitation came from the people living further away from the fort, the people at the camp went. They left Loom-Popyet to take part; my mother used to lead the women in the dancing. I remember when she would get up to join the women dancing I used to cry because I wanted to go with her. They held the celebrations in a place where there were no Bolivians, at the homes of one of the groups who didn't want to live near the military. They preferred to live among themselves.

■■■

We lived with the Bolivians but we didn't settle permanently at the fort. In the old days, the Enlhet didn't stay in one place; they moved continually. We used to go south and stay with other Bolivians at Na'tee-Ptelhla-Maaset, Fort Saavedra. It was a very big fort and a relatively large number of Enlhet lived there. We'd stay for a few days and visit the store and my mother would work for the soldiers.

Other times we'd go north to visit the camp at Yaatektama-Yelhem, Fort Arce, where there were also a lot of military houses. Likewise, the Enlhet who lived in Yaatektama-Yelhem would visit us at Fort Alihuatá. We travelled on foot, although my father carried me on his shoulders, just me. This happened before the war broke out. The Bolivians lived peacefully in their forts. When a Bolivian woman from

Yaatektama-Yelhem asked my mother to wash her clothes we would leave Loom-Popyet and go over there. The Bolivian chiefs had their wives with them to cook for them, but the common soldiers didn't have theirs.

■■■

We lived together with the Bolivians in Loom-Popyet, Alihuatá. The soldiers would come to our village to get women, which they would also pay for. The soldiers took advantage of Kam'aatko-Kvaanyam'. There were other women too, but I don't remember them. I know about Kam'aatko-Kvaanyam' because she lived with us; at that time she was young. The soldiers used to come to her and she received them. She didn't get pregnant; she couldn't have children. The Bolivians also used other women. I don't know about them myself but I used to hear my mother say about them, "The Bolivians taught her that."

I imagine the Enlhet didn't like their women getting involved with Bolivians but the women still went with them. They didn't come to my mother, though; they didn't go near women who had a husband. And besides, the apveske', the English *elle* leader, lived in Loom-Popyet and he probably said to them, "Don't go near the Enlhet women."

My mother didn't get involved with soldiers, she just worked for them in return for food. There weren't actually many Bolivians in Loom-Popyet and the situation was generally calm. There were not many Enlhet either, just one group of grass houses. There wasn't a great number of people.

After they arrived in Loom-Popyet, the Bolivians soon started to come to Kam'aatko-Kvaanyam'. This was before their chiefs, their apveske', were there. Once the chiefs came and the amount of soldiers increased considerably, they couldn't come to our village so easily. In reality they did use to come in the evening for the women, but they were very careful because if they were seen they would be reprimanded. Their apveske', a sergeant, used to follow them and they were afraid of him; they ran when they saw him.

Later, in Na'tee-Ptelhla-Maaset, Fort Saavedra, the situation was different (see also account 10). There they moved freely among our houses. The place was yellow with their uniforms (the Bolivians' uniform was light brown). The women received them and they paid them; they paid them with money. They came one by one to the village, under cover of the night. Their apveske', their chiefs, didn't allow them to touch Enlhet women and when they saw them they would send them away. They still came back again, but never as a group. Their chief warned us that we shouldn't stray too far because the soldiers would catch any women they found. They advised us to stay near them, near their houses.

In Na'tee-Ptelhla-Maaset, the Bolivians named my brother as a leader, an apveske', and made him responsible for watching over the women.

"Look after the women," the Bolivian chief, their apveske', ordered him.

And that's what he did; he walked around the village waiting for the soldiers. When the soldiers saw him they'd turn back and run away. When my brother came back from the Bolivian chief's house, any soldiers that were around our houses would run and even hide in the grass. They were afraid of him. The Bolivians made my brother an apveske', an authority figure for them. They even promised him that he would be given a vehicle after a certain time. That never happened, though, because of the way the war went. My brother spoke the Bolivians' language. He even knew how to use strong words to reprimand a soldier.

The Bolivian soldiers were forbidden to touch the women and when one of them was found with an Enlhet woman he was put in jail. That's why they were afraid of their leaders. The Bolivians respected their leaders. But the Paraguayans weren't frightened of their leaders. We realized that after the war when we had contact with the Paraguayan military. They don't respect their chiefs.

Account 9: With the Bolivians at Fort Arce
Maangvayaam'ay' [23]

The Bolivians chased Enlhet women constantly. That's what my mother and father told me. They used to hide the young girls because they didn't want the Bolivians to touch them. They disguised them as boys so the Bolivians wouldn't recognize them as women, so they wouldn't touch them, so they wouldn't mistreat them. They used to cut their hair the way the boys had it, and when they went to the fort they dressed as men. They wore a hat, pants, a shirt, and shoes, like the men did. So the soldiers saw them and thought they were men.

"Hey, boy!" they would say. A girl could approach the soldiers without fear of danger because they thought she was man; that's what my father and mother used to say.

One day at Yaatektama-Yelhem, at Fort Arce, a Bolivian soldier assaulted Luis Negro's mother. When her husband found out about this he told the apveske', their chief.

"That soldier touched my wife!"

"Right," said the chief, "I'll have him whipped." He called the soldiers together and the guilty man was pointed out.

"Was this the man?"

"Yes, that's him."

They took hold of him. "Whip him. Give him a hundred lashes." They whipped him and after that he never bothered another Enlhet woman. That's how it happened, because Luis' father was a sergeant. The Bolivians called him Sergeant Luis.

■■■

My father-in-law's father, Lamas, lived at Yaatektama-Yelhem. He used to carry water in big containers for the Bolivian soldiers in battle. Feliciano's grandfather Manuel did it with him. They would take the barrels of water to where the soldiers were, pour it into other containers and then go back to the lagoon. It was like working for a boss.

The water was transported in trucks with a Bolivian driver. "Carry the water. Go with the truck," was the order. "We're going to the party!"

They went willingly, because they thought it really was a party. But when they arrived with the water it wasn't a party, there were guns firing everywhere. They had no choice, they were already there.

"You're going to the banquet," they were told.

At first they thought that it really was a party because they didn't understand the way they spoke. It turned out that they called the war a party. They'd been talking about food for the soldiers. They lied to the Enlhet; they spoke nice words to them because they were worried they'd be afraid of the war.

When they got back to the camp they were told to go and eat the leftovers of the Bolivians' barbecue. There was a lot of barbecue, Lamas used to say, but they didn't feel like eating because they'd been so frightened of being hit by the bullets. It was impossible to predict when a gun would fire, when a Paraguayan would shoot at a Bolivian. They would be eating back at the camp while the soldiers shot at each other with their rifles. In any case, the Enlhet weren't in the middle of the battle, they were just made to carry water to the soldiers. That's what Lamas used to say. They carried it during battles but they didn't have to move around in front of the guns; the paths they had to carry the water along were in safe places. The Paraguayans brought their food along safe paths in the same way; they brought cattle to the front. The Bolivians took cattle to the front as well; that's what I heard.

Account 10: The Bolivian Retreat
Malhkee·tko-Ngkoyoy' [24]

We went back to Loom-Popyet, to Fort Alihuatá, but we only stayed a short time because soon the hostilities intensified again. This time the soldiers fired at each other ferociously; the first time the violence had been relatively limited. So when the Paraguayans came back we left Loom-Popyet; we moved to Na'tee-Ptelhla-Maaset, Fort Saavedra. The Bolivians themselves suggested we did it.

"You should leave. The front is getting near."

"They're advising us to leave."

So we left Loom-Popyet for good and settled permanently in Na'tee-Ptelhla-Maaset. There were certainly a lot of soldiers there! The Bolivians met there after taking back Loom-Popyet. We stayed for a time in Na'tee-Ptelhla-Maaset, but we never went back to Loom-Popyet.

Soon, though, the front was coming nearer again and the Bolivians warned us again.

"The Paraguayans are getting close. We're falling back."

So when the Bolivians retreated from Na'tee-Ptelhla-Maaset, from Fort Saavedra, my father decided to go with them.

"Go by the main road," one of the soldiers said to the Enlhet. "We're going to fight the Paraguayans behind you. Stay there, you'll be safe there." He was talking about Ayvompeen-Saanga, Fort Muñoz, which the Paraguayans call General Díaz.

We followed their advice, and the Enlhet who had been with the Bolivians left and headed west. We travelled all night.

"They're telling us to run," my father told us. "They're suggesting we stay in Ayvompeen-Saanga. We're going a long way away."

The valay, the Paraguayans, pushed the *yaamvalay*, the Bolivians, back toward the west. We heard the explosions constantly behind us.

"We're in a difficult situation," my father said. "I'm worried the Paraguayans are going to catch up with us."

We were spending the night on the road when two Bolivians approached us. "The Paraguayans are getting near. It's not a good idea for you to sleep here." We immediately carried on until we got to Ayvompeen-Saanga, to Fort Muñoz, and stayed there.

The Bolivians invited us to go with them to their country, to take the aeroplane they were carrying their soldiers in. They wanted to take my mother. The woman she had worked for insisted she go with her and work for her in her country. She was an *aveske'*, a leader, among the Bolivians. Even the women were chiefs, the wives of the chiefs.

"Come with us," she said to my mother.

But my mother didn't want to go with her; neither did my father. If they had, I'd be in the Bolivians' country now. My brother didn't agree either.

"I think it's better we go and live with the Nivaclé," he said. "They say there's an Englishman, an *elle*, who lives there." They talked about us getting on a plane and escaping with the Bolivians but my mother didn't want to.

Some of the Enlhet did go with the Bolivian soldiers, among them my uncle, Canuto's father, and others who'd lived in Yaatektama-Yelhem, Fort Arce. They travelled on foot. A lot of Enlhet went with the Bolivians, but none of them ever came back. Perhaps their children are still in that country. We lost them there; they died there. The only one to come back was Canuto.[25]

Account 11: Soldier in the Rearguard
Ramón Ortiz [26]

Life was hard during the war. Some of us were killed, some of us who went to the front. A brother-in-law of mine died like that, killed by a bullet, and two cousins. Bolivians killed them. Things were difficult during the war; we didn't know where to go.

The Paraguayans made me one of their leaders, an apveske'. They gave me a pistol and told me I should learn to be as furious as they were. That was in Haalhama-Teves, Puntarriel. That's where we were during the war. We worked hard there; I worked a lot, as a guard. Every time the train brought new soldiers, a lieutenant and the major ordered us, "Go and meet them! They're always deserting – if one of them runs, don't hesitate to shoot him."

I was prepared to do it because we copied the Paraguayans; we became like them.

Paraguayans, valay, often say that a lot of Paraguayan blood was spilled here in the Chaco. They only talk about Paraguayan blood. But it's not true; a lot of Enlhet died too, a lot of those who were forced to take part in the war against the Bolivians. The Bolivians nearly killed me too. It didn't happen in battle, it was during my work as a guard. Some Bolivian planes flew over Haalhama-Teves and dropped a bomb very near the camp.[27] The bomb left a big crater because the earth isn't very hard there. It almost hit me; I came within a hair's breadth of being killed. Luckily I only ended up covered in earth, like the Paraguayans who were with me. The lieutenant came running.

"Is everyone all right?"

"We're fine, we're alive."

"Good. Thank God."

We didn't know what God was. We just noticed that he said "Thank God." The major came quickly too, on horseback, Mayor Calabozo we called him, "Major Lock-up."

"Are you all right?"

"Yes, we're alive."

"Thank God," he said too. He was relieved.

The planes were still flying overhead.

"What should we do?" asked one of the Paraguayans.

The lieutenant came up to me. "Ramón!" I already had my name by that time. "Where did the chief go?" He was looking for my father.

"He's in the village."

"Run and find him, quickly. He has to help us, he has to kill those planes."

"Okay, I'll see if he can."

I ran off and met my father, who had come running after the bomb went off. "My poor children!"

The Paraguayan came to meet him. "Chief, help us! Kill those planes. Can you do it?"

"I don't know. I'll try."

He stood there with his back to the plane as it approached slowly. It was as if my father was bringing it; normally the planes went a long way away to turn around. We heard a noise above us, *clannng! clannng!* And the plane fell to the ground.

"Wait, don't go yet! It's got bombs inside."

But we could hear somebody shouting inside the plane. "Hallo! We want to become Paraguayans."

"Don't listen to them, that's a rabid dog talking. Shoot him!" And they killed them.

"Shut up, you dog!" said the Paraguayan.

They pulled the bodies out of the plane and dragged them away behind a truck and dumped them a long way off for the vultures to eat. That's what we experienced during the war; it was very hard. Even though I was still very young I developed an anger. I was very strong and moved easily.

I experienced something similar later when the Paraguayans fought against other Paraguayans during the revolution.[28] That time I was given a uniform again.

"Get back into battle!"

I was also given a pistol to carry on my hip.

"If they shoot at you and miss, pay them right back," were my instructions from the Paraguayan chiefs.

My father suffered after he killed the plane. Perhaps the power of his knowledge was not great enough to do it. A week later he became seriously ill and died. My father died. On reflection I think that he did have sufficient power because his grave glowed at night; his power didn't leave him after death. He died in Haalhama-Teves, Puntarriel. That's where we lived during that terrible time. My mother, on the other hand, died of the sickness, the sickness that made the skin fall off you in pieces and killed you so quickly, *nengyetyapma*, smallpox. If the sickness started at eight o'clock you would die at nine. Not one hour would go by before you died because your skin came off in pieces. A lot of Enlhet died from smallpox, an awful lot.

Account 12: The Civilian Population at Puntarriel
Seepe-Pta'heem-Pelhkapok [29]

Today I live in Peesempo'o, but that's not where I lived when I was young. When I was a boy, during the war, I lived in Haalhama-Teves, Puntarriel. I didn't take part in any fighting, I just saw the soldiers as they passed through on their way to the front. I remember it well; I would have been six or seven years old. My mother' brother Ramón Ortiz lived with us, as well as his elder brother Pantaa'e and another uncle of mine. He was the reason why we'd stayed there. The Enlhet all lived together; the Toba-Enlhet had its own group of houses.

Planes used to fly over Haalhama-Teves to drop bombs. Some soldiers kept watch over the camp, standing in a tall *meemong* tree to watch for planes approaching. When they saw one they'd shout and everybody would hide. One of these planes dropped a bomb on Haalhama-Teves. I wasn't nearby when it happened but we heard the explosion. Our parents were able to face up to the planes because they had the power of their knowledge: they could make the plane fall by blowing at it.

I remember Haalhama-Teves very well. I remember how some Paraguayans chased me, they were soldiers on the way to the front. These soldiers looked for women constantly and they used to come to our village. If they came and the Enlhet women didn't run away immediately, they would catch them quickly and throw themselves on top of them. I remember one day in particular like that. I was sitting in a *teves* tree a distance from the houses. Only the women were there; the men had gone out to collect honey. I'd sat in the tree, as children do, to watch what went on round about.

Figure 2.4 • Seepe-Pta'heem-Pelhkapok.

I was in the *teves* tree and in the evening soldiers came. They came from Puerto Casado and went to Kilómetro 160. That was the end of the railway line. Sitting in the tree I heard the train coming that brought the soldiers. When you're a child you don't think much about what might happen. As always, the train stopped in Haalhama-Teves, Puntarriel, and the soldiers got down. Then I realized some of them were hurrying toward me. There were four of them.

"Have they seen me?" I thought. I wasn't right next to the railway line, I was a good distance away. But there were no trees between them and me and they might have noticed me. I saw they were in a hurry and got down quickly from the tree; I jumped and fell. My kidney hurt a lot, but I ran. I ran toward the village and warned my mother and the other women.

"There are some soldiers, they're coming quickly." I ran to the houses and then I kept running to hide in the forest.

"Run!" We fled, my mother too, and went into the forest next to the *yengman*, the clearing.

There was a pregnant woman who couldn't run and she was left alone in the village. The rest ran to get away. When the soldiers arrived they grabbed her and raped her, even though her belly was already very big. They took turns to rape her; that's what they wanted. This woman was the mother of Layve's widow. She was the woman whose husband had been murdered by soldiers some time before. They raped her when she was pregnant. When they had finished with her they left her there. They didn't want to kill her; they were just after women. They heard the noise of the train and realized it was about to leave. They ran to catch it, got on board, and went on their way to Kilómetro 160.

We were in the forest when we heard the noise of the train setting off again for Kilómetro 160. We kept very quiet; when the train had gone my mother spoke.

"It looks like it's gone; the noise has faded. Let's go back to the village."

We went back cautiously and as we approached the grass houses we looked for signs of them, but all the soldiers had gone. Then we saw the pregnant woman. She was sitting there, not moving. They had raped her. She hurt all over because her belly was already very big. All this happened toward the end of the war. It was one of the last trains full of soldiers.

That's what they were like, the valay, the Paraguayan soldiers. They mistreated women. They were constantly looking for women. Even if the women were pregnant they raped them regardless. My uncle, Cacique Mita'i, was responsible for looking after the camp and stopping any Paraguayans that tried to enter; he had a soldier's cap and he wore the same clothes as the soldiers to protect us. But on that particular occasion the men weren't there; they were out collecting honey and didn't realize what was happening. That's how the valay are. If they don't know us they kill us.

SECTION 3
OUTSIDE THE FORTS

... illuminated its martial glory
Paraguayan national anthem

The following accounts are from the point of view of those Enlhet who did not live with the soldiers in the forts or who had left the military encampments.

Account 13: Flight to the Mennonites[30]
Savhongvay' [31]

In Kemha-Maaneng, Lichtenau, in the area that's Colonia Neuland today, there were no Paraguayans. It was only right at the beginning after they'd decided to enter our territory that some of them came with an Enlhet, with the intention of exploring our lands (Savhongvay', in account 3). That was a long time before the Mennonites arrived in the area.[32]

I feel sorry for these lands. They don't really belong to the Paraguayans' country. They're part of Enlhet territory, the true Enlhet. The Paraguayans lived in other lands. At best you could say that the Paraguayans took possession of these lands. But even so, all this belongs to the Enlhet. The Enlhet lived all around here. The Enlhet lived in Cruce de los Pioneros, for example; that land belongs to the Enlhet. At one time, all of this was occupied by the Enlhet; there were no Paraguayans or Mennonites. It's the Paraguayans' fault we left our homes, because they came first. It was only later that the Mennonites arrived. The first Mennonites to come to these lands were the *lengko pangkoo'*, the Mennonites of Loma Plata.[33] The *yaamlengko*, the Filadelfia Mennonites, came later.[34] We were afraid of them; I was afraid of them too when they first arrived. The same thing happened with the Paraguayans: the Enlhet were frightened of them.

The valay, the Paraguayans, ruined the Enlhet's territory. It's true they didn't get as far as Kemha-Maaneng, Lichtenau, only the two who came with an Enlhet did, and they proved not to be dangerous. But later the Enlhet heard news that made them abandon their homeland.

"The Paraguayans and the Bolivians are going to shoot at each other," they said. "Where can we go? People are saying it's going to happen here," they thought.

"How can we avoid it?"

"Let's go to the Mennonites." So we went to where the Filadelfia Mennonites were – it was easy for the Enlhet to move around because they didn't have many things, but when they approached the Mennonites and settled near their villages they had nothing to eat as they didn't have their plantations there. People said that after we left the Paraguayans came to where we'd lived; their road passed nearby.

When the Paraguayans started their war I was a child. We left our area and went to Lhaptaana, Friedensfeld [near Filadelfia] and Kemhaytaava-Amyep, Schönwiese. The Enlhet were afraid of the Paraguayans, who were fighting with the Bolivians. When they saw an Enlhet they didn't treat them well, they just killed them. The Paraguayans didn't interact with us, but the Mennonites did when they arrived. That's why when the war broke out the Enlhet decided to approach them. But it didn't work out well because when the soldiers saw them among the Mennonites they still killed them. That's the reason why the Enlhet fled again and retreated into the forest. That retreat to the forest was like a second flight. All the Enlhet fled; none stayed with the Mennonites.

Account 14: Like Jesus[35]
Savhongvay' [36]

I was with my grandfather when we met some valay, some Paraguayan soldiers that were on their way back from fighting against the *yaamvalay*, the Bolivians. They stopped in the *lengko* – the Mennonite's – village. There they saw my grandfather. They called him a Bolivian and then they murdered him. I'm talking about the father of Alhkahayaam'; she was from Matna-Maaleng, Schönbrunn [near Filadelfia].

The Paraguayans wanted eggs and they went into the house of the Mennonite that my grandfather was cutting firewood for.[37] I was with him and I said, "The Paraguayans are coming. Where should we run to?"

We tried to run away quickly, but they were on top of us and they caught my grandfather. The Mennonite didn't defend us; it wouldn't have looked good if he'd defended us. They would have killed him too.

They caught my grandfather and they caught me too, and they took us to a place between Kemhaytaava-Amyep, Schönwiese, and Matna-Maaleng, Schönbrunn. There they stood me at the side of the road and made me watch while they tied my grandfather's hands behind his back. They turned my head toward my grandfather.

"Look at him!"

They pulled him to make him move. I had to watch everything they did. Another of them pushed him from behind because he refused to move. He knew they were going to kill him. I had to witness them hang him between two *nempeena* trees. They tied one piece of rope around one of his hands and another around the other and hung him between the two trees. They hung him very high; his arms were open wide, like Jesus on the cross. They left him hanging there for a good while. He cried out; I imagine he must have been in a lot of pain. But his cries couldn't save him.

Meanwhile the soldiers went to tell their chief, their lieutenant, who was in the Mennonite's house.

"What shall we do with him?" they asked.

"Just kill him."

They went back and shot him. *Ba-ba-bang!* the shots rang out. They shot him in the chest, and he died. I had to watch it all, watch them execute my grandfather. I was terrified. "Grandfather is dead," I thought, paralyzed.

It was true, he was dead. But I was alive. They'd called me "son of a Bolivian" like him and they'd caught me. But they didn't murder me. They just made me stand next to the trees and watch. I must've been the age of my grandson listening to me here. I'd have been seven years old. Soldiers don't kill children that age.

They didn't murder me. Instead, the lieutenant became my father. "We're taking him with us," he ordered. He was a good person, he never lost control of himself. "I'm going to adopt him," he probably said. "Put him in the truck."

They threw me in the vehicle and put some dry biscuits next to me. They pointed to them and said, "Eat!"

Another soldier came. "Here's some sugar. Eat it with the biscuits," he must have said.

I didn't eat any of it.

▪▪▪

They put me in a truck that took me away. I thought they'd taken me to Asunción but I realized later I was in Ya'tempehek, Fort Trébol, to the east of Filadelfia.[38] I lived there among the valay, the soldiers. There were a lot of them. The Paraguayans had been living for a long time in Ya'tempehek. The first person to build a house there was called Patrón Carapé. He also dug a well. Other Paraguayans replaced him, large numbers of Paraguayans who occupied the whole edge of the forest toward Filadelfia. They cut a big open space in the forest and cleared it completely, with their hospital in the middle. I used to see how they brought people who'd been hit by bullets.

▪▪▪

I nearly went to the front to shoot at the Bolivians. If I'd been a little bigger I would have become a soldier.

"You're going to the front too," my lieutenant often said. I took this lieutenant to be my father. I've forgotten his name, but he was a good-tempered man. "You're going to shoot Bolivians too. We'll pay them back for everything," he said.

A lot of Paraguayans died, killed in the fighting.

The lieutenant used to take me with him when he went to the Mennonite villages. He put me in the truck they drove to collect bread to feed the soldiers.[39] When we got to the villages and the Mennonites saw the vehicle, the women would bring out their bread until the truck was full. That's how it was. I sat in the back of the truck and the Paraguayan gave me orders.

"You get the bread!"

"*Heey*', okay."

A rifle always went with us; the Paraguayans didn't travel naked. They always had a gun with them.

One day a Bolivian aeroplane came. The Paraguayans panicked. "The Bolivians are coming!" they shouted.

They picked up their guns and we ran to the trenches they'd dug around their encampment. I could have died that day. I'm lucky to be alive; the Bolivians very nearly killed me. But I never went to the place where they lived and I never saw a *yaamvalay*, a Bolivian, here in this area. I only met the valay, the Paraguayans, when they came into our land, into Enlhet territory.

▪▪▪

I was maybe eleven years old when the Paraguayans took me. I nearly had to shoot at Bolivians, very nearly. But I escaped, and I ran because I was scared they'd send me into battle against their enemies. I was afraid of dying at their hands and I fled. It scared me when they said, "You're going to be using a rifle."

I was given a rifle to use, a plate, a knife, all of a soldier's equipment, including boots. They cut my hair – that's how I got the nickname Looma-Apyeseem, Angry Hair.

"You're going to fire a gun," the Paraguayans said. "You're nearly twelve now."

"*Heey'*, okay." I accepted it. "*Heey'*, okay. Alright." I was ready to shoot at the Bolivians.

"We're going to go here, and there. The Bolivians are retreating and we're going to chase them." That's how they talked.

"*Heey'*, okay." But really, I was scared. Because I knew no one came out of those battles alive. I was going to die. So I escaped.

▪▪▪

I completely stopped using the Paraguayans' language, Guaraní, when I came across a Paraguayan. I was afraid they might recognize me. I just gestured, "I don't understand."

Nowadays, I occasionally use their language when I need to speak to one of them. It's only now that I sometimes speak a little in Guaraní. They love it when you speak to them in Guaraní!

Account 15: They Took the Boys
Metyeeyam' [40]

During the war the valay, the soldiers, used to come to where we lived to gather up the men and force them to go into their battles with them. They looked for young men. With that intention they came to Hemaklha-Maaset, to Neuanlage, and took away some of the boys, I think five. One of them was Yatka – his father was from there. They didn't take me because I was too young to be of interest to them. They took the five of them to Pongkat-Napoolheng, Campo Esperanza, with the intention of then moving them to Fort Boquerón, where they had their battle. As they always did when they captured an Enlhet, they gave them uniforms, nice clothes, and a poncho, a blanket as well. The rifle, though, would be given to them only on arrival at Nahangvet, Fort Isla Po'i. But the boys I'm talking about never got to Nahangvet: they escaped while the soldiers were asleep and by dawn they were back in Hemaklha-Maaset.

The soldiers took young men. Sometimes, though, they didn't get what they wanted from them because the Enlhet had their *apyo-bolhma'*, their wise men, who made them come back.

"Let them take them," the old men would say. "They'll be back soon."

But of the five, only four escaped. The fifth tried to hold the others back. "Don't go. I feel weak. I've got the flu." He was shivering. But the others didn't listen and they ran. He tried again to persuade his companions. "They're not trying to kill us. They just want to send us to Boquerón, that's all."

He tried to persuade them to change their minds, but they wouldn't listen and left him. They survived. The sick boy was not so lucky. When he ran, the Paraguayans shot him, and he died. This happened in Lhapo'o, to the south of Campo Esperanza. The Paraguayans had an encampment there. They had their encampments everywhere.

Account 16: Escape
Kenteem [41]

When the Mennonites had been in Filadelfia for two years the situation became much worse because the Paraguayans went to war and shot at other people like themselves. That was a very bad time for us.

Some Mennonites even fled their colony for fear they would die. They went back to the places they were from, but we're from here.

At first the Paraguayan soldiers had one fort at Alhvat, a place they called Guajhó. It was in a *yengman*, a low-lying clearing, a big *yengman*, and there were eels there. Alhvat is beyond Kemhaytaava-Amyep, Schönwiese [west of Filadelfia]. It was their first fort. They built it before the war and spread out from there. From there their road went west, where they had other forts.

Before the war the Enlhet used to go to the fort at Guajhó. At that time the valay, the Paraguayans, hadn't killed a single Enlhet. Instead, they shared food with them and the Enlhet could get things like biscuits and dried maize from them, for example. The Paraguayans are known as wild and uncontrolled, as people who killed us, but they did share their food freely. When they started their fight with the *yaam-valay*, the Bolivians, the Enlhet stopped going to Guajhó. By that time when the soldiers saw an Enlhet they wouldn't treat them well anymore. During the time of the visits to Guajhó, though, they weren't furious yet. It was because of the war that they lost all control.

When the war started, a large number of soldiers arrived. They'd made roads that ran across the open country; the roads kept to the open country and the soldiers had their encampments all along the road to the west.[42] One was to the eastern side of Yepooma, Friedensruh; the soldiers set up camp where the big *maaset* tree was. They had another on the other side of Yepooma, then the one in Alhvat, Guajhó, another in Kenma-Navsa and another in Nanaava'a,[43] all of them next to the road. Then there was another one in Maklha-Kenhek. I don't know the names they gave to these places. The camps followed the road all the way to Alkeete' and Havko'; they built Fort Toledo on those two places. Another military road passed through Vayna', Wüstenfelde, and also came out at Fort Toledo.

The valay had another camp near Lhamhapmek, Rosenort. They used to stay there for a short time and then carry on the journey. It was a stopping point on their way to battle. It sometimes happened that they would go into the forest at night to where the Enlhet lived, to kill them. But they didn't manage to kill anyone because the people all ran and spread out. The Enlhet moved very easily through the deep forest. They didn't get lost even at night; they always found each other again.

They whistled with their hands and you could hear it from a long distance away. That's how they met up again and they could be sure that no one had got lost. The women, who ran for fear of the Paraguayans, whistled like that to find each other again after the Paraguayans had separated them during the night. One would ask, "Are we all here?"

"Yes," said another.

None of the women died; none of the men were killed.

"We're alive," a third would reply.

That's how they found each other again. They never abandoned anyone; they wanted to make absolutely sure that everyone met up again. Once I was left alone during a night-time escape, but the soldiers didn't find me. When I heard the whistles I went in the direction they were coming from.

The Paraguayans had Enlhet experts who acted as their guides. One of these apveske', their chiefs, was called Maciel. He knew exactly what to do. He would go to where the Enlhet were living in the forest and warn them.

"You have to leave," he would tell them. "The Paraguayans want me to show them this place."

And the Enlhet would leave immediately, and that's how they survived and no one died, because another Enlhet had warned them that the soldiers were coming. So when he guided them to the place later there was no one there; they'd all run away.

My stepfather Aateng'ay' – the Paraguayans called him Sargento – also took soldiers to where the Enlhet houses were but secretly let the Enlhet know in advance. He would go to the village and say, "Run! The soldiers are coming through here." And they would run, because the soldiers used to kill them. They lived in constant fear. They were very strict with children who cried all the time; in some cases they even considered killing a child who wouldn't be quiet. So we retreated to Kaa'aok in the north where my uncle lived. The soldiers usually didn't go too far into the forest; they generally stayed where the Mennonites were. Other Enlhet retreated to the area of Apva'at north of Teniente Montanía, where there's nothing but forest. There's a deep riverbed there with lagoons that never dry out. People from different places gathered around these lagoons; they came to the water that there's so much of in the region. They weren't hungry either because in that area there was a lot to eat: honey, fruit, meat. They stayed for a year or maybe two years, and when the end of the war finally came they went back to their homes further south.

▪▪▪

Among my own people nobody died. But in Kemhaytaava-Amyep, Schönwiese, an Enlhet man died. Another died in Kemha-Paatelh, Kleefeld. They were killed by Paraguayans. They'd gone to the Mennonites and the soldiers found them there. In Kemhaytaava-Amyep, they murdered the father of Selhta'ay'. The place is to the west of Matna-Maaleng, Friedensruh, and the soldiers' road passed through there. So when he went to the Mennonites he met soldiers on their way back from the fighting. He ran away but it was too late. The soldiers saw him and shot at him; he was some distance away but they hit him. He still managed to crawl into a Mennonite sorghum field. He died in the field and nobody realized he'd been murdered. But the owner of the sorghum, a Mennonite, saw the vultures – those birds that eat dead meat – circling over his field and flying down all the time.

"What's that?" he wondered. "I'll go and see what it is that's died." He went and he found the body of the Enlhet. The other Enlhet realized that the dead man was the father of Selhta'ay', because he'd been missing and they'd had no news of him. He'd been left in the middle of the sorghum.

▪▪▪

Some Enlhet went into battle alongside the Paraguayan soldiers. My stepfather, Aateng'ay', fought against the Bolivians, but I didn't hear him talk much about those days. He had a lump on his head. He said the Bolivians shot him when he was fighting them and the bullet lodged inside. So Aateng'ay' didn't make it to the end of the war. He left the war before the end, unlike his younger brother, whose name was Panso. Panso stayed until the end of the war and came out safe and sound. He died a few years later when he was living with the Enlhet again. Panso is one of the winners. The Paraguayans often call themselves winners. I don't know why. If the Paraguayans had gone into battle alone they would have lost. They came out winners because of the Enlhet. The Enlhet are strong and they gave them help. The Paraguayans didn't go into battle alone. The Enlhet were with them!

Account 17: I Still Cry Today
Kaymaap-Takhaalhet and Kam'aatkok Ketsek [44]

Kaymaap-Takhaalhet
I know about the war. That shows how old I am. We lived in a state of anxiety; we were afraid of the Paraguayans, who were at war. Before, we lived peacefully in Nepolhnga'a, Heimstädt today, near Neu-Halbstadt. We had no contact with the Paraguayans, although we found out later that they'd been nearby in Yelhvayvoo-Pyettek, Fort Boquerón. The Bolivians were in Yaatektama-Yelhem, Fort Arce. They were in Savaayaamelket, Fort Yucra, too, and in Maaset-Yengman near Yucra, and Ya'kal'a, Fort Platanillos. From there and from Yaatektama-Yelhem, Arce, they came this way to found Nataayet, Fort Fernández. I don't remember these military movements myself but I learned about them when my father talked about the war.

We lived well in our home places, but then the war started and aeroplanes would fly over Nepolhnga'a. That's when we decided to leave the area. I couldn't tell you how old I was; I suppose a similar age to these children around here. At that age you're old enough to run. I would have been about ten, because I was able to run away on my own when we came across a group of Paraguayans. That encounter left us frightened and confused; several of us were killed. I wonder what would have happened if they'd caught me; I was only a child.

We left the region, left behind all the crops my father had sown and went to Nataayet, Fort Fernández, which was one of the Bolivians' forts. We wanted to live near them so they could give us shelter and protection; at least I think that was the reason – I didn't understand those things; I was still a boy. In any case our attempt to approach the Bolivians didn't work. We went there after the fighting and they had already abandoned the place, they'd run away themselves. Now the Paraguayans were in the area and we crossed paths with some

Figure 2.5 • Kaymaap-Takhaalhet.

of them. That day they murdered my grandfathers; they killed three of
the older people. We should have stayed in our homes; we'd have been
safe there. But we didn't know that.

Kam'aatkok Ketsek
When the fighting was over, our ancestors decided to go to the Bolivians and stay with them. The Bolivians weren't dangerous; they didn't

act against the Enlhet. The Paraguayans, on the other hand, the *sopkelloom* [literally, "furious, uncontrolled thing"] were terrifying; they killed us on sight.

"Let's go to the Bolivians' fort," they decided, those who are no longer with us.

But the Bolivians had fled. We got there too late; when we got to Nataayet, Fort Fernández, there was no one there. Even the Enlhet that lived there had left and gone back to their own homes. We set out toward Na'teem-Saanga, southeast of the fort, to try to find them, and took our goats with us. But on the way something terrible happened. We met death. Our Elders were killed. Paskomkom-Amyep, Laguna Verde, is the name of the place where they met their death.

Kaymaap-Takhaalhet

We wanted to go and live with the Bolivians but they had left. They'd gone back to their homes; they'd run away. So we left Nataayet, Fort Fernández, where there was no one now, and headed for Paskomkom-Amyep, Laguna Verde. We followed the road the soldiers had taken to battle. In one place we found a lot of used cartridges they'd left behind next to a big tree at the edge of the forest. When we went out into the open country at Paskomkom-Amyep we ran into some Paraguayans with livestock. They were on horseback. We were travelling on foot; we'd left our horses behind when we first ran from our home and went into the forest to hide. We only kept our goats with us.

So we came out into open country at Paskomkom-Amyep, which is on the way to Na'teem-Saanga, and we heard the Paraguayans shouting. They were soldiers herding livestock on their way back from the lagoon that's in that area. When they saw us they rode out ahead of their livestock and galloped to where we were. One part of our group fled immediately; my cousin Metaykaok'ay' ran into the forest.

Kam'aatkok Ketsek

I witnessed them murder our grandfathers. They died when the war was almost over, when the fighting had already stopped. We thought the soldiers had gone away, but we came across some Paraguayan, *sopkelloom*, that were still in the area. At first we thought they were Bolivians. One of them galloped over to us.

"There's a Bolivian horseman coming," our dead ancestors said.

I remember that. My cousin sent my brother Metaykaok'ay'. "Metaykaok'ay', go and ask him for water," she said. We were thirsty and the lagoon we were heading for was still a long way off. "Metaykaok'ay', go and talk to the Bolivian!"

So my brother went out to meet the soldier. The soldier stopped his horse and my brother asked him for water. But the valay, the Paraguayan, just shook his head; he didn't answer. Instead he asked, "Where are you going?"

"We're going to an Enlhet village," my brother replied.

The Paraguayan immediately turned and galloped at full speed back to his companions. "They're not Bolivians, they're *sopkelloom*! They're Paraguayans!"

We were thirsty.

"Run!" said the Elders who would soon be murdered. "Run!"

There wasn't much time; the Paraguayans came back at a gallop. We ran into the forest, me and my grandmother. It was me that took her to hide in the forest. "Grandma, into the forest! The soldiers are coming!"

I made her go into the forest. "Run, Grandma! Leave the goats where they are!" And so my grandmother was saved from being murdered.

"Hurry Grandma!" We went into the forest, but we could still hear the shots behind us. My grandmother picked me up.

"This way," she said. "Don't cry!"

We escaped into the forest. I might have been the age of this girl next to me here. She'd remember it too. I saw them shoot my grandfathers. We women escaped, but three of our Elders were shot.

When Kaymaap-Takhaalhet's father saw the Paraguayans galloping back toward us he shouted, "Run! The Paraguayans are going to shoot."

The boys started running straight away, my cousin Kaymaap-Takhaalhet, my brother Metaykaok'ay', another of my brothers, and my other cousin. Bullets flew past them as they ran. Each time a gun went off they fell to the ground and when they got to the forest they threw themselves straight into the thorns of the *bang* plants. My stepmother, Kaymaap-Takhaalhet's mother, ran toward the forest too, with one of my cousins. They shot my stepmother with a bullet that hit her above the chest. The other woman, my cousin, wasn't wounded. But my stepmother didn't die either because she was very strong. We were already deep in the forest when that happened.

Kaymaap-Takhaalhet

I didn't run immediately. My father and uncle didn't run straight away either, and neither did my mother or the Elders, my two grandfathers. But then they shot at my father and he ran. One of the Paraguayans fired at him from a very short distance. His rifle went off and I thought he'd killed him but he missed. So another of the valay pointed his rifle at my father and when it went off I thought again that he'd shot him, but he missed because my father had thrown himself on the ground. The Paraguayan had to reload his gun and my father stood up and ran. When he was more or less the distance from here to that *akpehek* tree over there, the Paraguayan fired again. Again I thought he'd killed my father when I heard the gun go off. But no. Again the Paraguayan had to reload the rifle, and at that moment my father escaped into the forest and they stopped shooting at him. I saw him running.

Then they fired at my uncle and hit him in the chest. The bullet entered his chest and came out of his back. But he still ran and escaped. We found out later that he didn't die at that moment. He was with the group for three more days. My father wasn't hurt but my uncle was breathing through the hole in his back.

I was still with my mother, my aunt, and my grandfathers. I saw my mother run and escape into the forest. The Paraguayans kept firing at her as she ran with her big bag on her back. One of the bullets hit the water gourd she was carrying in it, ricocheted off and destroyed her armpit. The bullet made a cloud of dust and I thought that it had smashed her whole body. But it only tore her armpit.

I lost sight of my mother and stuck with my grandfathers, with the goats by our side. I was with two adults, my grandfathers; I'd been left alone with them. At that moment a Paraguayan fired at one of them but his rifle didn't go off and they got into a hand-to-hand fight. The Paraguayan tried to hit him in the chest with a hatchet, but my grandfather blocked the blow and was about to take the hatchet off him – the

Paraguayan's hands weren't very strong – but at that moment one of the others shot at him from a distance. The bullet hit him in the face. He fell to the ground and didn't move.

My other grandfather was left alone, and me with him. He was the soldiers' target now. Another bullet came from a long way away and I saw him fall to the ground. I realized I was alone now and I ran. The goats – there were a lot of them – went with me and I ran into the forest; only the goats followed me. But it was easy to tell which way I was going because the animals bleated after me, and sure enough two of the horseman galloped in my direction. I looked around and saw a very big *peben* tree. I hid behind it. When they had gone past I went into a grove of *vaalha'a yetkook*. The goats followed me and bleated after me in the forest. When the Paraguayans heard them they turned their horses around; I guess they wanted to take the goats with them. They didn't find me because I'd gone a long way into the forest. I could hear the noise of horses' hooves on the sand in the clearings in the forest and I went further in. Then I didn't hear the horsemen anymore; I think they took the goats back out to the open country.

Kam'aatkok Ketsek

The Paraguayans turned their attention to the Elders. They murdered my two grandfathers. First they got into a hand-to-hand fight with them; they tried to hit them with a hatchet from their horses, and then they shot them. My grandfathers were strong; they were *apyo-bolhma'*, wise men, old men with knowledge. They made the bullets fall before they reached them. But when the invisible servants had no more power to defend them, their own powers failed and they died. The Elders were murdered, but we escaped.

We heard another rifle shot and we heard my uncle cry out as the bullet hit him. They shot him in the chest and the bullet came out of his back. But he didn't die immediately. He met up with us later in the place where we stopped to rest for a while in the forest. He was covered in blood and could hardly walk. They murdered us. They shot our Elders.

After witnessing the murders we hid deep in the forest, my grandmother and me. "Grandma, there's a *popom* nest, honey wasps," I said. The nest hung very low and I wanted to eat the honey the wasps made.

"Leave it, the Paraguayans will find us," my grandmother replied.

We kept running and slept deep in the forest. Even the goats were quiet; they ran away without making any noise.

There, in the middle of the forest, we found my father. We heard him calling. "*Sa'kok*! daughter! Are you there?"

So we met up again and escaped together. My father carried me on his shoulders. He'd protected us with the power of his knowledge so that the bullets didn't hit us. I knew my father, but I never knew my mother. The smallpox had taken her a long time before.

Kaymaap-Takhaalhet

Later, I found my mother's blood. I followed the trail of her blood; I followed the blood. As I advanced very cautiously I found my mother sitting under a *pang*, a cactus tree. "You're alive!" she said.

"Yes, but I've been through a nightmare. I was chased by men on horseback," I told her.

"I'm worse," she said. "Look at this." She showed me her underarm, torn apart by a bullet. The woman with her wasn't hurt, though.

We carried on our flight. We slept in the forest and when dawn came we heard the people who had run first whistling with their hands. We found them where they had spent the night. I found my father – he was alive! I saw my uncle there too, shot by a bullet in the chest. He could barely breathe; his breath came out of his back. We still had some of the goats with us when we found the others.

The next day we travelled on. We kept ourselves hidden in the forest and stayed in the clearings; we abandoned the plan of going to Na'teem-Saanga. After three days my uncle died. My aunt was alone now. He had stayed with us for three days, breathing through the hole in his back.

Kam'aatkok Ketsek

The place where they murdered my grandfathers is called Paskomkom-Amyep, Laguna Verde. That's where the Paraguayans killed our Elders. After that we stayed in the forest; we didn't go out into open country. There in the forest the Enlhet themselves killed a baby, the brother of Ay'ay, because he cried all night.

"He's putting us in danger. The Paraguayans might find us because of the noise he's making," was the reasoning of the people who'd survived the massacre. We were absolutely terrified. Constant fear overcame any compassion.[45]

"Uncle, kill this baby," said the child's mother. So they killed him; he was about a year old. One of the older people, my grandfather Kentem'-Pa'tek, hit him with his hatchet. The child was a half-orphan. His father was dead; smallpox had taken him.

Kaymaap-Takhaalhet
For a long time we stayed in the forest and in the small clearings inside it. There was no water to drink; instead we drank from the *pang*, the cactus tree, by scraping off the bark. At first we didn't leave the deep forest, but after a time we turned and headed for our own homeland and reached Kaymaan, southeast of Neuland. We came across Paraguayan soldiers again. One of the Enlhet in the front saw them.

"Paraguayans!" he said. But the warning came too late; they were already on top of us. They shot at us again, but we all managed to get away with our lives. As we fled I ran into someone else and fell into a thorny *bang* plant. I got up again and ran. I ran with the rifles firing behind me.

We went back into the forest again. This time we stayed in the area southwest of Lajkat, the place the Mennonites call Sandhorst. There were no Paraguayans there but still, we moved very cautiously as we went about our daily tasks, my father collecting honey, my mother preparing the fruit of the *maaneng*. It was a long time until we went back to Nepolhnga'a, Heimstädt. By that time the Paraguayans, the soldiers, the war, had gone away. There were no more soldiers in our region and we settled down again. We formed a large group again; we moved around in peace, recovered our good life. But to this day I still feel like crying when I talk about what happened. Many of our older people cried when they talked about the war.

Account 18: Fear
Kooneng-Pa'at [46]

I do remember a little about the war. I remember going with my father when he used to go to Ya'tempehek, Fort Trébol. He would carry me on his shoulders to the Paraguayans' fort to get food for me; the fort was near Toopak-Amyep, Gnadenheim, where we lived. The soldiers had invited him to get clothes there. Many times the Paraguayans' behaviour put my father in danger. But he had the power of his knowledge to keep him safe, and the valay didn't kill him. Besides, he was an apveske', a person with authority, and had the protection of the Paraguayan.

There were a lot of people in the encampment, really a lot of people. Everywhere was white with people and white with the corpses they brought. They must have buried them later. The Bolivians killed nearly all the Paraguayans; they almost wiped them out completely. In the battles they used cannons that made a very loud noise. Even though the battlefield was quite a long way away we could hear the cannons fire, they were like thunder. It was a time of a lot of fear. When the soldiers came back from fighting they would come to Ya'tempehek, to the fort, to drink water and eat. They were tired, but they would go back to the battle soon after. By that time very few Enlhet were left alive. The smallpox had killed them. One of its victims was my mother.

■■■

Later the soldiers came to Toopak-Amyep, Gnadenheim, to get sweet potatoes from the Mennonites, and watermelons and sorghum. By that time, though, when they came to the Mennonites, they didn't share their food with us anymore; they were furious and tried to kill us. They would find us sometimes around the Mennonites' village and when they saw us they called us Bolivians to insult us.

"Hey! Bolivian, Bolivian!" they shouted and made signs with their hands.

The soldiers used to kill us. They didn't treat us well. They shot at the Enlhet. They killed them without a second thought. We didn't know where to go. So we retreated into the forest, to Vellejey, Wiesenfeld.

We didn't move; we were afraid of the Paraguayans. In Toopak-Amyep their trucks were everywhere, everywhere was green with vehicles. Those people killed us, they weren't our people. You remember there was no water during the war,[47] and so the Enlhet women had no choice but to go and fetch water from the Mennonites' well. They went at midday when the Paraguayans slept their siesta. They came out of the forest, very frightened that the Paraguayans might catch them. The gourds they used for carrying water made a lot of noise as they approached the well running in fright. They didn't have buckets; the containers they used were made from the trunk of a young *naamok*, the bottle tree, tied around with string made from *tamam'a* fibres. They took them to use as buckets to the Mennonites' well. They would pull out the water quickly; they were terrified the Paraguayans might appear on the road. They warned each other. "The trucks are over there on the road." When the women had filled the gourds they ran back, and they were very relieved to reach the forest.

▪▪▪

We were hungry during the war because the Enlhet were afraid to move around. Even though my father was an apveske', a person with special authority, and he had the protection of the Paraguayan apveske', we didn't go to Ya'tempehek, Fort Trébol, anymore. We had no plantations of crops anymore either; it was only after the war that we were able to plant again. I'd say you could compare that time with today; we live with almost nothing again.

We were hungry, and the Mennonites didn't share their food with us; they kept it for themselves. The women were very afraid but they were driven by hunger to the Mennonites' village. Hunger made them take rope made from *tamam'a* to the Mennonites. The Mennonites would give us stale bread in exchange, or they would trade sweet potato peelings for it. The women didn't refuse the potato peelings they were offered in exchange for their *tamam'a* rope.

We were hungry. It was hard to get food. The valay, the Paraguayans, were furious and the women couldn't even prepare *kentem'* to eat. You had to burn off the green leaves of the *kentem'* plant on the fire to eat the heart, but they didn't want to do that because they were afraid the Paraguayans would see the smoke. So they cut off the leaves and buried the stem under the hot ashes to cook it, but you can't cook a large enough amount like that.

The Enlhet made sure they weren't seen; they lay low in the forest. They were very frightened; they were afraid the Paraguayans would kill them at any time. They didn't eat honey because the Paraguayans might hear the axe when they opened a hive in the trunk of a tree. "The Paraguayans might follow the sound of the axe," they said.

They couldn't eat anything in the forest because of the Paraguayans' war. If they saw us the Paraguayans would kill us immediately. They're not our people, they're not neighbours. When they saw us they would shout, "Bolivian, Bolivian!"

They called us Bolivians. They grabbed children too; they put them in their trucks and took them away. I'm scared of Paraguayans to this day. Because they killed Enlhet. They murdered an Enlhet who was taking rope to the Mennonites, and after that the Enlhet retreated even further. A bullet took off the ear of another Enlhet, Haanmon's father; he was lucky not to die. I remember these things happening. That shows how old I am.

SECTION 4
PARALLEL EVENTS: THE SMALLPOX EPIDEMIC

The right of Indigenous peoples to preserve and exercise their ethnic identity within their habitat is recognized and guaranteed.
National Constitution of Paraguay, Article 63

At this point it is necessary to discuss an event that took place in parallel to the Chaco War and was as much a determining factor for the future of the Enlhet as was the war itself. This event was the traumatic smallpox epidemic of the summer of 1932–33 (Anonymous 1933; M. Friesen 1997, 306; 2016, 250). In a few short months, it took the lives of over half of the population.

Account 19: The People Fled
Yamasma'ay' [48]

After the war, the great sickness came; the smallpox epidemic. We called it *nengelyeetapaykam'* [literally, "we break"].[49] It started in a battlefield in the area of Teena'avhat [the speaker is referring to the battle of Toledo]. Later it arrived where my father lived; it arrived in Teejela'. When it fell on our houses, it left a bright streak across the sky like a meteor and soon the women and the men started falling sick. First they got big spots on their skin and then the skin broke into pieces. I was infected too but I survived; the spots on my skin stayed small. The sickness wiped out the Enlhet; it wiped out entire villages. Our people died everywhere; a lot of people died. People fled when the sickness appeared; they tried to take refuge in the area where the Mennonites were. We went there too, and over time we stopped going to Teejela'; it was as though the virus chased us out of there.

Account 20: Vaccination
Malhkee·tko-Ngkoyoy' [50]

The Enlhet came to the conclusion that it had been the Bolivians themselves who had spread the smallpox. They argued that the Bolivians had been able to protect their own people through vaccination. The Bolivians were vaccinated.

"A Bolivian said to me, 'There's a sickness coming,'" my brother warned us. "The doctor said, 'There's going to be a serious sickness.'"

They protected us too and they vaccinated us. They gathered together the Enlhet who lived with them; I was very small, I would've been about so high, up to my hand. "Go to the hospital; they'll vaccinate you," a Bolivian ordered us.

That was their plan: they wanted to spread the disease. "This is going to be a very serious sickness," they said. People said that it was the Bolivians who started the smallpox. It happened after the fighting; it was during that time that the great sickness appeared.

At Loom-Popyet, Fort Alihuatá, there was a hospital.

"Tell your people," they said to my brother. "They must get together and come to the hospital. We're going to vaccinate them because a serious disease is coming." So we went and they vaccinated us. I was still small.

"I'm going to give you an injection," the Bolivian said to me. "It's to protect you against the sickness." The Bolivians vaccinated all of us who lived with them. They didn't use needles. Instead they used a small blade, a knife; they used it to cut the skin on your wrist. They lifted up a little piece of skin, put some powder underneath, and closed it again with liquid. We thought it was the juice of the sickness. I didn't want to let them touch me, the way children are, but in the end they stuck the little piece of skin back down on my arm. I've still got the scar. It must have been the right cure for the sickness; that's why we survived.

■■■

We witnessed the moment when the sickness arrived. It happened in Vaetke-Ngkennavo', south of Paratodo. We'd gone to visit my father's relatives. While we were there people started to get sick and die. I was near the sick people, I went over to where they were lying. I was just a little girl so I didn't think about what I was doing; I played with the infected children. I felt sorry for them when I saw how their skin fell

Figure 2.6 ▪ "We fled back to Loom-Popyet." When the Enlhet moved from one place to another, the women carried their belongings on their backs in large bags made from *tamam'a* fibres.

off and nobody could do anything to save them. When my mother found out where I'd been she was startled. "*Sa'kok*, daughter! Don't go near them!" she shouted.

Even though I was with the sick children I wasn't infected. My father didn't catch the sickness, and my mother wasn't infected either, or my brother, because we had the Bolivians' vaccination in our arms. That's why we survived in spite of having mixed with the sick. It was horrible to see them; no one was saved. There would be many more Enlhet today if the sickness hadn't killed them.

People around us were dying and we fled back to Loom-Popyet, Fort Alihuatá. The Bolivians were still there; it wasn't until later on that the Paraguayans would push them out (see account 10). When we arrived the first thing they did was to ask us, "Are you hungry?"

"Yes, we're hungry."

"What did you see where you've come from? Did you come into contact with the sickness?" My brother acted as translator; they'd made him an apveske', a leader for them.

"Yes, we were in contact with the sickness. There are no people left in the whole region," he told the Bolivians.

The Bolivians' doctor, after he'd scanned us with his machine, realized that we were about to become infected. "Right," he said, "I need to give you some more medicine." This time he gave us pills. There were pills too against the sickness. We survived.

Account 21: More and More People Died
Haakok Maaset [51]

First there was a battle at Yelhvayvoo-Pyettek, Fort Boquerón. Then the soldiers left the area. Behind them, the Enlhet lands were left stripped of everything. Soon after, the sickness appeared. It was the soldiers' blood, people said. We'd been to visit the *lengko pangkoo'*, the Mennonites of Colonia Menno, and on the way back we stayed in Yaameklhenaamok, to the north of Ya'alve-Saanga. There was food there, the fruit of the *yaayet* tree. But during our absence from Kemha-Paapeyav – which is inside what is now Ya'alve-Saanga – the sickness had appeared without us knowing. So we travelled on toward Kemha-Paapeyav. On the way through Lheknemesma we came across a small hole dug in the path. In it someone had put some *aktam* and *tamsava'* leaves. These small holes were the way the Enlhet communicated over long distances, and my grandfather understood that what we were looking at meant a grave.

"The sickness has arrived here," he said. "Look at this hole."

We were very alarmed. "Let's go back!" We went back to Yaameklhenaamok and we ate the fruit of the *yaayet* tree again. While we were there the wise men used the power of their knowledge to understand the situation.

"We see the sickness. It makes smoke that is coming towards us," they declared. They explained that the sickness looked like smoke as it approached. The wise men can see these things using their knowledge. Then they sang through the night.

In the early morning the sickness attacked my elder sister. She was the first victim. We saw the skin on her stomach turn red, very red.

"Does it hurt?"

"Yes, it hurts."

Then her stomach turned black and before long she died. She died after a very short time. I think her death took less than an hour to come. When she died we ran; we abandoned her without burying her. We retreated into the forest beyond Yaameklhenaamok. There another woman got sick. Again, she died immediately. And so it went on; somebody would die and we fled. We went further and further away, running from the sickness.

We fled because we wanted to escape the sickness. We didn't realize that it had appeared everywhere. We ran from the sickness but it always found us again. The Enlhet died; they died on the journey. They were able to walk a hundred metres and then they lay down and died. They died as they walked; that's usually how it was. There was nobody left to bury them; the vultures must have eaten them. The terror people had of the sickness made them behave like that. Our custom was to bury the dead, but they were afraid of this sickness that made your body turn black. The disease is called nengyetyapma, smallpox. First, small lumps come out on your skin and the skin turns red. And then abscesses appear and the skin turns black. Then the person dies. But if the lumps are big the person will survive. Some survived. This terror began when the Paraguayans were fighting in our country and stripped it of everything. The Enlhet were left with nothing, and then the sickness came. This sickness was caused by the blood of the Paraguayans, people said. That's what the Mennonites used to say.

My father didn't get sick: he'd washed with the fibres of the *aktam* tree. I'd washed with the juice of the same fibres too. My father also burned the leaves of the *aktam* and the *tamsava'* plant, and we stood in the smoke; that's why we didn't get infected. But other Enlhet died on the journey. They died continually, one, then another. We fled and didn't stop until we reached the place where the Mennonites lived. There we joined up with other Enlhet and formed a big group with them, a group of sick people; five died in Nanaavhak, Blumengart. We carried on running until we got to what's now the Rodeo Tréhol, near

Loma Plata. We stayed in the *yengman,* the open space they use today for parking cars, near a watering place in the forest. We only stayed there for a very short time, because soon another person died and we continued our flight. And that's how it was to go on until there were no more Enlhet left.

In the place where the Rodeo Trébol is today a lot of Enlhet who came from different places met, running from the sickness and frightened. In the end, we formed a group that was very big and quite mixed. My father put up a grass shelter. That night it rained hard but we didn't get wet, unlike a lot of the people who were with us. *Boom!* went the thunder all night long. My father's fire didn't go out, and after a long night, morning came. As the sun came up we heard an Enlhet shout from a way away.

"More dead!"

There were so many! Perhaps thirty people died in a single night. Every time someone died we heard thunder, like you hear after lightning. That night was nearly the end of us.

That was where my mother became infected. Blood came out of her body. She was red with blood; she died because of the blood. She stood up – my father didn't see her because he was collecting firewood – and tried to hold on to the branch of a tree, but she collapsed and fell into the fire. She burnt herself on one side and died afterwards; there was nothing to be done. I remember it; I was there. My mother died in Rodeo Trébol. That's where the sickness caught her, the great sickness.

When my mother died, my father left. "Stay with your uncle," he said to me. He left, and I never saw him again. I don't know what happened to him, whether he died as well. At that time, the sickness hadn't infected him, he was healthy when he left. From that time on I stayed with my grandfather and I was nursed by one of my cousins. I remember my mother's death. She fell in the fire and then my father left us. I never saw my father again; I don't know what became of him. Maybe he died too, of the sickness. But he was healthy when he went away.

My mother died in what would later be called Rodeo Trébol. Today people often think it's the old Fort Trébol, the Paraguayan encampment. That's called Ya'tempehek, though, and it's near Savak'e,

Lichtfelde. The place where my mother died doesn't have a name. There was no Enlhet settlement there, it was just forest. The soldiers built the camp at Ya'tempehek because there was a *yengman*. Before the soldiers, the Mennonites, when they arrived, had camped there. The Paraguayans arrived second; the Mennonites arrived first.

■■■

We continued our flight after my father abandoned us. We kept a certain distance; another man was infected and died soon afterwards. It was always the same. We came out to a small clearing, and another person died there. Before he died he went mad and everybody was afraid of him. He ran around, fell on the ground, then carried on running, until he died.

We kept moving and got to Ya'hello', Schöntal. We camped under an *alhpong* tree there; it gave good shade. "We'll stay here."

Another woman fell ill in that place. She had a son who had just started to walk. He ran around his mother, his feet going *patter, patter, patter*. He would come back to his mother and sit down on her. It was in the evening. In the end, when the skin started to come off her belly, the woman cried out, "Why does this have to happen to me? This child's pulling my skin off. Kill him! Please, he's killing me." Her husband stood up, picked up the child by the feet, and dashed his head against the *alhpong* tree. The child cried out at first; his brains came out, but he didn't die straight away. It was going dark and his brains shone white. After a time, he died.

Once it was dark, the man left; the others had demanded he burn the body.

"Burn it."

"Alright."

"Take it away and burn it," they told him. It was already very dark. Night had fallen and the dead child's father took a burning piece of firewood into the forest.

He shouted from a distance, "Am I still too near?"

"You're too near. Take him further away and burn him!" they said. He was carrying fire with him into the forest. "You're still too near.

Further!" He went even further away until they couldn't hear him anymore. They quickly hid the axes and the knives because they were afraid he might come back in the night, made mad by what had happened.

"He might kill us in the night."

But he didn't come back. They waited but he didn't come back. They needn't have hidden their weapons. He probably died in the forest; he'd already shown the first signs of the sickness when he left. Or he went mad when he killed his son. His wife also died. All of the skin fell off her.

The sickness, *nengelyeetapaykam'*, the smallpox, wiped out the Enlhet. People said it was the blood of the Paraguayans. The fear of smallpox drove us far away, but fear was of no use to us. They ran, but the smallpox wiped out the Enlhet; it was everywhere. Only now are the Enlhet increasing in number again. After the great sickness there were no Enlhet left. But I was never infected. I'm still healthy today.

▪▪▪

We moved, but again only a short distance; we went to another shade tree, still around Ya'hello'. A man who the sickness hadn't killed went to the *lengko*, the Mennonites, there. He knew their language. I think it was Kalape'e – he was the only one who could speak their language at that time; he was the first person to have approached them. So he went to the Mennonites' village and talked with them. Then he came back to our people.

"One of the Mennonites has asked us to visit him. He wants us to do the *maaneng* dance. He'll take the sickness out of us."

The Enlhet agreed right away. "He's got sweet potatoes and *seppo*. He invited us to take food from his field." We quickly set off for the Mennonite's house, with the sick among us. The women went to his field.

"Bring sweet potatoes, but don't bring *seppo*. *Seppo* is poisonous."[52] The women pulled the sweet potatoes from the earth and cooked them in the embers, the Mennonite's sweet potatoes. There were two Mennonites, Penseem-Pophehek, and Alyav'atee-Pmankok, who the Mennonites called Abram Ratzlaff, and Abram Unger. We were to see them again later as missionaries at Ya'alve-Saanga. They lived in Ya'hello'. Later they would set up the Ya'alve-Saanga mission. That meeting with us marked the beginning of their work.

In the afternoon, we did the *vayke-neeten* dance. "They want us to dance *vayke-neeten!*"

The Enlhet danced, but instead of a drum they used an old tin bucket; they didn't have time to prepare properly. Meleklama-Pakanma, the father of Aayat, played that drum. Even the sick danced; they danced without stopping until dusk. Meanwhile, one of the Mennonites sat on a wooden box.

"He's going to put the sickness inside that box," Kalape'e explained. He spoke the Mennonites' language. Then the Mennonite took out a camera. The Enlhet were very afraid of it, but Kalape'e reassured us. "The Mennonite says there's no need to be afraid. He's going to scan you with this machine and pull out the sickness. We'll be cured."

The Enlhet overcame their fear of the machine. They thought it really could take out the sickness. In reality, it was a photographic camera.

When the photographic plate was full the Mennonite said, "I'll carry on later."

The Enlhet rested and the Mennonite took the plate out of the machine and put it in the wooden box. The Enlhet watched as he opened it.

"Watch, he's opening the top." That's how they talked. "Look, he's putting it inside."

They commented on what they saw. We thought that he really was putting the sickness inside the box; we didn't know that the black things we had seen in the box were photographs. The Mennonite, when he finished changing the photograph, asked them to dance again.

"Another."

The Enlhet danced again. They danced *maaneng* and *vayke-neeten* until the evening. In the evening, we went back to our homes. We had got a lot of sweet potatoes. When we got to our village, we found it was true: no one had died.

Next morning, at first light, an Enlhet cried out, "How can it be? Not a single person has died?"

"We're all healthy," came the answer.

"It seems it was true. We should go back to them."

"You see? He told us we'd be healthy."

"He invited us to go to his house again. He said he was going to finish his work," said the Enlhet who could speak the Mennonites' language.

"Let's go back."

We went back to the Mennonite's house. We danced *maaneng* and *vayke-neeten* again. We ate sweet potatoes again. Again we stayed until the evening. When we got back to our village, the Enlhet were all in perfect health; nobody was dying anymore. Still, the solution had come late: the Enlhet were nearly wiped out.

Someone made a suggestion. "Let's split up. I'm going home. It looks as though we're cured."

The Enlhet dispersed and each went back to their home. We came here, to Kemha-Paapeyav, which is now in Ya'alve-Saanga. I was very young but my uncle picked me up from time to time on the way and put me on his shoulders. I don't know how old I was when my mother died. She died, but I was healthy. I've been healthy ever since I was young; the great sickness didn't infect me.

Account 22: Kenaateng
Metyeeyam' [53]

It's difficult to explain. Even the *apyoholhma'* died, the wise men. Their knowledge wasn't powerful enough to resist the sickness. The Enlhet vanished; a lot of them died, everywhere. Everything changed; there were no more people. There used to be so many of us! They lived all over this region in a lot of fairly big villages. But even the *apyoholhma'*, the wise men, with all their powerful knowledge, couldn't stop the sickness. Only one of them survived, the father of Haakok Melketna'ay'.

The man who brought the sickness came to Nalhpaateng, Halbstadt, south of Loma Plata. The soldiers left the area and then he arrived. It was never clear what he was. He was probably a *yaame'elle*, a North American, although the Mennonites didn't know if he was one.

"Where does he come from? Is he a *nolte*, a North American?" my uncle Lospata asked one of the Mennonites.

They said he wasn't an *elle*, an Englishman, either. Perhaps he was a Bolivian, or he came from above, an *enlhet-neeten*, one of the beings who live in the space above us.

"He's not a North American," said one of the Mennonites. "He doesn't speak like the *nolte*."

"There's going to be *sembengkok*," said the stranger. Nobody understood this word. They thought he probably meant *maaneng askok*, the master of the dance.[54] He kept repeating it. "There's going to be *sembengkok. Sembengkok!*"

Later people concluded that he was talking about smallpox. They supposed that the smell of the blood of so many dead people had risen up to the place where the *enlhet-neeten* live. So the epidemic was payment for the rotting corpses, for the valay, the Paraguayans who fell, and the dead *yaamvalay*, the Bolivians.

It was evening when a Mennonite we called Lengko Peya brought the stranger to our village. The stranger brought two big suitcases with him full of *apaava*, fabric, clothes.

"Dance," the Mennonite said to us. "This man is asking you to. He wants to take photographs of you."

He suggested the women take off their clothes. "Lospata, tell the women to take off their clothes before they dance. He's going to take photographs of them."

The Enlhet spoke to the women. "Take off your skirts. This man wants you to dance naked. He's going to give you the *apaava* that he's brought in exchange."

But the women paid him no attention and ran away into the forest. They were not accustomed to showing their genitals. At this negative reply, the stranger sucked his finger – he was a short, fat man – and spat blood into his hand. Then he ate the blood. Everyone was astonished. He didn't spit the blood on the ground. They had no idea why he did it; later they thought that perhaps he was trying to spread bloody diarrhea.

The Mennonite spoke again, this time to the men. "He's asking the men to play their *kaaya*, their gourd rattles," my uncle Lospata translated again. I propose we play them."

"*Heey'*, alright."

Figure 2.7 ▪ "Once he had taken his photos the stranger opened his suitcases."
Meeting between Mennonite immigrants and the Enlhet in Matna-Maaleng,
Schönbrunn, 1931, soon after the arrival of the Fernheim colonizers.

The men were prepared to show him their rattles; some waved ostrich feathers with their hands as they sang. They gave a demonstration for the stranger and he set a tripod near them and took photos
with his camera. At that moment, another of my uncles arrived,
Yohoon Kela's father. He had been hunting *maapa'*, moles, and had
brought his catch; his bag was full of them. He showed the stranger
how he caught them; again, the stranger took photos of him. There
were a lot of people; we were a big group. The sickness would soon
wipe them out.

Once he had taken his photos, the stranger opened his suitcases
and took out cloth of different types. He also had needles. The man
who spread the sickness was giving out cloth, very beautiful cloth. So
he opened the suitcases. There were a lot of people; a lot of people
lived in Nalhpaateng. He opened these big suitcases, both the same

size. The women were watching and when they saw the fabric they came nearer. That's women, they forget themselves when they see nice clothes. They'd run away at first, but when they saw the clothes they got over their fear.

The stranger handed out the fabric. He gave some to everyone; there was a lot of it. The women were happy. That's how they are: when they see nice clothes they forget where they are. They took the fabric – but it was sickness. He gave nothing to us; my mother didn't take anything, neither did her mother. He didn't give anything to my uncle Lospata, who was sitting next to him, or to Vaaso, Cacique Vaaso. I guess he realized they were *apyobolhma'*, wise men, and they would quickly understand what his intentions were. Most people, though, accepted his cloth, that large group of people. He gave it all out. At that time only a few women wore clothes; the Mennonites had only recently arrived. I was very young and I didn't wear anything. My testicles hung for all to see.

At dusk, my father stood up in the middle of the open space between the grass houses. That's what the apveske', the leaders, did in the old days when they were about to speak. He spoke up and everything went quiet. "This giving out of clothes doesn't smell right to me. I suspect the cloth is full of sickness," he said. "I see the smoke of the sickness here among our houses."

Everyone was quiet as they listened to his words; they fell completely silent. "I'm leaving. I'm going back to where I'm from. There's a bad sickness coming."

"He's right," said the other Elders.

My uncle Vaaso took the floor.

"It's true. I'm coming with you, brother-in-law," he said. "The sickness has already started to spread."

"I'll follow you later," said his brother Lospata.

Everyone was quiet as they listened to my father. We left; that same night we went back to our home land.

We spent the next night in Na'tamaaphek. Then we spent a day there and ate *peyem*, iguana. Those were the days when there were still a lot of *peyem*, before the Mennonites took over the whole place. The sickness didn't attack the Mennonites, or the Paraguayans. This sickness sought out Enlhet places; it called out to us as it approached: "Vaa, lengvaaa!"[55]

It sounded just like a Mennonite boss calling us. In reality, though, it was the sickness calling from inside a whirlwind before it fell down on the people. When that happened, they fled immediately.

▪▪▪

We travelled on, and stopped beside a watering place to collect eggs. After the war, it had rained a lot and there were plenty of birds' eggs. In that place we saw the sickness coming down; it fell like a bolt of lightning, with thunder, *crack*! The ends of the branches of the *aykaaba* tree lit up.

"Run!" shouted my father.

At first the whirlwind carrying the sickness stood still, like a *naamok*, a bottle tree, but then it leaned down and started looking for our tracks. When it didn't find them it jumped into the water, *splash*! The sickness could move; it chased us.

We ran and didn't stop until we were a long way away. We went to Hemaklha-Maaset, Neuanlage. My uncle Vaaso, though, went to Ta'ne, Gnadenfeld. There he discovered that nobody had survived. He caught up with us during the night.

"There's no one left alive in Ta'ne," he said. "The sickness has taken them all."

My father was a very wise man. He gathered the people together next to our houses; he didn't sleep. "I'm not going to let my children come to harm," he said. "I can see the sickness."

All night he waved branches from an *aktam* tree. His relatives were very distressed; they asked him constantly, "Brother, what's going to happen? Is it going to take us too?"

"No, that's not going to happen. I can see it; I put up a barrier around us." And so my father reassured them. All night long he walked around the people and waved the *aktam* branches. He didn't sleep. And no one died; we were better off than people in other places.

But then, there in Hemaklha-Maaset, the sickness caught a man in our group too.

"There's a strange smell," said the man. "I think a *teme'es* has bitten me." He thought it was a *teme'es*, those small insects that live in the water and bring out little blisters on your skin; you shouldn't go in the water when they're there.

"I don't think it's that," my father replied. "There's a light all around us, like the light that the sickness has."

My father tried to cure the sick man, but afterwards decided, "I'm taking the children away from here. We can't fight the *nengyetepma*."

We left at first light. We reached Samaklha-Ngya'alva and stayed there a few days. Then we retreated further, to Kenmaa-Paapen', Lindenau. Yetna-Haapen' is the name of the exact place we stopped. The next day, my father went to Kenmaa-Paapen' but no, there was no one left alive.

"They've all gone," he told us when he came back. There had been a lot of them. But there was no one left. The sickness killed them all. The next day my father went to another village a little further away. The sickness hadn't reached there yet and my father saw a person waving *aktam* branches so that it couldn't attack them. Early next morning, my father went to another village. But no, the sickness had wiped them out; no one was left alive in the village. "There's nobody there. There's only us left."

The next day my father went again to another village. Again he found only a mosquito net flapping in the wind. The dead were lying under it, the sick infected by *nengyetepma*. The day before, they had been working harvesting beans, and in the evening they'd still been healthy. But they fell ill in the night and died soon after. The disease was extremely violent; it didn't allow life. It left mosquito nets alone in the wind.

My father came back. "They're dead. They've all gone. All that's left are the mosquito nets," he said.

Around Kenmaa-Paapen', Lindenau, there were three Enlhet villages populated with people from the north. They were all left empty. The same thing happened everywhere. In some villages the sickness would leave one person; in another, two and in another, again just one. There were no people left, there was nobody to bury the dead. The *maama*, the vultures, circled over the villages like they do when they see dead cattle. The smell was horrible. While the vultures ate the corpses, other birds, the *kenaateng*, ate the flies that covered the dead bodies. They looked like the vultures; the grass houses were black with *kenaateng* that came to eat the flies. To this day I don't hunt *kenaateng*.[56]

■ ■ ■

A lot of people also lived in the region of Pa'aeklha'pe', Loma Plata. But the sickness wiped them out, even such a large number of people. Smallpox killed immediately. The *apyoholhma'* themselves, the wise men, died. Women who considered themselves strong, adolescents, they all died. The area was left without inhabitants. The same thing happened in every region: before the epidemic they'd been densely populated areas! I often think about that; I talk constantly about it. The sickness called out to the Enlhet as it looked for them. People said that it was an *enlhet-neeten*, an invisible being, who sowed the sickness; he put it on clothes that he handed out; this happened after the war. Some people also said a sickness like this will appear again in the future.

The suffering was so great that my father decided to take his people to the world beyond the lagoons. I don't know the exact place where that happened.

"We'll go there," he said to the people with him. "I'm going to take everybody. It's a dark road; we have to pass through a tunnel. But when we come out the other side, everything will be light and the people there will come out to greet us. They have enough to share."

My father intended to take us under the earth to the other world. I don't know the reason why he changed this mind.

Account 23: The Invisible Beings
Kam'aatkok Ketsek [57]

My mother was infected with the sickness, *nengelyeetapaykam'*. I remember something about her death, but only very little as I was very small. She lay down under a *nempeena* tree and they left her there alive because her skin was stuck to the deerskin she was lying on. The deerskin stuck to her own skin.

"*Meeme, meeme!* Mummy, mummy!" I cried.

"You don't have a mother anymore," they said to me.

"Your mother isn't here. We left her behind," my aunt told me, the mother of Kaymaap-Takhaalhet. "We left your mother behind."

My mother didn't call after us when we abandoned her; her whole body was breaking. We left my mother behind and went to another place, fleeing the sickness, *nengelyeetapaykam'*, terrified. It's a terrible thing to abandon someone, but there was no choice. It was very difficult for my father. I remember my elder brother talking to him."

"Daddy, don't think anymore about what happened," he pleaded.

"I know. We left her behind. She's dead," replied my father.

Now I had no mother. My father collected honey; he got *ya'alva*, armadillo, for me so I could suck one of the bones. When he killed a deer he was the one to cut a piece of meat for me because my mother was dead. He made a little container for honey for me out of the skin of a deer. He put honey in it for me from the *peeyem* bee. *Peeyem* honey doesn't give you stomach ache, not like honey from the queen bee, *yaamyavheene'*, or from the *yavhan*. He put the honey of the *popom* wasp in the container as well.

They told me I caught the disease too. But my father treated me with the root of the *pehen*, tree, and I was cured. You scrape the roots and cook the skins. Then you paint the liquid onto the lumps on your skin. People who survived the sickness had bathed with this liquid. I only remember a little about all of that; it happened a long time ago.

■■■

The great sickness, smallpox, appeared. The old people, who aren't here anymore, called it *nengelyeetapaykam'* [literally, "we break"]. They said that before it came there used to be a lot of Enlhet. But this disease wiped the people out. It came after the war; it was started by the soldiers. Above us live other Enlhet, the invisible beings, *enlhet-neeten*; they were not pleased that the creoles shot at each other in our lands. They could not allow so much killing. So when the blood of the soldiers rose up, they made the owners of the lands pay. They paid for it with the smallpox. If a person was infected with the disease their skin would be completely covered in blisters full of liquid. It was

Figure 2.8 ▪ Kam'aatkok Ketsek.

liquid, it wasn't pus. When the sick person lay down their skin stuck to the animal skin they were lying on and came off their body. It was as though their body was breaking. It was the *enlhet-neeten*, the beings above, who brought this sickness. The massacre that the creoles committed made them act against the people who shared the region with them, the Enlhet. The Enlhet didn't prevent the killing and so another death came to them.

▪ ▪ ▪

The *enlhet-neeten*, the invisible beings, followed us as we moved. They would sit on a *yaatepvatahap*, a jatropha plant, and we would hear them playing the guitar, *twang! twang! twang!* They would make noises with their mouths too, *pssst!* The older Enlhet, those who had survived the massacre (see account 17), could see them and knew how to contact them; we called them fathers of the *enlhet-neeten*. An old man once showed them to us. It happened after the death of an uncle of mine.

Those who were infected by smallpox were abandoned while they were still alive. People would leave them a little water and flee. We left my uncle in Ya'yeem-Paatelh. "We have to leave him behind; he's got the disease. He might infect us; we're still healthy," said my father.

We left at night and he stayed behind under his mosquito net; he died there with his skin stuck to the animal skin underneath him.

That same night – we camped some distance away – we saw a bolt of lightning strike where we had left my uncle; the sickness fell like lightning. We heard thunder behind us too, like the thunder that comes with lightning. We got up straight away and ran all night without stopping; I remember it. We went to Sengkenmelh, near Neu-Halbstadt. That's where we heard the *enlhet-neeten*, the invisible beings, playing the guitar. There was nobody there, but we could hear the guitar being played by the ones who brought the sickness.

"Girls, listen," said another of my uncles. "The ones who bring the sickness are playing."

We went to bed hungry, but we accepted that we just had to bear it.

SECTION 5
UNBRIDLED VIOLENCE

For three ill-fated centuries a sceptre
oppressed the peoples of the Americas.
Paraguayan national anthem

The following accounts deal with the brutality to which the Enlhet
were subjected by the Paraguayan military.[58] It should be pointed
out that the Enlhet accounts do not contain references to similar acts
perpetrated by the Bolivians.

Account 24: They Wanted His Wife
Sa'kok-Nay' [59]

In Kemha-Paatelh, Kleefeld [near Filadelfia], an Enlhet was murdered,
a cousin of my father, at the very beginning of the war. He wasn't from
Kemha-Paatelh, he was from Pa'aeklha'pe', Loma Plata, but during a
yaanmaan, a female initiation celebration, in Pa'aeklha'pe' he married a woman from Kemha-Paatelh and went with her to her home
region – women took the men with them when they married. There
the valay, the Paraguayans, murdered him. They wanted his wife.

The murder happened when the couple took *tamam'a* rope to the
Mennonites to sell to them. They'd been told, "Go to the Mennonites."
They say that at that time there was only one Mennonite living in
Kemha-Paatelh. "Take the rope and trade it for bread," the couple had
been told.

When they arrived at the village they met some *sopkelloom,* Paraguayans [literally, "furious, uncontrolled thing"] on mules. They
wanted to have the woman, but her husband did not want to hand
her over; they had only been married short time. So they murdered
him to get the woman. They shot him and, after they had killed him,
they grabbed her. They put her on a mule and took her to Mariscal
Estigarribia. Later, during the night, she managed to escape. The soldiers were sound asleep. When they got up she was already a good
way away. She knew how best to run; she stayed next to the road but

Figure 2.9 ▪ Kooneng-Pa'at.

in the forest so that nobody would see her. When she reached where her people were, her feet were very swollen.

When the Paraguayans wanted to have a woman the men were in a dilemma. If a man refused they would kill him, even if he was an apveske', a leader. The Paraguayans had no qualms about shooting an Enlhet. They didn't treat us well. It's no coincidence that, to this day, I don't go near Paraguayans. Even if they bring food I don't go near them.

Account 25: They Shot Him
Kooneng-Pa'at [60]

The valay, the Paraguayans, really weren't people like us; they killed. One day a man who had recently got married went to the lengko, the Mennonites, to sell them rope. He didn't have children yet when the Paraguayans killed him. The soldiers killed him at the entrance to Toopak-Amyep, Gnadenheim [near Filadelfia], in front of the Mennonites. The Mennonites didn't care about the Enlhet man's body; it was left there in the road. The Paraguayans buried it themselves later in the Mennonites' cemetery.

The victim was the uncle of the wife of Laava-Pmenek. He knew something was going to happen. "Uncle," he said to Seepe-Pmommaap's grandfather, "I dreamt I was bathing in the resin of the nempeena tree; my skin was red all over."

"Then why do you want to go?" he answered.

"I need to go; we're hungry."

He took the rope that his wife had made and left. When he got to the entrance to the Mennonite village he looked around carefully to see if anyone was there.

"There are no Paraguayans," he said.

He was taking rope to exchange for sweet potatoes. Suddenly the Paraguayans shot him from a distance and he fell, right at the entrance to Toopak-Amyep. He was a big man. The women that were with him ran. After that happened, the Enlhet retreated into the forest between Toopak-Amyep and Ya'tempehek, Fort Trébol.

Account 26: Like Dogs
Maangvayaam'ay' [61]

I also heard people talk about Galeano's mother, who died here in Campo Largo. It wasn't just the yaamvalay, the Bolivians, who were always persecuting the women, but the valay, the Paraguayans, too. Some of them almost broke Galeano's mother's legs when a group of them raped her when she was a girl, when she didn't have a husband. They found her somewhere – it happened in the area around Kemhaklha-Yaanava, Straßberg. They tied her feet; they tied one foot on one side and the other on the other so that her legs were wide apart, like when you kill a sheep. With her legs wide apart one Paraguayan after the other raped her; they took turns until they were all satisfied. She twisted to try to get away, but they'd tied her tight. When they had all had her they untied her feet. They didn't kill her. But she wasn't well; she walked with a limp until the day she died. That's the story I heard the Enlhet tell. The Paraguayans were like dogs.

Account 27: Don't Cry!
Kam'aatkok Ketsek [62]

The *sopkelloom*, the Paraguayans, killed our old people, and when they went back to their fort they took a woman with them, my aunt. They took her daughter too; she was a young girl, like my grandchildren here. I'm scared of Paraguayans to this day; I'm very scared of the *sopkelloom* because I remember what happened that day as though I was seeing it now.

It seems the soldiers had run out of bullets, because their rifles stopped firing. Then they started to chase us and they caught two women who had escaped into an island of forest. They surrounded it, caught them, and put them on a horse. The girl cried as they were taking them away.

"Don't cry!" her mother told her. "Don't cry. These Paraguayans won't think twice about killing us. Remember how they've killed others," she said to quieten her. Her daughter didn't listen and kept screaming with fear of the Paraguayans.

They took them to their camp. The terrified girl kept crying. So they made her stand in front of a *maaset* tree and shot her to kill her. It bothered them that she wouldn't stop screaming for fear of them. The Paraguayans, the *sopkelloom*, executed the little girl. They put her in front of the *maaset* and murdered her. Her mother watched it happen. They didn't kill the mother, though; they just fell on her and raped her. She let them do what they wanted with her and so she survived.

Figure 2.10 • "I'm scared of Paraguayans to this day." During the annual dry season, the Paraguayan State distributes food to Indigenous families in the Chaco. Each recipient must sign a receipt. Those who do not know how to write their name sign with their fingerprint.

My aunt stayed some time with the valay because it took her a while to find a way to escape. She let them fall asleep; she waited until they were sound asleep. Once they were snoring – they had lain down around her – she got up quietly and ran. Very carefully she got out from among them and ran away where there was no path; she fled into the depths of the dense forest. She met us again later. She had survived; she was alive. The Paraguayans didn't kill her because she escaped when they were sleeping. But they murdered her daughter, the young girl.

Account 28: There She Is!
Sooso' [63]

From Poy'-Aava-Ya'teepa the group went to Lheyaaho'pak, which is between Poy'-Aava-Ya'teepa and Lhepasko', Rancho Quemado. The Enlhet planted crops there and they intended to harvest sweet potatoes. They guessed that there would be no movement of soldiers in that region; that nothing would happen to them. As they were harvesting sweet potatoes, they heard the call of the ibis, the *moktak*. That's what my mother said. It was before I was born but I know about it from what she told me.

"The ibis is calling," said one of the children.

This happened in the region of Lheyaaho'pak, where they had their sweet potatoes. The Paraguayans didn't usually go there and the Enlhet paid no attention to the *moktak's* calling. They went on pulling their sweet potatoes out of the ground and only glanced occasionally toward the ibis. They were busy with the sweet potatoes.

"What's going on over there?"

"What can the ibis see?"

The ibis kept calling until finally one of the women got up to look toward the edge of the forest.

"Who's that? They're dressed in white!" she shouted. These Paraguayans were wearing light-coloured clothes, my mother said. The Enlhet had no clothes; they wore only skirts made from animal skins.

"*A!* Let's hope they're not Paraguayans!"

"Get up! Look, they're valay, soldiers!" It was a small group of soldiers. They were soldiers searching the area for Enlhet. They came from Rancho Quemado, my mother said. Suddenly they heard the sound of a rifle shot. That's how my mother remembered it.

"They're soldiers! Run!"

Immediately the women ran. They left the sweet potatoes behind; they didn't take them with them. One of the women also got separated from her daughter; she thought she'd gone with another woman.

When the soldiers left, the Enlhet went back to look for the girl. They saw her standing a distance away.

"They didn't kill her! She's looking at us," one of the women shouted.

They got to where she was but no, she was dead. The Paraguayans had stuck a branch into her body so that the corpse stood up in front of the tree. That's why, when they saw her from a distance, she gave the impression she was alive. That's how my mother told it. It turned out they'd murdered her. The Paraguayans killed the girl who got lost when the women ran away from collecting sweet potatoes.

"What a relief!" her mother shouted when she saw her standing there. "She's alive, Look! There she is by the tree."

The Enlhet retreated again. They lived in constant terror and flight. They didn't take revenge yet. Only later would they react.

SECTION 6
REACTIONS

PEACE AND JUSTICE
Motto on the reverse of the Paraguayan flag

The following accounts describe Enlhet reactions to the violence. These accounts show them to be actors even in the midst of severe difficulties.

Account 29: They Laughed at Us
Sooso' [64]

It happened in Tekses-Saanga, south of Lha'akma-Phaymaka'aok, where the Paraguayans' road passed through. One day valay arrived, Paraguayans; a truck full of soldiers. They came from Tomaklha-Pook-Maama, Fort Cabeza de Tigre. They got down from their vehicle and went straight over to a young girl they wanted to take. But when they saw her they stopped suddenly. Her hair was cut like a boy's.

"It's not a girl," they said.

That's what my father said.

Then they looked at Antolín's mother. My father didn't want to give her to them; she was his cousin. He went to face them.

"Go and face them, they want to take the orphan girl," said the women.

"Talk to the Paraguayans! Send them away!"

My father had more power, more knowledge than the others.

"Go and talk to them," the other men said.

My father explained what he was going to do. "I'll give them my machete. They'll like it when they see it and they won't do anything. These Paraguayans just like to look strong. They don't have knowledge," he said as he stood up.

And that's what he did. It wasn't my mother who told me this; my father told me about that day.

My father took them his machete. But he didn't go naked; he was a man of knowledge, a wise man. He greeted them.

"*Kellheep nak*! It's you!"

"*Ko'o*, it's us," they answered.[65]

My father took out the machete. "Do you want this machete? I'll give it to you if you want it."

The soldiers, the *sengelpelhteetamoo* [literally, "they catch us"], looked at the machete. "It's nice." They took it in their hands and examined it more closely. "Very nice."

"Keep it."

They laughed at the machete; it was very ugly. They found the situation very funny. "We'll be back. Your knife's very nice," they said. "Start up the vehicle!"

They were still laughing inside the truck and looking at the machete. They'd never seen anything like it; it was broken. But it was no accident that the *sengelpelhteetamoo* laughed like that; my father had acted so that his power went with the machete to lessen the soldiers' anger and the danger. And it did lessen: they found the machete ridiculous. Their laughter was the product of my father's actions.

"They're on their way, but their vehicle will break down on the road," my father declared.

They left and, as they drove away, my father turned his power toward their truck.

"I'll hurt their vehicle. I'll make it turn over." As the truck drove away, my father killed it. The soldier's vehicle turned over. It was completely destroyed and its occupants were killed; they never reached their camp. Through his knowledge my father had followed the soldiers and made their vehicle turn over. He destroyed the truck; he often told us about it. They didn't steal the woman; my father had protected her.

"If they come back we'll kill them all."

Account 30: They Became Furious
Seepe-Pyoy' [66]

My father stayed away from the Paraguayan camps, but he was known to the military chiefs as an apveske', a chief, and they treated him well. When he lived in Lha'akma-Mpenek, to the south of Paratodo, for example, a group of soldiers came to our village one day. They were interested in women, the same reason they always came.

"What news?" my father asked them. He could speak Guaraní.

"Nothing, all quiet. We're just looking for women. We'll pay for them."

"We'll give you them," my father answered, as he was the apveske', the leader.

"We'll pay you for them." They brought five bags of dry biscuits to pay for the woman they were to be given. They only got one: there was a woman among the Enlhet who had abandoned several husbands and went with other men, and besides she couldn't have children. She was the one they handed to the soldiers. They used her as protection; it wouldn't be so hard for her to give the Paraguayans what they wanted.

"Yes," said my father. "Of course. There's a woman here for you."

The soldiers came looking for women. They usually gave them only one, and the soldiers paid for her.

So the valay, the Paraguayans, took her, just that one woman. They made her lie down next to the village and threw themselves on her, all of them, the whole night long. There must have been fifty soldiers my mother said. The woman was used to these things and wasn't afraid of the soldiers. Besides, they had paid for her; they paid ten bags of biscuits. Afterwards, the soldiers were happy and expressed their good will toward the Enlhet.

"We're not going to treat you badly," they said.

They paid for the woman; twenty bags of biscuits they gave to the Enlhet. My father experienced these things and told me about them. The situation was calm, it seemed all was well; but it was very difficult. Deep down they didn't want to hand over the women. But it was impossible to refuse the Paraguayans' demands. They would have been furious. That was the Enlhet's reasoning, because they knew the ways of the Paraguayans. That's why, in the end, they handed her over to them.

■ ■ ■

At first it seemed the situation was under control and that calm would be maintained. But things soon got worse. The Paraguayans nearly killed two Elders when they went to the fort at Poy'maalhek, Pozo Blanco.

"Let's go to the soldiers' camp," they said. "We'll see if they'll share some of their food."

They went, but the soldiers spoke angrily about them.

"Let's kill them!"

They understood what they said because our grandparents could speak the Paraguayans' language, Guaraní.

"Let's kill them!"

The two Enlhet got on their horses to escape and the soldiers chased them on their mules. The Enlhet rode as fast as they could and got away from the soldiers; the soldiers fell behind perhaps a hundred metres. Suddenly one of the horses tripped and its rider fell. He got back on quickly and spurred his horse, and they escaped. That day the Enlhet started to become furious, and the moment would soon come when they would kill Paraguayans too.

That wasn't the only bad thing that happened. Benítez' father, who spoke Enlhet and Nivaclé, and also Macá, was another apveske', a person with authority; he was one of the Paraguayans' apveske', a leader for them. But the moment came when they turned on him. He lived near the Paraguayan fort at Tomaklha-Pook-Maama, Cabeza de Tigre. One day a military chief wanted a woman and came to the village to find one.

"I want a woman."

There were women with Benítez' father, but he refused to give one of them to the Paraguayan. "I'm not giving you any women." He stood up to the military chief.

"I'll kill you," was the reply.

My mother was there – she wasn't married yet – but she knew what to do. "They're sure to kill him. I'll escape, I'll run away on my own. I'll go to another village," she thought.

My mother ran because she saw the argument between the leader and the military chief.

The following night the Enlhet was murdered. The motive was women. At first light the Paraguayans surrounded his house and killed him because he hadn't wanted to give them any women. The people that lived with him fled; they only caught his sons and took them with them. Many years later one of them, Benítez, came back, but only him. He couldn't speak Enlhet anymore and he looked like a Paraguayan.

■■■

A short time later a Macá came. He lived in Maklhavay. When the Anglican missionaries left the mission at Nanaava'a, Nanawa, and handed it over to the Paraguayan military [who used it as a fort], some of the Macá, Nivaclé, and Enlhet that they'd gathered there left with them. This Macá had come to visit Benítez' father, who was a relative of his. He didn't go by the soldiers' fort, but went straight to the Enlhet camp next to it; he had a feeling something bad had happened. He reached the camp, but nobody was there. He saw that everything had been scattered around.

"There's obviously been a murder."

At that moment, an Enlhet from another place arrived. His name was Pataam-Tata'a. The Macá spoke to him but he didn't understand what he was saying.

"I'm going to the fort," he answered.

The Macá tried to stop him. "Don't go. Something strange has happened. I think my brother-in-law's been murdered."

But the Enlhet didn't pay any attention and went to the camp. He didn't understand what the Macá had said to him; they didn't speak the same language.

When he left, the Macá climbed an *aykaaba* tree to watch him from a distance. The soldiers saw the man approaching and stood up.

"What does he want?"

"Let's wait and see."

They grabbed him; apparently their chief wasn't there.

"We'll keep him here tonight," they said. "When our chief comes back he'll tell us what to do with him. He'll probably tell us to execute him."

Pataam-Tata'a lay down; he had a mosquito net with him. One of the soldiers kept watch over him so that he couldn't run away; he stood next to him. Night came and it was about to rain so, as usual, the soldiers were busy collecting up their things. Pataam-Tata'a took

Figure 2.11 ▪ Seepe-Pyoy'.

advantage of the moment of confusion and ran. When they realized he'd escaped they switched on the headlights of a truck, but he'd run into a grove of thorny *moktek* trees, to safety. His things were left with the soldiers, though.

■■■

A short time later, they murdered another Enlhet, a preacher named Haakok Toolhay. He was Enlhet and had a Macá father. He came from Maklhavay and was going toward the region of Nanaava'a to spread the Good News. He arrived at the fort at Cabeza de Tigre, which was on the side of the road, and they killed him. I don't know the reason why; the Paraguayan soldiers just killed anyone. Perhaps his death was connected in some way with the murder of Benítez' father.

Another Macá, who had found out about the murder of Benítez' father, travelled west with the news.

"They killed one of our people. And they murdered a preacher."

The news spread, and the Enlhet began to think differently. "Now it's our turn to murder Paraguayans. They treat us very badly." They argued like this in the region south of Paratodo – the Enlhet, Nivaclé, and Macá who lived there and had always been closely connected.

"We'll even up the deaths. We'll take revenge."

And that's what happened.

"We're going to kill Paraguayans too." They talked about killing like the Paraguayans did; in the old days the Enlhet knew how to kill. Many Enlhet were murdered by Paraguayans, and in the same way they killed many Paraguayans. The Paraguayans would come back from the front in small groups. Sometimes five, sometimes three of them. They were deserters returning from the front without permission; they didn't come back on their chief's orders. They tried to join the Enlhet, but they couldn't, they were killed. When they went into a village to ask for water they were killed. They were blamed for the behaviour of Paraguayans in general. In the region of Paratodo the Enlhet killed Paraguayans.

Account 31: "They're Going to Kill Us," They Thought
Maangvayaam'ay' [67]

When the fighting started, the Enlhet ran to the forest; they went to the deepest parts of the great forest. They were living in Loom-Popyet, Fort Alihuatá, when they made the decision. "The *yaamvalay*, the Bolivians, are going to start fighting the valay, the Paraguayans. We should shelter in the forest."

The Enlhet retreated into the forest. I wasn't part of that, but my father and mother always talked to me about the war when I was maybe fifteen years old. They said that the Enlhet moved into a large area of forest in the region of Ta'malmaa-Yman, where there was no open country. They stayed in a small clearing with a little watering place. They drank the water from there. I never went to Ta'malmaa-Yman; I know it only by name.

They lived there for a few weeks; about two weeks I think. They ate honey; they weren't hungry. In fact, the only thing they ate was honey because they couldn't hunt animals; the soldiers would have heard the gun shots and found them. My mother used to tell me about it. One day, three Paraguayans suddenly appeared at the edge of the clearing. It was too late to run; they already knew the Enlhet were there because the dogs had started barking straight away. One of the Paraguayans fired at the dogs; the dogs were next to the women and the bullet almost hit one of them. At that the Enlhet started arguing.

"A! The Paraguayans are furious; they're dangerous."

"Good. Let's kill them all," someone suggested.

"They started it," they argued.

"Let's get all three of them."

The Enlhet surrounded the Paraguayans; one of them started to speak and greeted them. "Kellheep nak lha! It's you!"

"*Eebe, nengko'o*, yes it's us."[68]

"Do you have honey?" they asked.

"Yes, plenty." They prepared three gourd containers full of honey for them.

"Sit down." The soldiers sat on the ground. They were very hungry and they devoured the honey gladly.

"These Paraguayans look as though they want to kill us," thought the Enlhet. "Get ready!"

They picked up their tools – hatchets and machetes – but kept them hidden.

The Paraguayans ate the honey. Each of them leaned over his container of honey as though nothing was wrong. Then the apveske', the leader, gave the order. "Now!"

In an instant they cut their throats with their sharp hatchets; they cut the heads off two of them completely. With the third, the hatchet didn't cut through and his head was left hanging on his chest. He ran, even though he had no head. He bumped into trees but he kept running until he fell. Then they killed him where he had fallen. That's what my mother told me happened. The things my mother and father told me about were astonishing.

After that the Enlhet moved on. They were afraid more Paraguayans would come. They took refuge in another place in the middle of the forest. All the same they came across two more Paraguayans while they were out collecting honey. The Paraguayans had got lost and were thirsty, very thirsty.

"Do you have water?" they asked the Enlhet.

"No, we're collecting honey," they answered.

"We're hungry."

"You can eat the trunk of the *pa'ang*, the forest palm," they told them.

These Paraguayans didn't behave threateningly; they were just asking for something to eat. So the Enlhet gave them the trunk of a *pa'ang* and watched them. You have to cook the *pa'ang*, then it tastes good and fills you up. But if you eat it raw it's poisonous and it can even kill you.

"They're going to eat it. They're going to eat it all; they're hungry."

And the *pa'ang* did poison them. They'd eaten it when they were very hungry. They fell over and stood up again as though they were drunk, and went away like that. The two of them died alone in the forest. That's what my mother told me.

I don't really know how many months the Enlhet stayed in the forest; perhaps five. During that time they didn't go out into the open. But after a time, the Paraguayans went away. One of the men went out into open country to investigate the situation and found everything very quiet: the soldiers had gone, they'd gone back to where they were from. He came back to the others.

"We can come out of the forest," he said.

"Let's go!" They went out into the open country. In the forest they hadn't eaten meat. They went back to where they'd come from, to the places they had fled from. They took up their good life again. They were able to find different kinds of pigs again. They stayed alert, but no, everything was calm.

"Things are back to normal," they said.

Again they hunted in peace; they could find everything they wanted, ostrich, anteaters. That's what happened in the Enlhet country.

Account 32: The Haircut
Yamasma'ay' [69]

I experienced the war in the Chaco. I was a boy; I'd have been six years old. We heard the gunfire.

"What's that?" wondered one of the Elders.

We heard shots; the Bolivians were fighting against the Paraguayans. All night we listened to the sound of the guns.

"Listen! Let's hope it doesn't come this way," they said.

My father's home, Teejela', is fairly close to the road from Mariscal Estigarribia to Kilómetro 180, perhaps five kilometres to the north.

"Stay alert!" said one of the Elders. "The explosions could come near where we live." The gunfire was continuous, day and night.

Some time later, a *yaamvalay*, a Bolivian, came to our village in Teejela'. We often met Bolivians who had deserted.

"Look what's coming!"

The deserter arrived in our camp. He had only a mosquito net with him. He had no weapons; he was on the run.

"It's a Bolivian, a deserter."

He lived with us for a time. He was so hungry he ate meat raw; he took it out of the pot before it was properly cooked. He ate raw anteater meat; he ate raw venison. Nobody stopped him; he was starving. They let him eat raw meat. One day the women were cooking fruit from the *maaneng* tree, and he went over to the pot again to pick it out raw. He ate it before it was ready, before the poison had come out of it – the fruit only loses its poison after it's been cooked for a long time. He ate the fruit, started to groan, and died. The *maaneng* fruit killed him, it poisoned him.

I saw Bolivian deserters, and I saw the Bolivians working on building the road from Teniente Montanía to Mariscal Estigarribia. I saw it as a boy. The *yaamvalay* built that road. The Paraguayans put a lot of Bolivian prisoners to work. They carried the earth to build the road. Teejela' is near the road, I'd say about five, six kilometres to the north. The soldiers lived near Teejela'; their encampment was on the road.

■■■

While the Paraguayans and the Bolivians were fighting we stayed hidden in the forest; we kept out of sight. But when the war was over we came out, and we went to the Paraguayans' camp. They wanted to shoot at us, but in the end they didn't. My father raised his hand and shouted, "We're not Bolivians!"

"Come here!" answered a soldier.

In those days, after the war, we didn't understand the Paraguayans' language.

From that time on the Paraguayans would give us food and provisions when we went to their camp. We would get biscuits, dried maize, rice, and sugar. They asked us for hammocks too. They traded a rifle for just one hammock. They weren't Paraguayan rifles, they were Bolivian rifles that the Paraguayans had captured. Around that time our fathers began to prefer rifles and stopped using their bows. They had plenty of rifles; they could get rifles and bullets in exchange for hammocks.

We used to go to the fort to get supplies. The soldiers became our neighbours. Still, it was dangerous to be with them because they were still prepared to kill us.

"Where are you from?" they would ask us. We were afraid they would call us Bolivians and kill us; the Bolivians came from the north. So our fathers would answer, "From the south, from Paraguay."

We didn't really understand their language.

"Good. Then you're one of us," they'd say.

At first, the Paraguayans would shoot us on sight. If they saw a man with long hair they were likely to kill him out of hand; in the old days Enlhet men had long hair. But they didn't kill us if we cut our hair like theirs.

"Cut your hair," the Paraguayans ordered the Enlhet. So our fathers cut their hair. Now they had haircuts like them.

PART THREE
IN DIALOGUE WITH THE
ENLHET ACCOUNTS
HANNES KALISCH

In the following pages, I make some observations on the accounts in the previous section, augmented with information from external sources where appropriate. These notes do not constitute an exhaustive systematization of the accounts, nor definitive conclusions on their content. It is not my aim to offer a detailed analysis of the question of the Enlhet and the Chaco War or to analyze in detail the specific role of the war in the process of colonization of the Indigenous population in general.[1] Instead, the discussion focuses on providing ways into the issues and on highlighting questions that offer a way toward opening new communication – novel interaction – with the Enlhet based on their own voices, voices that speak of things that have never been heard outside their own society and come, therefore, from hereto unknown perspectives.

THE ESTABLISHMENT OF VIOLENCE AS A MEANS OF RELATING

The Mennonites just came. They came third.
The Paraguayans were the second to arrive.
The Enlhet, though,
the Enlhet have always been in the Chaco.
It is their natural homeland.

Haakok Metaykaok [2]

Initially, the few military explorers who came to the region behaved prudently in relation to the native inhabitants. They were unsure as to how they would react to their presence. They also depended on Indigenous knowledge to study the region and establish their forts in places with water, a resource whose presence defined the strategic value of any position. At this stage, the encounter appears balanced for the Enlhet, equal to equal, leader to leader, as Sa'kok-Nay' points out (in account 1). From the point of view of the military, however, inequality was inherent from the beginning. As the Mennonite immigrants would later state repeatedly, they considered the Enlhet inferior and saw it as natural that the Enlhet should live in a state of subordination.[3] This perspective legitimized the subjugation of the Enlhet and initiated a pattern of growing violence.

Deceit

The first level of violence takes the form of the instrumentalization of gestures of friendship: these were calculatedly false. The simulation of friendship (still a frequent characteristic of relations with Indigenous Peoples today) was motivated by an interest in the other not as someone with whom to articulate, but as a resource: the Indigenous possessed essential knowledge and served as labour (Malhkee·tko-Ngkoyoy', accounts 2 and 8). In account 4, Ramón Ortiz confirms that the military "deceived" the Enlhet with their gifts; the Enlhet interpreted these gifts as the act of sharing through which a balanced relationship was maintained.[4] Belatedly – perhaps many years later – the

Enlhet will have realized this was not the case; that they were actually a means of capturing them. However, whether or not these gifts fulfilled the intention of the intruders, even today the Enlhet find it difficult to understand violence that consists of the negation of the other as a person; more exactly, it is difficult for them to assume the idea that the white man is guided by the presumption of a natural imbalance between himself and Indigenous Peoples. This is why Ramón Ortiz states, more in the tone of a credo than a convincing argument, that "The Paraguayans didn't reject us and we hadn't refused them" (page 38). Although he appears to refer to a situation of equilibrium, this supposed equilibrium is founded on a systematic difference in appreciation and power. Whether knowingly or not, Ramón Ortiz relies on a concept of equilibrium that does not correspond to the historical Enlhet arrangement for constructing harmony, *nengelaasekhammalhkoo* (Kalisch 2011b). He bases himself on a concept of equilibrium that is broken (as is shown linguistically by the fact that he defines it as the absence of rejection and not as the presence of respect).

The use of the word "deceit" is justified not only by the simulation of friendship. There is another deceit – another betrayal – in the fact that, during the first encounter, the military used other Enlhet, people contacted previously, to avoid a hostile reaction among those who had not yet been contacted (see also Savhongvay' in account 3). This use of Enlhet agents was common during the establishment of relations; many of these agents were people occupying a non-central social position within their group, which facilitated the military's access to them. This is illustrated clearly by the case of Cacique Kalape'e,[5] who died in 1993 in Ya'alve-Saanga. Kalape'e was an important mediator between the military (and Mennonites) and the Enlhet in the area around present-day Filadelfia. However, biographical information about him indicates a certain social distance from the group for which he mediated: he was from the area of Neuland and lost his parents as a child. He lived for some time in Puerto Pinasco (for which reason he spoke Guaraní) and later married in Gnadenheim, *Toopak-Amyep*, on the outskirts of what is Filadelfia today. However, his wife died of smallpox soon after. As an orphan, outsider, widower, and in addition a young man, his position in his group was relatively marginal. This would be a common characteristic among early mediators (Richard

2008). Despite this, his role as an intermediary gave him some importance among his people, reflected in the title of *cacique*, "leader" – apveske' – that the white men gave to him and many other agents in those early days. In general, for a better understanding of the exact role of the people who served the military as mediators, their biographical details and the specific social context in which they lived should be analyzed in each case.

Women

As the military consolidated their presence in the Chaco, their readiness to act with violence against the Enlhet increased: the violence implicit in the encounter became more and more visible. In account 5, Seepe-Pyoy' highlights the fact that the Enlhet knew, initially, how to calm that implicit violence. At the same time, he alludes to a central thread in the accounts regarding relations with the military: their interest in women (Seepe-Pyoy', in account 30). In the view of Kenteem (account 6), this interest in women – manifested as violence toward them – transcended the Enlhet-military dynamic and was the motivation for the actions of the enemy armies themselves: Kenteem describes violence against an Enlhet woman as the reason for the confrontation between the two creole groups. It is important to see that, according to Kenteem, the Bolivian reaction was not motivated by violence toward the Enlhet in general, but toward their women. Thus, the attitude of the soldiers to Enlhet women crystallizes as the symbol of the Enlhet way of relating with the military, be it the Paraguayan or the Bolivian. These relations developed along the dimension of violence, with its varying degrees of visibility. In this regard, Kenteem is clear that it was not a question of defending women but of possessing them: in the symbol of the Enlhet woman, the power imbalance between the Enlhet and the military is made manifest.

Against this background, the prostitution of women at the forts, which took place in front of their husbands – although Malhkee·tko-Ngkoyoy' omitted to say so, and even denied it, other female relators remember that her mother was also prostituted – can be read as an attempt by the Enlhet to limit violence against them through domestication and control of that violence.[6] However, although prostitution

at the forts left them more margin for reaction than did rape and killing, both alternatives fit the same idea of relations on the part of the
military (on both sides), based on a dimension of violence and contempt. Undoubtedly, sexual morals among the Enlhet followed guidelines different from those of the known Western tradition, which
complicates an understanding, from our viewpoint in the present, of
the symbolic underpinning of their decision to prostitute themselves.
However, occurring as it did under conditions of imbalance, contempt, and violence, this can only have been a traumatic experience;
indeed, it was shrouded with silences. Concomitantly, relators who
were children at the time of the war make surprisingly few references
to prostitution at the forts. They must have seen it; however, since it
did not appear in the adults' accounts, they could not develop an account of it themselves. This is why Malhkee·tko-Ngkoyoy' does not,
in fact, know – rather than *not wishing* to know – about the prostitution of her mother in front of her father, despite the certainty that it
happened in front of her also. With the origin of accounts concerning
the phenomenon thus obstructed, the memory of the reasons for the
trauma was suppressed utterly and silence prolonged indefinitely.[7]

The Creole Perspective

Enlhet descriptions can be contrasted with those of Arturo Hoyos,
a Bolivian doctor arrested by the Paraguayans and whose notebook
was published in 1932 in Asunción.[8] It is quoted here without further
comment (compare also Seepe-Pyoy' in account 30):

> In 1924 another incident occurred with the savages. Life with
> them suddenly became intolerable. The leaders' women were
> taken indiscriminately by the officers, and in the presence of
> their husbands; they were attracted by money ... When the situ-
> ation with the natives, far from improving, became worse and
> worse, they took reprisals, and in September of that year some
> indians killed two boys, one of seven and one of fourteen years
> of age. The people who brought the news said they had cut
> their throats and then thrown the bodies into a well. The boys
> were sons of a local [Argentine] settler, José Palacieni ...

In response, Commander V.B. ordered Lt. C.C. to go to the village with an intelligent indian and ask the leaders who the culprits were in order to punish them, and to tell them that only thus would the rest of the tribe be pardoned. The officer went to the village of *cacique* Leiva, who was a good friend of ours and lived near the fort. Having been unable to find any sign of the authors of the crime, Lt. C.C. resolved to bring *cacique* Leiva and eight other indians to the fort ... It was in these circumstances that they were killed mercilessly on the road. On returning to the fort Lt C.C. reported that Leiva and other Indians had been made an example of and executed on the road ... Because their presence [that of the Indigenous population] was essential to us, as we put them to work on the hardest and least pleasant tasks and sent them on the most difficult errands, as well as using them as guides, one day we went to seek them out, Major S.R., Sub-lieutenants R.S.C. and U.E.M. and myself, to try to win their trust. The moment they saw us they took fright and fled, terrified. But as we showed sincere friendship to those we were able to reach, several of them came back and approached us, and each of us brought back a pretty indian girl to his hut at the Fort. The women behaved like old friends, and little by little the rest of them came out of the forest and came to us, hesitantly ... We paid no attention to the men; we just caressed the girls ... We continued to enjoy all the women we found among the tribes. (Hoyos 1932, 1–2)

Life at Fort Boquerón became impossible. On three occasions I left to avoid getting into a fight. The officers even quarrelled over girls; they threatened to shoot each other. In that regard, one day a *cacique* was punished terribly for not having brought girls to Lt. L. A group of soldiers was immediately dispatched to the village and sixteen of the best indian women rounded up. They were fairly good-looking and in the end quite happy when we showed them the good life to be had among civilized people. They were eventually made to stay and wash clothes for the soldiers, the officers having cast them aside since they now had new women, a behaviour which caused another near-fatal incident: one of the tribes became insubordinate and decided to seek the help of the Paraguayans to attack our positions. Fortunately it all ended well and life returned to normal. (Hoyos 1932, 10)

All the officers were fond of [Fort] La China because they went there to enjoy themselves.[9] The women were all depraved. They took every pleasure. *Coca* and strong drink ... The Indian tribes ceased working or making any attempt to earn their livelihood. It was easier to bring their women there and, while they gave themselves to pleasure, the Indian men would receive a ration of food, get drunk and dance all night. (Hoyos 1932, 11)

Actors

Let us return to the gifts given by the explorers to the Enlhet during their first encounters.[10] The Enlhet accepted and understood these gifts within their logic of sharing: the act of sharing, which is based in reciprocity, implies two actors and means that they become *engmook* – relatives, allies. It is a key mechanism and a necessary condition for the creation of the equilibrium that is so valuable to them within their philosophy of relating.[11] This explains the great symbolic value for the Enlhet in the fact that the intruders gave them their things and shared food: they appeared committed to equilibrium.

The importance placed by the Enlhet on the symbol of sharing is reflected in the insistence with which the relators state that they received from the intruders *in abundance*. For example, Sa'kok-Nay' (account 1) reports that her father "got a lot of food" from the explorers: "*seppo* [mandioca] flour, wheat flour, dried maize, all kinds of things. He got sugar, soap, shoes. They gave him everything, blankets, mosquito nets" (page 31). This image of abundance is in contrast to the statement that the explorers came with a "little truck" (page 31); they cannot have been carrying a genuine abundance. In addition, this insistence in the accounts contrasts with what we know about the perspective of the intruders, for whom there was certainly no commitment to equilibrium; quite the opposite.

To understand this insistence on a supposed abundant sharing, the brief exchange "Are you hungry?" "Yes, we're hungry" included by Malhkee·tko-Ngkoyoy' in account 20 is important (page 78). This dialogue appears repeatedly in Enlhet accounts of the initiation of communication with the intruders, whether military, civilian, or missionary, Mennonite or creole (whereas it is not used during an Enlhet-only encounter). At first, when encounters still appeared balanced, the Enlhet understood the question "Are you hungry?" as expressing the goodwill the strangers lacked on so many other occasions; they understood it as a greeting that initiated an act of sharing. Thus, they naturally responded positively, though their doing so did not imply a necessity of the food being offered. Indeed, they lived in what they perceived as abundance and shared what they had with the intruders, as is stated for example by Malhkee·tko-Ngkoyoy' (account 8). For their part, the strangers, who did suffer many unmet needs in that hostile and unfamiliar environment, assumed that, like them, the Enlhet lacked basic necessities; that they were poor and hungry, needful of everything (see Kalisch and Unruh 2014, 540ff; 2020, 546ff). Their prejudice blinded them to an understanding that the interest of the Enlhet in their belongings and food was not the result of material poverty. Instead, their selective perception confirmed the intruders in these prejudices, and, as we will see later, as this continued to happen, their reading of the situation began to impose itself on events. In sum, the same interactive act was motivated and read – experienced – in a radically different way by the intruders and the Enlhet.

▪▪▪

The accounts demonstrate that violence soon increased both on the symbolic level and in attitude and action. In the years following the war, generalized discrimination of the Enlhet became systemic and their access to their resources diminished rapidly. The fragile initial equilibrium – though in reality, it is not possible to speak of equilibrium since there can be no equilibrium without communication – was destroyed and rules were put in place for relating that no longer allowed for sharing (Kalisch 2014a; 2014b; 2019). In parallel, the function of the formula "We are hungry" changed. It ceased to be a reply to the white man's greeting and became an expression through which the Enlhet themselves initiated an encounter, thus giving the impression that they had opted to rely on charity. However, and this

Figure 3.1 ▪ "The function of the formula 'We are hungry' changed." A hunter brings home on his motorcycle an anteater he came across on the road. This is an unusual event, as hunting has become difficult, and many young people no longer like to eat meat hunted in the forest.

is crucial, from their viewpoint, this formula still did not express a material need, but a means of relating. They perceived relations with the intruders as violent, but the intruders' giving of things – sharing, from the Enlhet perspective – appeared to overwrite the perceived violence. That is, reliance on supposed charity was seen by the Enlhet as the only form of communication with the intruders through which they could maintain the illusion that the intruders were acting in good faith; of maintaining the appearance, at least in their own eyes, of the continued applicability of the logic of sharing so as not to renounce belief in the possibility of the equilibrium that was so valuable to them.

This strategy of applying their own reading to the encounter with the intruders – a strategy that remains common today in relations with the other, even though the other may see it as a simple interest in their things – is not without ambiguity. The Enlhet perceived the intruders' attitude of exclusion clearly. For this reason, the relators' contradictory insistence on the notion that the intruders shared abundantly (Sa'kok-Nay', account 1) or that they were concerned with equilibrium (Ramón Ortiz, account 4) allows for two readings: from one viewpoint the relators deny, and from the other they avoid conforming to, the attitude of exclusion that is so obvious to them. As a strategy for denying the obvious, their approach is something akin to closing their eyes to reality. It goes back to the idea that it is extremely difficult for them to accept that the white man is guided by the presumption of a natural absence of equilibrium between himself and Indigenous Peoples (page 115); that the notion of successful shared living is no longer applicable. However, as a strategy for avoiding accepting the obvious, it reflects a decision not to define and understand themselves, despite having been dispossessed and subjugated – defeated – by the other, as his victim. It thus aids in resisting the temptation to feel bitterness, while nonetheless constituting an implicit claim against the intruders.

The decision of the Enlhet to not consider themselves victims is highly significant. In today's world, a victim possesses moral authority and has, in theory, the right to *receive* reparations for the suffering caused (Todorov 2000). However, this is not an authority that the victim can exercise. It is symbolic authority based on the mere *hope* of the restitution of his rights. It is thus an authority that induces the victim to rest upon it. It leads easily to a situation where the victim does not repair or reconstruct and so continues to be the object of the predispositions and actions of others; of the victors. On the other hand, the fact that the Enlhet refuse to accept the condition of the victim, the passive condition, the condition of object – a refusal that shows through all the accounts – clearly implies that they continue to be actors, subjects (page 6).

The possibility of reconstructing ways of relating with the intruders on inclusive terms does not depend solely on the Enlhet. However, if they were to consider themselves victims, they would lose this possibility permanently. That is to say that it is precisely through this form of resistance to representing – the refusal to see – the other as an aggressor that they keep open the option of a future for themselves, the option of one day regaining their liberty. At the same time, through their strategy of not assuming the obvious imposed by others, they retain great potential for contributing to the reconstruction of their own and others' lives, a potential that would develop quickly if the intruders accepted the open hand they extend.

▪ ▪ ▪

The prejudices of the intruders did not change, and the processes of reduction and dispossession did not slow. In time, the phrase "We are hungry" lost its original meaning and became a formula by which impoverishment and dependency were assumed. As a synonym for "We are poor," it has come to form part of the current self-description of the Enlhet. It is a statement that still does not make victims of them, but could become a step toward it. To escape the trap concealed in these readings and counter-readings, it is essential to return to the resource of the memory of the people, which remembers the Enlhet as actors and can suggest new horizons. Let us now explore this question.

On Memory

Kenteem's account (account 6) illustrates the difference between a chain of events and what constitutes memory (page 11). Kenteem presents an episode woven around reliable facts: a known place (or region), known people, and an identifiable moment before the war.[12] In parallel to this, he highlights certain dynamics and processes. He refers to the movement of the Paraguayan military and describes their attitudes; he implies that the Enlhet maintained communication with the Bolivians. On the same narrative level, he also explains the reason for the start of the war. His explanation does not coincide with narratives in the societies of the warring states, who, for this reason, might accuse him of an unjustified leap from record or report to conjecture on the connections between historical facts. However, in the formal structure of the account, there is no such leap. Kenteem presents his personal interpretation of the Bolivian capture of Fort Toledo in July 1932 (a fact the dominant view *would not* question) like any other fact:

that the Bolivians were informed of the capture of an Enlhet woman and that they responded to it (a fact that the dominant view probably *would* question). That is, the existence of a leap can only be postulated if other narratives are known and are considered to be more accurate regarding the trigger for war (although the reasons for the war are many and varied, and nobody can say for certain what caused it). This poses the question of the reliability of the account.

I will not discuss here whether the Bolivian attack on Fort Toledo was the result of the causes Kenteem reports (without plausible arguments we should not question his interpretation of the facts). Rather, it must be remembered that he, like the other relators, treads the fine line between what is a record of facts and what is memory (page 12). Memory, in describing *reasonably* the connection between the relator and his people's past, creates an additional layer of meaning that transcends simple facts. In other words, the accounts are more than the presentation of mere facts (or less, if facts constitute the audience's only interest). This, however, does not affect their reliability; it does not even raise the question of reliability. For reliability should be defined in terms of the coherence that an account has or does not have with respect to other Enlhet accounts.

■ ■ ■

Kenteem, a participant in Enlhet memory, discusses in his account the connection of his people with their past and the actors in it. He makes clear that the Enlhet needed to be defended from representatives of Paraguayan society by the enemies of that same society, the Bolivians. He thus highlights a clear divide between the Enlhet and the society of which they were obliged to form part; the society that usurped their own. He also concurs with other relators in that the Paraguayans – the valay – are to be feared (Sa'kok-Nay', accounts 1 and 24; Kam'aatkok Ketsek, account 27). They are to be feared to this day because there is no current narrative that proposes a different solution, a solution other than continued submission. This statement requires explanation.

Fear of Paraguayans is very visible in the life of the Enlhet today. It is evidenced in interaction with a concrete Paraguayan individual, for the Paraguayan is assumed to be superior, an assumption frequently

reaffirmed by their attitude. In an even more paralyzing way, it manifests itself as the fear of an abstract Paraguayan, one who might be
out on the road, for example, even if there is no interaction with them.
This fear activates an imaginary state that leads to a perception of con-
jectured dangers as a real, concrete disaster from which one only just
escapes. Of course, in the great majority of encounters with Paraguayans, the eventuality so feared by the Enlhet is not realized. However,
it materializes in the constant creation of accounts of near-fatal encounters that circulate and dictate feelings, perceptions, and the very
way in which the Enlhet see themselves in the world. Rumours arise
regularly, for example, of Paraguayans passing through communities
to steal children. Even though no child ever disappears, the feelings of
terror these rumours produce are very real.

As the accounts make clear, these fears are the consequence of concrete historical experiences. However, as Enlhet memory has gradually become clouded, awareness of their origin has been obscured.
Although the Enlhet could still find knowledge of these origins in the
remote corners of their people's memory, those who transmit and
those who receive the fear no longer know how to give it words. Thus,
it is a fear shrouded in silences that simultaneously disable listening
(Hassoun 1996). The accounts might suggest that the fear is specific
to a moment in time, but the inaccessibility of the accounts themselves – whether due to the effect of their having ceased to be shared
or because of an inability to hear what is being shared – brings about
a situation where domination by fear becomes as invisible as the air
around us. It engenders a world impossible to imagine without fear.
Fear has become normal.

To interrupt this normality and find words to break the silence,
the activation of memory takes on importance. The voices of memory
facilitate appreciation, for example, of the origin of fear, so that its
contours are revealed. That is to say, seen from the viewpoint of
memory, normality – that which seems obvious – appears in light
and shade, and tensions are created that encourage differentiation
and questioning based on one's own experience and ways of expression. New options for contextualizing the present appear. Thus, if a
people maintains or regains access to its memory, it can revisit and
update the fact that it is a community of actors and thus be authorized

for action and interaction. It can, at the same time, face its pains and sorrows – among them, fear – long suppressed and hidden by profound silences and vain chatter. We are used to the idea that interest in Indigenous history is motivated by the acquisition of knowledge – an important pursuit within the Western tradition – or an attempt to find, or even restore, a better time. However, a return to memory, which can only be undertaken by a people for itself, seeks something different: it makes it possible to change in one's present some of the consequences of the past (Dening 2004, 37).

▪▪▪

This much may be said, on the one hand, regarding fear of the Paraguayans. On the other hand, it should be pointed out that many Paraguayans continue to behave toward Indigenous people in a way that does make it prudent to beware of them. For example, attitudes such as the ridiculing and questioning of the Indigenous world, mistrust, contempt, and arrogance toward people so different from them, remain very much alive.

Expropriation

With his reading, Kenteem presents us with a hypothesis as to the start of the war. In account 3, Savhongvay', who describes the arrival of explorers in Kemha-Maaneng – Lichtenau, in the region of present-day Colonia Neuland – presents a further hypothesis on the same subject that is no less revealing, considering relations between the Enlhet and Paraguayans, than that of Kenteem and the two are not mutually exclusive. Savhongvay' maintains that when the explorers arrived in the region, the decision to expropriate the Enlhet had already been made. He explains that both Paraguayans and Bolivians argued their right to the land by the assertion that they had brought Indigenous people, the original owners, with them (page 36). It can be understood that, by this argument, the Paraguayans recognized the rights of the Enlhet over the land. However, at the same time, they declared them citizens of the State and thus assumed their rights over the land as rights of the State. They dispossessed the Enlhet without the Enlhet realizing it (page 35). As Savhongvay' points out, this usurpation is manifest in the Paraguayan names given to places in Enlhet territory (page 36).

The assessment of Savhongvay' coincides with information we have from the Paraguayan State itself. During the government of Carlos Antonio López, the Supreme Decree of 7 October 1848 was promulgated. It "declares to be Citizens of the Republic the native Indians of the twenty-one peoples of the territory of the Republic" (article 1) and "property of the State the goods, rights and actions of the aforementioned twenty-one native peoples of the Republic" (Article 11; Supreme Court of Justice 2003, 13). However, the Indigenous Peoples did not receive the rights of the citizenry in exchange for dispossession. On the contrary:

> The process of loss of their territorial rights would later be compounded by the absolute exclusion of the Indigenous from the political life of the country when in 1852 the same government under Carlos Antonio López reformed the Law on Reglamentation of the Administration of the Republic, establishing the condition of "landowner" as a prerequisite for access to …
> the condition of citizen, [depriving the native peoples] of their rights as citizens. (Ayala 2014, 66)

To this process corresponds the fact that the opposing sides in the war never understood their war as a colonial war against the true owners of the region. For them, it was an international dispute over creole rights claimed by each side for itself (Capdevila 2010a). Different Enlhet hypotheses regarding the war, its origins, its development, and its effects are shared, with variations, by several relators. I will leave a systematic analysis of these for another occasion.

Bolivians and Paraguayans

In this collection of Enlhet accounts, there are very few references to Bolivian exploration.[13] This may be because Bolivian explorers came from the west and were led by Nivaclé guides. The Enlhet and the Nivaclé shared a broad strip of territory from north to south within which they maintained extensive family ties and where the majority was bilingual. It was, therefore, easy for Nivaclé guides to reach the eastern border of this shared strip and even beyond it. The line of forward forts maintained by the Bolivians in 1932 – Camacho/Mariscal Estigarribia; Loa; Huihay/Carayá; Yucra; Arce; Alihuatá; Saavedra/Ávalos Sánchez – reflects this. In keeping with the fact that this line follows approximately the western limit of the Enlhet territory (see map 1.3), Enlhet accounts of encounters with Paraguayans are noticeably greater in number than those of encounters with Bolivians.[14]

SECTION 2
DILEMMAS

It was wonderful how mutually inclusive the Enlhet were;
they treated each other with attention and respect
Metyeeyam' [15]

With the arrival of large numbers of Paraguayan troops in 1932, the situation became tense, as these Paraguayans "wanted to kill us."[16] As a consequence, the Enlhet abandoned and avoided the Paraguayan forts.[17] Only some of the rearguard forts saw their continued presence.[18] At the Bolivian forts, on the other hand, the large-scale arrival of soldiers did not have the same effect (Malhkee·tko-Ngkoyoy', account 8) and the Enlhet only abandoned these when the Bolivians themselves retreated, in many cases leaving with them (Malhkee·tko-Ngkoyoy', account 10). It should be noted here that, generally speaking, the Enlhet present contact with the Bolivians as having been less violent and less dangerous than contact with the Paraguayans, although it was certainly not free from violence.

Relations with the Forts

Some Enlhet groups avoided the forts; others visited them sporadically to meet the new arrivals or to exchange articles with them; others lived more or less continuously with the military, on the dimensions of work for the men, and prostitution of the women.[19] Here I mention only in passing the lines of reasoning applied by the distinct Enlhet groups to resolving the dilemma between approaching the forts and retreating. It is probable that there was a range of localized reasons, for example, the individual wishes of a leader. However, many processes, lines of reasoning, and decisions were repeated in a similar way in different areas. For instance, many forts were built in places with more or less permanent water and were strategic for the Enlhet. One motive for living alongside the soldiers at the forts, then, was dependence on water, which was scarce at certain times of the year. Another, related, reason was the fact that groups did not easily abandon the places they occupied by preference and which served them in a way as "symbolic centres" (Malhkee-tko-Ngkoyoy', account 2). Another was avoidance of the immense violence of encounters outside the forts.[20] It is precisely the experiences of those who did not approach the forts that allow us to understand cohabitation with the soldiers – and in particular prostitution (pages 116–17) – as a strategy to control the military through face-to-face relations, through the establishment of social relations. This control mechanism was relative as, not only outside but also inside the forts, more or less explicit violence caused constant fear. Differences in criteria for judging whether to live alongside the military or abandon the forts during the different phases of the war corresponded, to a large extent, to the concomitant intensity of this fear of Paraguayans.

These criteria were not linear, however. This is illustrated by the fact that some Enlhet continued to live in a fort even after the violence they experienced there increased significantly (Seepe-Pta'heem-Pelhkapok, account 12). Ramón Ortiz' explanation in account 11 implies that dependency links had been established – both ideological and physical, and whose nature will be examined elsewhere – which made it difficult to abandon the place despite the adverse conditions they experienced. For example, both Paraguayans and Bolivians named certain Enlhet as intermediaries between the civilian Indigenous population and the military and gave them a military rank, serving the military's vested interest in maintaining a minimum of order in the forts to continue to benefit from the presence of the Enlhet.[21] This practice, apart from creating a feeling of protection among the Enlhet, gave the appearance of a certain social matrix and made separation difficult.

Enlhet Fighters

Another issue, and one that would merit closer consideration elsewhere, relates to the fact that many Enlhet took part in military activity, especially on the side of the Paraguayans.[22] In this regard, Ramón Ortiz says in account 11 that not only Paraguayan blood was shed (page 50). Other Enlhet relators go much further than this statement and insist, like Kenteem in account 16, that the Paraguayans would not have won the war without the participation of the original inhabitants of the region, the Enlhet (pages 64–5). This statement of having been part of the victory is, at its heart, a claim on participation in a shared historical project. It is a claim that the Enlhet maintain to the present, though today they express it in other words. Nevertheless, it continues to be disparaged and even denied by national society.

MOVEMENT UNDER PRESSURE

That's how it was. It was terrible, really terrible. Compared with that experience, today things are very good. In fact, I often worry that the Enlhet might be persecuted again.

Savhongvay' [23]

From the point of view of those Enlhet who did not live with the soldiers at the forts, various relators in the present collection illustrate the constant danger they faced of falling victim to violent attacks by the military. The situation produced constant fear that triggered distinct patterns of movement: people stopped visiting the forts, approached the Mennonite settlements, although they did not find refuge there either, or withdrew to places not frequented by the military despite the real risk that they might suffer from restricted access to water. In short, it became impossible to live in a satisfactory and reasonable way; it was dangerous even to collect food in the forest.[24] These conditions resulted in the hunger that the Mennonites still perceive today as a central characteristic of the traditional Enlhet way of life (Kalisch and Unruh 2014, 504; 2020, 506–7).

Profound Change

The movements of Malhkee·tko-Ngkoyoy' (accounts 2, 8, 10, and 20) during her childhood serve as a paradigmatic illustration of the fact that the war changed traditional patterns of displacement within her territory completely (see also Savhongvay', account 13). During the first years of her life, Malhkee·tko-Ngkoyoy' lived at the Bolivian fort of Alihuatá, Loom-Popyet,[25] and in the surrounding area; the group would make visits from there to the region later called Paratodo and from which her father came. However, toward the end of 1933, she and a relatively large group of Enlhet accompanied the Bolivian retreat as far as Fort Muñoz, Ayvompeen-Saanga,[26] where they parted company with the Bolivians and went to live with the Nivaclé at the German oblate mission of Escalante, Aalha (Malhkee·tko-Ngkoyoy', account 10),[27] because the father of Malhkee·tko-Ngkoyoy' had Nivaclé relatives, some of whom lived there. They stayed for some time at Escalante before returning to Fort Muñoz, which by the time of their return was under Paraguayan control. With a military document in their hand to protect them, they then headed east, taking the military road from Fort Muñoz to Fort Nanawa, Nanaava'a. Malhkee·tko-Ngkoyoy' recounts this journey, and their encounter with the Paraguayan military during the journey, in great detail, although her accounts are not included in the present book. Her group finally settled on the ranch named Pozo Colorado, Vasee-Yaamelket, belonging to the North American George Lohman, Yoyi Looma (page 17). For a time, they also lived in Maklhavay, the principal Anglican mission among the Énxet, further east again. There, Malhkee·tko-Ngkoyoy' learned the Énxet language.

Only when she was an adolescent did she and her group return to her father's home in the present-day area of Paratodo, where she married. By 1948, when the Mennonites began to populate the region, Malhkee·tko-Ngkoyoy' had two children. The immigrants soon occupied her family's traditional places and the foreign settlement of the region led her to find another place to live. A few years later, she and her husband moved to the north of Fort Alihuatá to live on the edge of another Mennonite Colony, Neuland, which had been founded in 1947. In 1962, the Mennonites established the Campo Largo mission in the same area, near Fort Boquerón.[28] Malhkee·tko-Ngkoyoy' belonged to the first group to be settled there, and she died there in 2016. She never returned to the region of Alihuatá.

SECTION 4
A PARENTHESIS: EVENTS PARALLEL TO
THE WAR

They were not allowed to travel their own path
to understanding and comprehension to its end.
Their way of life vanished.

Vena'teem [29]

In parallel to the Chaco War, two events unfolded that would be as important in determining the future of the Enlhet as the war itself. First, a traumatic smallpox epidemic in the summer of 1932–33, and second, from 1927, Mennonite immigration. Contact between the Enlhet and the Mennonites became firmly established during the war.

The Victims of Smallpox

As well as being extremely virulent, smallpox is highly contagious. For this reason, the Enlhet strategy of fleeing when it attacked them made them a vector for it spreading more quickly. Ten days after infection with smallpox, a rash appears on the skin. This turns into pustules that join together to form large blisters. In the later stages, the skin begins to detach from the body and death occurs within a week (Oeser 2008, 44–5). In the case of haemorrhagic smallpox, which is the form described by the Enlhet, the blood vessels burst under the skin, making it look black. Smallpox did not affect the Mennonites, as they had been vaccinated against it. In addition, Europeans have a natural immunity to smallpox that the Enlhet did not.

In respect of the neighbouring Énxet population, Grubb (1914, 202–3) reports that as early as 1884, a third of the population had died from smallpox. According to Grubb, the proportion of victims reached two-thirds in some villages. In Enlhet accounts, there are indications that there had also been outbreaks among their population before the Chaco War. Indeed, the combined factors of the high contagiousness of smallpox, high mobility of groups, and close relations among them facilitated the spread of the disease to the whole region.[30] We know for certain that the epidemic of 1932–33 spread throughout the whole

Figure 3.2 • "The skin begins to detach from the body." Unknown Enlhet man, 1940s, a survivor of smallpox, with smallpox scars.

of Enlhet territory and, as the Elders attest, left it depopulated. In support of their testimony, Siemens (1943, 5) mentions that animal skin traders travelling in the area told him that "about 25 years ago, the population was fairly big; the current generation is only a shadow of that." Indeed, it is known from outbreaks of smallpox in Europe that the death toll reported by Grubb, who mentioned losses of up to two-thirds of the population, is not an exaggeration (Oeser 2008, 45).

Such a severe reduction in population in only a few months makes estimation of the number of people in the Enlhet community before the Chaco War difficult. In 1943, the Mennonites carried out a census of the Enlhet in the area of Filadelfia and Loma Plata and counted 625 individuals (Siemens 1943, 5). This figure is still cited today in popular Mennonite discourse for the time of their arrival. However, Siemens (n.d., 11–12) himself estimated a figure of 1,000 Enlhet at the time of the census since, he argued, a large part of the population was to be found in the Mennonite colonies only at harvest time and was, therefore, not included in the census. Even this correction, however, remains far below the real figure. On the one hand, at the time of the census the Enlhet still led a very mobile life, which made it impossible to survey them accurately. On the other, only a small part of the population went to work for the Mennonites, who at that time occupied a relatively small area of land in the northern part of the Enlhet territory. Stahl (1980, 157) and Schartner and Stahl (1986, 73) not only fail to question these aspects of the 1943 census but compound any error by extrapolating from the 1943 estimate, without adjustment, to arrive at an Enlhet population for 1930, for which they give the same figure of 1,000, taking no account whatsoever of the disastrous effect of smallpox and other deadly diseases.[31]

To arrive at a more realistic approximation of the number of Enlhet before the Chaco War a different method of calculation is required. Here only an indication of the parameters of such a method can be given; it is not possible at the current stage of research to link it to specific numbers and, indeed, this will probably remain the case since the necessary historical data was not recorded. Nevertheless, bearing in mind that the Enlhet census was carried out in a region covering one-fifth or less of their territory and that, at a conservative estimate, smallpox claimed the lives of half the population, a figure may be reached of 6,250 to 10,000 for the year 1930, still without challenging the results of the Mennonite census. This figure does not include victims of other epidemics or war; nor does it reflect the fact that during the war very few children were born alive (Siemens 1943). In synthesis, the true number of Enlhet in the year 1930 must have been higher than 10,000. If it is also taken into account that occurrences of outbreaks of smallpox previous to this date are highly probable, then for the year 1900, a much higher figure still can be estimated. By contrast, the 2012 National Census reports around 8,200 Enlhet (DGEEC 2014, 78). That is to say that these are losses from which the population has not yet recovered.

War, Smallpox, and Mennonites

The traumas inflicted by the smallpox epidemic and by the Chaco War inevitably combined.[32] Many Enlhet relators identify a causal relationship between the war and the appearance of smallpox.[33] In addition, both events contributed toward the same result, the subsequent subjugation of the Enlhet by an alien society arriving to settle in the midst of their territory. Some relators describe smallpox as the initial reason for their approaching the Mennonites, while others identify the Chaco War as the motivating factor.[34]

Indeed, the early relationship of the Enlhet with the Mennonites can be understood only against the backdrop of the war and the smallpox epidemic. These events set the course for the meeting of the two groups, without the Enlhet having discussed in depth with the immigrants the question of possession – and use – of their land. However, in the difficult situation imposed by military hostilities, the Mennonites appeared to be their allies, even though, in reality, there was no alliance. On the contrary, the Enlhet's need for refuge – which the Mennonites did not offer other than in a few isolated cases – ran contrary to the strong vested interest of the immigrants in populating the region and becoming its owners.[35]

Under constellations so prone to non-equilibrium, and at a time of additionally marked hardship for the Enlhet, the incipient economic relationship with the immigrants – manifesting itself, for example, in the sale of *tamam'a* rope[36] – led to the creation of a contact discourse that was based unilaterally on the thinking of the outsiders and was difficult to revise after the war. The difficulty of renegotiating terms of cohabitation was aggravated by the fact that the group of Mennonites in Fernheim showed a marked interest in evangelizing the Enlhet – in "converting" them and "civilizing" them, to use the terminology of the 1935 statute for the missionary work of the Mennonites, *Light to the Indigenous* – in changing them at all cost.[37] Thus, while the situation was very favourable for the Mennonites to begin and carry out their enterprise of colonization, it was fatal for the Enlhet.[38]

Smallpox as a Vehicle for Subjugation

Haakok Maaset (account 21) does more than to give a simple illustration – in astonishing detail – of the terror caused among the population by smallpox. He explains the connection between smallpox and subjugation. He mentions two Mennonites who demonstrated their amazing power to save a person from the certain death the plague brought. It is much more than a detail that these two men were shortly thereafter among the architects of the effort that would organize the subjugation of the Enlhet people by Mennonite society, namely the missionary work begun in 1936 at Ya'alve-Saanga (Kalisch and Unruh 2014; 2020).[39] Like all people with power, these two men merited reverence and inspired respect. Fearing them as they feared all powerful shamans, the Enlhet were swift to attend to their wishes to avoid any offence that might incur their anger.[40] In other words, as a result of their experience that these men could save people from smallpox, any inclination among the Enlhet to defend themselves against the men's missionary attitudes and activities was dispelled.[41] Haakok Maaset refers to this connection between smallpox and subjugation when he concludes that the powerful action of the two Mennonites on smallpox "marked the beginning of their work" among the Enlhet (page 84).[42]

The connection between the smallpox epidemic and subjugation is repeated in the Enlhet accounts in a considerable number of variations[43] (see also Kalisch and Unruh 2014, 202; 2020, 201–2). An important aspect of this connection is the fact that smallpox took a lesser toll among those who submitted to being vaccinated by the military, while people who attempted to maintain their independence – those to whom Malhkee·tko-Ngkoyoy' refers in account 8 – were affected far more severely. To highlight the importance of this observation, it is useful to summarize an account by Melteiongkasemmap (2016) regarding Toba-Enenlhet history. Although some Enlhet relators give similar accounts, Melteiongkasemmap demonstrates especially clearly the implications of the choice between submitting to vaccination and resisting it. These are implications beyond a simple question of life or death. He states that the smallpox epidemic of the 1930s was sent by the creoles to oppress the Toba-Enenlhet.[44] However, it was these very creoles who offered vaccination against the disease. Thus, the offer posed a dilemma to the population: to allow themselves to be vaccinated by those who wage war using an epidemic, which means to accept defeat, or to refuse and die an almost certain death. One part of the Toba-Enenlhet population submitted and was saved; the other resisted and died. With their physical disappearance, resistance itself was extinguished. From the time of this episode onward, Toba-Enenlhet tradition has survived basically through the accounts of those who took the decision to submit. The DNA of defeat has become part of Enenlhet memory.[45]

Salvation and Capitulation

A January 1933 article in the *Mennoblatt*, a bi-weekly periodical published in Filadelfia in German, mentions smallpox among the Enlhet:

> Haemorrhagic smallpox. This plague has appeared in some Indigenous settlements belonging to the Lengua (Enlhet) tribe. Increasingly, the war has displaced the poor from the colonies. One of the causes of this dreadful epidemic may be that they live only on roots and the fruits of the forest, as they no longer dare to seek beans, sweet potatoes and bread in the Mennonite villages or to go hunting in groups in open country as they used to. Consequently, they often go hungry. The people in the village of their leader Chief Alemán near Friedensfeld [Lhaptaana] have been almost wiped out. For fear of infection they do not even bury the dead; they even abandon the sick to suffer, impotently, a slow and horrible death from hunger, thirst, and insects. (Anonymous 1933)

The article confirms entirely what the Enlhet relators say about the extremely high death rate caused by smallpox. As to the causes of smallpox, however, the writer of the article presents an unusual hypothesis. He suggests that the epidemic arose because the Enlhet did not have access to the Mennonites' food and consequently lived "only on roots and the fruits of the forest." There is no doubt that the war radically altered the daily existence of the Enlhet and that they suffered hunger (Kooneng-Pa'at, account 18). However, Mennonite immigration occurred – it is important to note – less than three years before the journalist wrote these lines. Before and after the arrival of the Mennonites, roots and forest fruits constituted a fundamental part of the Enlhet diet. That is, the writer of the article refers not to Enlhet reality, but to the Mennonite perception of it. His comments reflect the fact that the immigrants considered themselves – after barely three years – crucial for the survival of the Enlhet. Indeed, in the common Mennonite view it was not the arrival of diverse groups of intruders that threatened the integrity of the Indigenous population.[46] In their view, the Enlhet "were almost extinct" long before the occupation of their territory by outsiders began (Redekop 1973, 315).[47] That is, in the article above we see an early reflection of the incipient Mennonite narrative according to which the immigrants saved the Enlhet from extinction;[48] in the words of Redekop (1973, 315), "[they] have enabled tribes to develop autonomy for survival in a modern world culture."

The concept of the salvation of the Enlhet is fundamental to the Mennonite narrative for two reasons. On a very immediate level, the immigrants used it to make sense of the suffering they themselves had experienced under the Stalinist terror, and to justify their presence in Enlhet territory with the argument that God had sent them to these lands for no less a purpose than to save its Aboriginal inhabitants (P.P. Klassen 1991, 130–1). On a less visible level, the significance of this notion of salvation is related to Mennonite dispossession of the Enlhet. Their flight from the Stalinist terror, which is a cornerstone of the Mennonite narrative – in particular for those in Fernheim – led them to see themselves as dispossessed. A few years after this flight they settled in the heart of Enlhet territory, their consolidation occurring, in addition, at a time when horrific suffering made all notions and practices of normal life impossible for the Enlhet. The immigrants became aware of the situation of the native inhabitants,[49] but the suffering of the Enlhet, though comparable to their own recent experiences under the Stalinist terror, did not become a shared dimension on which to establish relations in equilibrium. On the contrary, as has so often happened, victims within one framework became aggressors within another (Todorov 2002): the Mennonites, the dispossessed, became dispossessors. Despite the fact that the immigrants were conscious of this constellation,[50] they did not question it, but legitimized dispossession of the Enlhet with the argument that, since they had been dispossessed themselves and had no place in the world to live, they had no option but to carry it out.[51] Thus, in addition to transferring to the Enlhet their condition of dispossessed, they adopted a very particular conceptual stance regarding the dispossession they were protagonizing – they declared this dispossession an act of salvation from continual hunger, sickness, death; in short, from extinction.[52] They have reduced this reading of dispossession to a simple formula: the survival of the Enlhet – they say, speaking in place of the Enlhet – was much more important than the loss of their independence and sovereignty.[53]

Thus, the settlers themselves implicitly propound the notion of Enlhet capitulation (which is central to an understanding of the history of the Enlhet after the war), although the word itself does not figure in their vocabulary. For capitulation is precisely that: the surrendering of independence in return for survival, the assumption that life is so valuable that it is better to live in submission than to die. Capitulation, the final defeat of the Enlhet, began toward the end of the 1950s when, through the symbol of mass baptisms, they renounced their world and placed themselves at the will of the immigrants.[54] This defeat marked the culmination of a process described, paradoxically, as peaceful.[55]

Failure of Duty

We have considered different hypotheses among the Enlhet as to how the war began (page 126). These hypotheses were always within the human – the social – dimension. However, hypotheses explaining the arrival of smallpox go beyond references to the social dimension:

in the Enlhet view, all illnesses have a direct link to a dimension beyond man – the spiritual dimension. Malhkee·tko-Ngkoyoy' (account 20) for example, indicates that the epidemic was caused by the Bolivians (page 76). A very particular line of reasoning leads her to this conclusion: smallpox can only be prevented by one who is able to cause it. Thus, the observation that the Bolivians had the power to stop the outbreak implies that it was they who were the cause. The notion of cause and control on which Malhkee·tko-Ngkoyoy' relies here is not one linked to physical or biological laws. It is based on the logic of the power of the Elders, which follows the spiritual dimension. Other relators' references to the spiritual dimension are much more explicit in referring to smallpox, and their accounts therefore contain very dense symbolism (Metyeeyam', account 22; Kam'aatkok Ketsek, account 23).

■■■

Subjugation, once achieved, produces a state of submission to the new power group, to new social and economic conditions, and to a new regime of possession and use of geographical space and everything within it. This submissive state is not only reflected with respect to the subjugators but has become crystallized within the symbolic constellations of Enlhet society itself. This is exemplified plainly in account 22 by Metyeeyam' and even more clearly in account 23 by Kam'aatkok Ketsek. Kam'aatkok Ketsek explains that the Enlhet shared their territory with invisible beings. These invisible masters of the land made its human masters, the Enlhet, pay for the terrible bloodshed the war brought. They had to pay, through a smallpox epidemic that killed over half their people, for having failed to maintain equilibrium in their lands, even though it was not they who had destroyed it but the Paraguayan and Bolivian armies at whose hands they suffered so grievously.

This reasoning reveals a constellation of which the Enlhet were, and are, very conscious: to live harmoniously in their lands it was essential to maintain good relations with their invisible cohabitants. They had developed means of communicating with them and thus of maintaining equilibrium with them; the invisible beings had become *engmook*; relatives, allies. However, the fact that these allies turned against the Enlhet meant that every step they took from then on became potentially dangerous and the movement of the people within their own territory was severely hindered. When added to the profound disruptions of the time and their consequences, this very grave rupture between the Enlhet and the space in which they lived could not be compensated. On the contrary, the Enlhet felt that as the traditional relationship with particular places and their invisible inhabitants became increasingly damaged, the invisible beings' displeasure with them grew and it became more and more dangerous to travel through such areas. Through constant reinforcement of this rupture between the group and its territory, the rupture came to be a part of the Enlhet symbolic map in the form of a negative territory (Kalisch 2021). A familiar and welcoming backdrop was inverted to become one characterized by vague but constant danger. This inversion was and remains highly instrumental to the interest of the settlers and colonizers in occupying, and maintaining the occupation of, the land, for it favoured and continues to favour not only abandonment of the territory but also the silencing of possible claims of the Enlhet on their lands.

Responsibilities

The importance of Kam'aatkok Ketsek's account is not limited to drawing attention to the inversion of the concept of territory. Above all, she reveals a concept of relating to space that is completely different from that of the colonizers' world. She demonstrates that the Enlhet have an existential need to influence events in their territory that is not oriented toward control but toward the continual reconstruction of equilibrium within it. In parallel to this, Kam'aatkok Ketsek's reflections do not raise the issue of recovery of their lands. Indeed, this is not a frequent theme in current Enlhet affairs, though a definitive renouncement of the physical recuperation of their territory would have serious implications: it would admit an idea of cohabitation in which the price of possible reconciliation between the Aboriginal People and the incomers is paid exclusively by the dispossessed while the dispossessors go free of the cost of healing the consequences of their past actions. It would once again constitute subjugation or, from the opposite view, a surrendering of the self. It would be the antithesis of an articulation oriented to equilibrium between the two groups.

However, although Kam'aatkok Ketsek does not touch on the theme of physical recovery of their lands, she does not propose surrender. Rather, she repositions the theme on a new dimension of arguments and reformulates it on new lines: with her orientation to equilibrium she gives greater relevance to the exercise of responsibility for cohabitation in the territory than to the stating of a claim to it in a material or physical sense. She thus alters the focus of prevailing discourse and overturns current notions of development. Concomitantly, she does not refer to the subjugators' concept of responsibility, which is of a responsibility upon the subjugated to fulfil the demands of those in power and so play their part in maintaining the status quo. She is referring to a responsibility for equilibrium that, in order to be such, can only be a responsibility *in* equilibrium, a responsibility shared with other social actors. This is why the notion she proposes, which is a traditionally Enlhet notion, is not one of surrender. On the contrary, she speaks of a right to responsibility that is simultaneously the right to protagonism on one's own terms. When the Enlhet are in a position to take up their responsibility in this way, they will protagonize the redefinition of their territoriality between what it was, what it is, and what it could be, and the multiple superimposed territorialities within their historical territory, in an unprecedented way. It will be a redefinition oriented to equilibrium and will, therefore, inevitably affect discourse and practice around access to, and use of, territory. However, this will happen using categories other than those currently in use and will lead as a result to hitherto unimagined solutions. Kam'aatkok Ketsek's account opens avenues that merit further exploration.

■■■

The outbreak of smallpox is a tragic demonstration of the result of the Enlhet not being enabled to respond to the imperative for responsibility for equilibrium in their lands that their tradition proposes, their memory yearns for, and their daily life continues to manifest. At the same time, the episode of the epidemic allows an understanding of the tension that the failure to fulfil their responsibility places them under, a failure they see before them every day and are unable to remedy. This tension explains their practice of not assuming the exclusive attitude of the other despite perceiving it so clearly (page 122) but instead reaching out their hand to those who control everything. It explains the fact that they have invested more effort than all of their neighbours in continuing to construct harmony in their territory.

As long as the Enlhet are held in the lowest regard within the current interethnic system and have no convening power beyond their society, their practice of continuing to invite the other to the construction of new channels of communication could be mistaken for a lack of awareness, a lack of adaptation to reality. However, their insistence in this practice shows them to be enactors of their historical convictions. They know that if they reject concord there will never be harmony in their lands. Without them, there will be no peace. Conversely, as long as they continue to consider themselves as actors, as long as they hold out their hand, a reasonable vision of, and option for, peace remains. In the practice of not accepting the obvious – which constitutes an important act of resistance and requires considerable effort – they nurture significant potential for reconstruction of relations in equilibrium with the intruders. They do so looking forward to the day – which may come, let us hope – when the intruders open themselves to such an option.

SECTION 5
VIOLENCE, NEITHER NECESSARY NOR ACCIDENTAL

Then we left our home lands. We did it because of the Paraguayans.
The valay, the Paraguayans, ruined the Enlhet territory.
What happened to these lands is a shame.
This is not the Paraguayans' country. This is the Enlhet's country;
There's no question that this land is ours.

Savhongvay' [56]

Military violence perpetrated against the Enlhet for the pleasure of it is a constant feature of the Enlhet accounts. At certain times and on certain occasions some military chiefs acted to curb the violence, as Maangvayaam'ay' (account 9) and Seepe-Pta'heem-Pelhkapok (account 12) report. The reasons for such intervention are not made clear in the accounts, but the fact that the military at the forts took advantage of Enlhet women and the labour of the men is certainly highlighted and they even had Enlhet men among their ranks.[57] Thus, it is reasonable to suppose that they had some interest in maintaining a minimum of order between the soldiers and the Enlhet, so that the situation of exploitation could remain stable.

However, as we have seen in relation to the prostitution of Enlhet women at the forts (pages 116–17), the question of violence against the Enlhet is more complex than casual, preventable aggression. The acts of aggression reported were unnecessary: the Enlhet were not adversaries in military terms and did not provoke violence. Nevertheless, violence against them – against the civilian population – was not casual; it was systematic. The few instances in which officers tried to attenuate the violence (in cases where there was a certain social matrix between the Enlhet and the military, page 130) are in contrast to the many instances where acts of violence brought no consequences for their military perpetrators. Indeed, these acts of violence, carried out not in battle but against civil society, had strategic value. They were a clear message – a strong symbol – that the presence of the military contradicted, inverted, and eliminated the fact that the Enlhet were the sovereign inhabitants of their lands, members of an independent people. In this sense, violence against the Indigenous population –

especially violence against women and children – must be given a very precise reading. In its official *representation* and the conscious of the warring nations, the Chaco War was an international war (Capdevila 2010a). However, within this war another, non-military, war was fought, an asymmetric war (Richard 2007). In its *articulation*, the Chaco War was not only an international war but also a colonial war.

The pleasure taken in cruelty demonstrated in the accounts remains to be considered. Colonial wars facilitate violence and massacre because they are fought a long way from centres of power and "the moral principles that previously ensured the cohesion of the [colonizing] group have been abandoned"[58] (Todorov 2010, 177). Nevertheless, there is another more important reason explaining unrestrained violence intended not simply to defeat the other but to destroy him cruelly. Although this reason is related to the difference perceived between the self and the other, the violence is not rooted in ignorance of what the other is, which would make it susceptible to avoidance through better knowledge of him. Rather, it is generated in the radical difference that obstructs adaptation of the other to the categories of one's own *imaginary*, and thus an *understanding* of him as an element of a shared social system and so, ultimately, the *feeling* of him as part of a shared humanity (Todorov 2010, 178). It expresses a denial of the condition of the other as human, a condition that is, de facto, not in doubt, through treatment that does not simply kill as one might kill an animal. Rather, the brutality of the killing corresponds here to an attempt to pervert and contradict something that – despite all differences – remains obvious: the humanity of the victim. Thus, for the killing to be given a reading that transcends the simple elimination of the other, it needs to be reinforced by unprecedented cruelty. The Enlhet understood this constellation. That is why, as I have mentioned, they sought to establish social relations as a strategy for self-defence regardless of the high cost to them (page 130).[59]

The Conquest Again

Unconstrained violence and pleasure in cruelty for its own sake have gone hand-in-hand with conquest since the earliest times. Bartolomé de las Casas described it in detail in his *Short Account of the Destruction of the Indies* in 1552. However, it is not necessary to go to Central

America to find such unspeakable violence. González (1556, 607–8), for example, records the following regarding Asunción, seat of governance of the Viceroyalty of the Río de la Plata:

> Captain Vergara ... ordered women to be brought, not only for himself but for those he wished ... [their children being] at the breast of the women as they were carried away, and the children were left in that place ... The Indians seeing that they were not returned to them ... the mothers, aunts and relatives, [and] knowing that they were in the hands of the Christians, the lamentations were so great day and night that from pure passion and from not eating, they finally died, men and women alike.
>
> And of the Indian women taken by the Christians many were so oppressed that, seeing themselves in this condition, some fled to their country, and being brought again, were whipped and mistreated; others seeing themselves exhausted and desirous of their children and husbands, and unable to go to them, hanged themselves; those who did not, gorged themselves with earth, for they would rather kill themselves than suffer the life that many gave them; besides this, others were kept so locked away that the very sun hardly saw them, and should the Christians they were with see any thing which did not seem to them right, even though what seemed to them were not so, from pure jealousy they would kill or burn them ... [Some time ago there were among the Christians] almost fifty thousand Indian women at the least; and now at present there must be among the Christians fifteen thousand, and all the rest are dead.

In short, the middle of the twentieth century in the Chaco saw a repeat of attitudes and strategies established at the very beginning of Paraguay's colonial history. Just as the dispossessed Mennonites became dispossessors (page 141), the colonized Paraguayans became colonizers. However, much remains to be considered regarding the violence linked to the Chaco War, its causes, its effects, and the reactions it generated in turn. In this regard, it would be especially interesting to know more about the perspective and objectives of those who perpetrated it:[60] a better understanding of the Chaco War as a colonial war is needed. The following section addresses this.

SECTION 6
ACTORS

They were all very frightened, full of fear of the Paraguayans.
Taalhe-Ktong [61]

As time went on, the military began to sever the few ties they had established with the Enlhet and to increasingly sow terror. Seepe-Pyoy' (account 30) identifies this as the reason the Enlhet began to defend themselves and to seek revenge; the reason was not, for example, the threat of possible dispossession, which at that precise moment in history still constituted a fairly abstract possibility.[62] Seepe-Pyoy' even identifies the specific moment the Enlhet decided to respond to the violence of the military with the same physical methods as those used by the soldiers, and to kill them.

The Power of the Elders

Before this decision, the Enlhet defended themselves exclusively through the power of communication (Seepe-Pyoy', account 5) and through the shamanic power of their wise Elders, the *apyobolhma'*: the "people with powerful knowledge."[63] By the application of their power, the wise men commanded potential for defence through which they could even cause the destruction of the other. Although the effects they produced with their power were visible to the common people, the power operated in a world invisible to them. Thus, when it was employed in a violent way[64] – to punish or avenge, or for other specific reasons, causing, for example, a sudden death, an illness, or a misfortune – the relation between the actor and the result of the action remained hidden and could only be perceived by other wise men. In such cases, the wise men responded to the initial aggression again within the non-visible sphere. In this way, the visible social context remained free of the necessity for acts of violence. In parallel to this, all physical or verbal aggression was held in very low regard by Enlhet society. The practice of delegating the exercise of violence to the wise men had a pacifying effect on society as it avoided the escalation of violence in the visible social sphere by means of extended response and counter-response within the invisible sphere.

However, a limiting factor operated on the efficiency of the wise men's actions against the intruders. For the Enlhet, the invisible power of the wise men existed as fact because they knew how to read the signs indicating that it had been employed. For example, for them, the overturning of the military truck in account 29 by Sooso' was the result of a specific action by a wise man with power. Fear of the power they perceived was the incentive for the avoidance of any kind of aggression in the visible sphere. This avoidance – the pacifying of society once again – was another of the principal functions of the notion of power. The soldiers, however, were unable to read the signs (although the existence of powerful people was not an idea alien to the traditions of their own culture) and would have understood the crash as an accident. As they were not party to the logic of the Enlhet wise men, they did not fear it. In consequence, and despite the shamanic power having real effects on concrete incidents (effects which could not be read as such by the outsiders), beyond Enlhet society it could not fulfil its most important function: that of avoidance. In this way, its effect was greatly reduced; the moment arrived when the Enlhet had to use a language the soldiers would understand and began to react in a physical way to the violence they perpetrated. We see again in passing that the appearance of violence is related to the lack of a shared social matrix (pages 130, 147).

Symbols of Subjugation

Acts of physical vengeance took place once the battlefront had moved on. They were directed at small groups of soldiers, whether deserters (Bolivian or Paraguayan) or Paraguayan garrison posts controlling occupied territory. Although the actions of the Enlhet appear cruel and deceitful, they were no more brutal or insidious than the violence of the military toward the Indigenous population. Nevertheless, one aspect of these compensatory acts is noteworthy. Similarly to the military, Enlhet recourse to vengeance was not oriented toward specific individuals. Rather, all members of the enemy band were targeted. In contrast to the behaviour of the military, on the other hand, the level of violence inflicted by the Enlhet in a particular act depended on the degree of provocation enacted by the victim.

The existence of these acts of revenge – and of other forms of re-sistance such as that exercised through the power of the wise men – indicates clearly that the Enlhet, though victims of military violence, did not surrender to it.[65] In fact, the notion of capitulation – of final defeat leading the people to renounce their own world and place themselves at the will of the aggressor – only appears two decades later and is combined with the baptism, within a very short time, of the entire Enlhet people (page 141). However, although capitulation came later, Yamasma'ay' (account 32) remembers that at the end of the war a clear symbol of subordination was imposed: the cutting of hair. The account of the hair cut – a metaphor for the exclusion of the In-digenous world and the simultaneous assimilation of the Indigen-ous People – indicates that Enlhet society perceives clearly that the condition for participation in Paraguayan society is submission. In this account, Yamasma'ay' sets out the terms that since that time have defined the identity of Enlhet people who assume life in Paraguayan territory (because they have no choice): negation of themselves. At the same time it makes clear that it is an identity constructed not only on the exclusion of their world, but also on the fear summarized in the words, "I'm afraid of them to this day."[66]

Capitulation and Memory

Relations with Paraguayan society ceased after the war because its representatives withdrew almost completely from the Chaco. It was only with the fall of the dictatorship of Alfredo Stroessner in 1989 that Paraguayan society once again emerged as an important and visible actor for the Enlhet. Their relationship with the other intruder soci-ety, the Mennonites, by contrast, intensified rapidly after the war. It was consolidated in the postwar years on axes such as the significant reduction in the Enlhet population caused by smallpox; the traumas suffered by the people; social transfiguration into new, local groups; territorial reconfiguration in the new context and, later, on those of continued loss of space, loss of access to resources and the impossi-bility of keeping goats and sheep and, finally, the concerted efforts of the Mennonites to christianize them.[67] The intensive phase of the colonization of Enlhet society ended with mass baptisms of the entire

Enlhet people at the end of the 1950s, an event that marks and sym-
bolizes the aforementioned capitulation of the Enlhet, the decision to
opt for the path proposed and imposed by the Mennonites (page 141).

Capitulation caused a change so radical that the Enlhet themselves
assumed, within the framework of the mission, the version of history
promoted by those who had defeated them: the notion that they had
been saved by the Mennonites.[68] However, this imposed reading of
Enlhet history is based on uninformed hypotheses about the past and
cannot be corroborated in the accounts that represent the memory
of the people. On the contrary, it very much contradicts them. It is
here that the activation of memory becomes crucial to overcome a
condition of submission that appears eternal because the criteria for
understanding it as related to time and place are lacking. It is here
that memory contains invaluable potential for liberation. It is the potential for understanding oneself as an actor in processes and not as a
victim of results. It is the potential for new visions.

▪▪▪

The processes and dynamics in the years after the war that I have summarized here do not belong to the account of the Chaco War itself and
are not the subject of this book. However, this limitation should not
lead us to think of the processes of the Chaco War as separate from the
dynamics of the postwar period. It is the combination of the two that
describes the violent wave of colonialism that swept over the Enlhet
people. I have explored this combination in other work.[69] This observation concludes the historical part of the present book. From this
point on I will explore the importance of the memory of the Enlhet,
not only for their own society but for all of Paraguay.

PART FOUR
A FURTHER REFLECTION: THE ENLHET ACCOUNTS AND PARAGUAY

HANNES KALISCH

For three ill-fated centuries a sceptre
oppressed the peoples of the Americas;
But one day pride arose to cry:
Enough! ... and the sceptre was broken.
. . .
Paraguayans, Republic or death!
Our spirit has set us free;
Neither oppressors nor slaves enter
Where unity and equality reign.

Paraguayan national anthem

Kaymaap-Takhaalhet has related his narrow escape from a massacre committed by Paraguayan soldiers (account 17). He is now close to ninety years old.[1] However, he is not at peace. His past has caught up with him and has become his present. Separated from his surroundings by deafness, he continually hears the voices of Paraguayans pursuing him to murder him. He lives in constant fear. Only his constant movement among the houses in the village allows him to combat his fears. With slow steps, he attempts to escape the violent death he fears might overtake him at any moment. He is weak and cannot get up unaided when he falls along the way. Yet only by this interminable flight does he feel he can save himself. Kaymaap-Takhaalhet, the cousin of Kam'aatkok Ketsek, was also the cousin of my wife's grandfather. His experience, which is the experience of all his extended family, is my daughters' history.

Kaymaap-Takhaalhet often visits us during his restless journey. He stays a few hours; sleeps in his chair. As soon as he wakes he hears the voices of the Paraguayans. He gets up and continues his perpetual flight in slow, short steps. As he leaves, he meets my younger daughter, in Enlhet terms his niece. She has just started school, where each morning they sing the national anthem as the flag is raised.[2] They see

Figure 4.1 ▪ "Ten kilometres from our community lies Fort Boquerón." Enlhet girls at the former Fort Boquerón during the 2019 annual official ceremony, attended by the President of the Republic, to mark victory at the so-called Battle of Boquerón on 29 September.

each other and exchange a smile. All the while she hums the tune of the national anthem, with its difficult words in a language that is not her own. She repeats the ones she remembers: "oppressed the peoples of the Americas ... Where unity and equality reign. Unity and equality. Unity and equality."

Ten kilometres from our community lies Fort Boquerón.[3] I pass by there when I visit the neighbouring community of *Ya'alve-Saanga.* This afternoon my daughter is with me and she asks if we can stop at the old fort. She loves to walk along the high bank built within the precinct as a sort of monument. As I wait for her to come back I look at the Paraguayan flag flying on its pole. In the strong wind, I can read clearly the words on the emblem: *Paz y Justicia* (Peace and Justice).[4]

Words Unspoken

Kaymaap-Takhaalhet has not moved far from his place of birth. However, he will not die in the country where he was born. In his country, territories were not managed by a central power as in nation-states. It was said – it is still said – that for this reason, he was not born in a country. People called it a no-man's land. It was also said – and is still said – that he had no society until he was made to join Paraguayan society. People said the Chaco was an uninhabited desert.[5] It is true that he was born with no citizenship. However, the citizenship he will die with is one that he neither understands nor embodies. He suffers it. It is a citizenship that does not consider him a citizen.

They said there was nothing although there was. They say there is nothing because they do not know what there is. How easy it was and is, in this imagined nothingness, to impose the self on the other, for any imposition appears to create values where there were none and thus to be for the supposed good of the other. The Mennonites gave clear words to this pattern when they declared that the process of dispossession of the Enlhet was in fact their salvation (page 141). In the case of the state, the model is repeated. In exchange for dispossession – almost all of their territory has been taken from them (see map 1.2) – it claims to take responsibility for them through its institutions: responsibility for their health, their education, and their economic well-being. Housing is built for them, but territories are not restored. Schools are built that, it is argued, prepare them for life in the modern world but that, instead of opening up possibilities for their participation as protagonists, are a means for their submissive integration (Kalisch 2010a; 2020). In sum, what appears charitable arises in fact from the arrogant premise of being able to decide for the other society what is best for it. It is an expropriation of the responsibility every society has for itself, a usurpation that allows the manipulation of a society by external interests. In short, to state that the Indigenous people lack everything and need someone to take responsibility for them is the ultimate act of colonization because it legitimizes their dispossession, their reduction, their exclusion, and their marginalization: their continued submission.

The accounts in this book speak of the most overt and intense stage of colonization, which included the military invasion of Enlhet territory and the consolidation of the Mennonite colonies. As has been seen, however, actions aimed at the subjugation of the Indigenous Peoples are not limited to these historical events, and the violence reigning in their lands did not end with the cessation of military hostilities. The concept of violence is not limited to bloodshed; it includes the act of imposing one's interests without articulating them with those of others. In this sense, both Mennonite and Paraguayan societies continue to commit marked violence today,[6] albeit with varying degrees of subtlety.[7] Both said there was nothing although there was. Both say that there is nothing so as to destroy what there is. The massacre that Kaymaap-Takhaalhet so narrowly escaped rendered this logic physical, in the deaths of the older people, and it is the logic under and within which he has spent his life; under and within which he had to reshape his life. Separated from his surroundings by his deafness, he sees more than other people. His restless journeying is not the whim of an old man who has lost touch with reality: for good reason, fear of those Paraguayans will not let him rest, even at ninety years of age.

■■■

Two centuries ago, Paraguay gained independence from Spanish dominion. For the Indigenous Peoples imprisoned in the interior of the country, independence brought a change in the protagonists of the colonization of their lands, but that is all. During the government of Carlos Antonio López, the Supreme Decree of 7 October 1848 "declare[d] Citizens of the Republic the natural Indians of the twenty-one peoples of the territory of the Republic" (Article 1) and "property of the State the goods, rights and actions of the aforementioned twenty-one natural peoples of the Republic" (Article 11; Supreme Court of Justice [of Paraguay] 2003, 13). This decree referred to the twenty-one Guaraní peoples of the Franciscan reductions (Schvartzman 2015, 207), but demonstrates the line of discourse that later came to form the ideological and legal matrix to be applied to the entire Paraguayan territory and to all the peoples living in it (page 127). The occupation of the Chaco territories, in the present case, happened only eighty years later with the Chaco War (Savhongvay', account 3). In the name of the defence of national sovereignty, the war served to crush the Indigenous Peoples of the region who had until that time been independent (pages 127, 147). The colonial enterprise was thus able to proceed on several fronts through Indigenous territory without significant resistance.

With regard to the colonization of Enlhet territory, in particular, the Paraguayan State formed an alliance with the Mennonite colonists. In addition to protecting and aiding the immigrants, it granted the Mennonites a kind of autonomy that it never considered granting the Indigenous Peoples, whose right to a space and to their own protagonism is still not recognized today. On the contrary, the current National Constitution refers to the territories of the formerly independent peoples – peoples "pre-dating the formation and organization of the Paraguayan State" (Article 62) – as simply a "habitat" (Article 63, for example). The term *habitat* lacks any political connotation: these peoples – "defined as cultural groups" (Article 62) – are not understood and treated as political subjects. Clearly, the independence of Paraguayan society from the Spanish crown was never accompanied by independence from the logic of subjugation. Paraguayan society remained trapped by this logic (page 148).

■■■

During the intense stage of colonization of the Enlhet territory, Indigenous society suffered the rapid disarticulation of its various, complex autonomous political systems.[8] The process that led to this disarticulation was full of internal contradictions; the polyphony of the accounts of the Chaco War reminds us that the experience of the different groups that we call today the Enlhet was multifaceted. Within groups, there were arguments and controversies where differing options were projected. Thus, there were different ways of responding and reacting to the state of war and to the violence experienced that, in addition, manifested themselves in each group differently and at different times. Within a few years, however, the violent pressure from outside left gradually less space for this diversity of responses, and the capitulation of the Enlhet toward the end of the 1950s (pages 141, 151–3), which marked the culmination of the most intense phase of colonization, produced a relatively homogenous result:[9] the baptism of almost all the Enlhet within a few years and their subsequent settlement in the so-called missions, protagonized by the Mennonites.[10] Under these circumstances a common formula for shared living with the Paraguayans also crystallized, based on fear of them and still in operation today: *Don't cry. Keep quiet. Bear it.*

■■■

The testimonies of the elder Enlhet generation were given from a perspective opposed to that of the reader. They demonstrate clearly that here, "perspective" means more than the position in space and time from which one observes. It implies a way of seeing and of speaking, a way of understanding the world. One of the themes that will be investigated in the following pages is the implication of the fact that radically different perspectives do exist.

It is common for radically different perspectives to collide. Here, however, the question is one of a collision between people of differing viewpoints that occurred and occurs within a marked imbalance of power. From its privileged position, the colonial dynamic, which presumes the existence of a single reading of the world, threatens the perspective of the other extremely aggressively, and the violent impact of this causes words to die before they can be spoken: colonialist society produces, above all, silence in the societies it attacks. Indeed, the Enlhet observe from silenced perspectives; some are perspectives that were disarticulated and others have taken refuge in silence. There are also silences by decree: all reference to collisions has been removed from communicative circulation in order to feign a prevalence of harmony. The meaning of the accounts – another theme that will be explored later – must be defined within this context of amnesia caused by overlapping silences.

Facts and Experiences

An interest in history might be based on an eagerness to know the past in order to learn from it and behave more appropriately in comparable future situations. However, given a past that produces silences in the present, my dedication to the past of the Enlhet has another motive: the need to find tools to aid in working on the consequences of past facts on the present (Dening 2004, 37). It is in this sense that I have argued that memory constitutes the building of bridges from the present to one's past (page 11). But then, if memory does not look from the past but from the present, what are the *facts of the past*?

Let us look at three cases. The Enlhet claim that they lived in abundance (Kalisch and Unruh 2014), but the foreigners say about them that they lived in poverty.[11] This judgement reflects, in part, simple ignorance of the physical circumstances of Enlhet life and, in part, the value criteria that the immigrants applied. For them, the Enlhet were poor because they did not have flour and rice; because they did not have clothing and other things that the Mennonites considered essential. By contrast, they did not see the wealth of the region that the Enlhet knew how to use perfectly and which was thereby the Enlhet's wealth. They did not see it but even had they seen it, the Mennonites would not have considered it wealth[12] (see the words of Anonymous 1933, page 139). In reality, the very opposition of categories wealth/poverty, which describes relatively stable conditions, was not an Enlhet idea; they would have used instead the concepts of abundance/hunger (Kalisch and Unruh 2014, 64), which describe conditions of juncture. Additionally, their values preferentially emphasize non-material aspects of life such as equilibrium and harmony (Kalisch 2011b). Immersed in these two different, and barely reconcilable, perspectives, Haatkok'ay' Sevhen makes an observation that throws this into stark contrast: "We may have been poor, but it wasn't a burden for us" (in Kalisch and Unruh 2014, 61).

Few might doubt that the descriptions "wealthy" and "poor" depend to a high degree on contextual and cultural circumstances. In the case of a concept such as hunger – the second case – the question is less obvious, as the term appears to express a bodily state that has physical consequences outside our control. However, despite the fact that hunger produces a weakness experienced by all humans, the concept of hunger cannot be defined solely by absolute, measurable criteria either. For example, Heeva'ay' (in Kalisch and Unruh 2014, 309–10) mentions that Enlhet children went hungry in the first Mennonite residential school in the 1940s. Indeed, this experience is a common theme among Enlhet relators. When the account of Heeva'ay' was first published (Unruh and Kalisch 2002), an old Mennonite missionary explained to me with some annoyance that "if they were hungry, we were all hungry," because, he said, both pupils and teachers received the same amount of food. There is no reason to doubt his word, and his annoyance illustrates the point that the concept of hunger can only be defined on the basis of a particular society's reading of the constellations it experiences. In the same way, the fact of the feeling of hunger does not exist outside the perspective from which it receives its meaning.[13]

Let us take as a final case the smallpox epidemic. Both the Enlhet and the intruders were able to observe the physical evolution of this event. Indeed, descriptions among the two groups coincide to a large extent. Beyond these coincidences, however, for the intruders it is an illness they explain through causes and effects occurring at the physical level: their actions in response to it were solely at this physical level, for example through vaccinations. For the Enlhet, in contrast, smallpox represented an explosion of their universal order, not in the sense of a metaphor for the disaster, but in the sense of an explanation of it (page 142) that defines the framework for what they felt and the way they responded to the epidemic. Thus, if we read the words of Kam'aatkok Ketsek (account 23) in a metaphorical sense, we do not take them seriously;[14] we devalue them instead of attempting to understand not only her position but also the meaning of the fact that this position exists and that it implies a specific perspective.

■■■

The radical difference between the two perspectives on the epidemic is usually interpreted through differentiation between reality itself and discourse about it – representations of it. From the idea of different representations of the same reality it is a short step to questioning, from a hegemonic perspective, the appropriateness of the other perspective on reality and to qualify it, with varying degrees of condescension, as metaphorical, mythical, unenlightened, and superstitious, so as to declare it irrelevant out of hand, an obstacle it is typically proposed can be overcome by the usual call for "more education." However, not only the intruders but also the Enlhet speak, each from their perspective, of the *fact* of the smallpox epidemic. That is, the Enlhet too maintain that their perspective equates to reality, not simply to a discourse related more or less arbitrarily to it. Thus, the option clearly exists to understand the other as a person who inhabits a metaphorical world whose connection with reality is of doubtful value. However, if we do not wish to go down the path of accusing the other of being mistaken before having fully understood his position, we must assume that we have before us a radical difference that will not disappear simply because somebody declares unilaterally that the existence of other valid perspectives is impossible. If we do not wish to cure our ignorance by discarding what escapes our knowledge or even our perception – such an attack on difference would make us good colonizers – then we must attempt to understand the background to such a radical difference.

■■■

Each side speaks from its own perspective about the *fact* of the smallpox epidemic. For both, however, the facts – in the case of the present book, historical facts – do not exist independently of the memory of them. I do not mean that we have knowledge of facts only through memory; there are other ways of being aware of past facts. What is important is the evolution of the facts. The following paragraphs will explain this.

I have defined memory as communication in progress (pages 11–12). It is not a simple record in which experiences are stored. In this communicative definition, the concept of memory is not limited to the facts of the past but includes all senses that *circulate* in society and the meanings society gives to the world. With these characteristics, memory plays a crucial role in the experiencing – be it the protagonizing, feeling, or observing – of any event.[15] As has been illustrated in relation to hunger, a person experiences and communicates an event according to the readings his or her society gives it – the readings that society causes to circulate through its memory. He or she enacts processes of signification from the perspective implied by those readings. That is, an event – for example, suffering from hunger or the spread of smallpox – receives its meaning from humans; it has no inherent meaning, no meaning in itself. In other words, if nobody

Figure 4.2 ▪ "Memory is communication in progress." Solely through self-initiative, over the last few years community FM radio stations have been set up in different Enlhet communities. These have changed the dynamics of communication within them greatly.

perceives this event (be it as an actor or witness, or from the traces it leaves behind it), it has no meaning (although it still has consequences). Nor does it have essential sense. This said, if it is a human being that signifies the events, and if the meeting point of events in the manifest world with their perception by that person is mediated by the readings he or she shares with society, then there are (at least) as many ways of signifying as there are societies. For example, death has the same consequences for all: the end of a life. However, readings given to this event and its consequences – readings that in turn have consequences of their own – vary enormously from society to society.

For as long as we know only our own perspective in depth, it appears absolute to us (indeed, in our daily life, it is). We are thus unable to see what is under discussion here: that as humans, our awareness of facts – or of what we call reality – is mediated by our perspective; that real facts do not exist for humans beyond their awareness of them. That is, facts are always experiences (experiences can be understood as facts intertwined with the readings according to which they are perceived and communicated). This statement does not deny the reality of facts. Rather, it takes into consideration that the same fact is never a single fact because it is subject to perspectives and, therefore, depends on how it is seen and how it is spoken of. In short, it is understood that to draw a difference between reality itself as existing independently of humans – a single reality – and the various discourses around it is not a productive exercise. Rather, in the same way that a fact is never a single fact, neither is reality ever a single reality. It is not the same for all: every tradition constructs its own reality, its own world. This construction is based on certain axioms. To use other axioms would be to create another reality and another world.[16]

To synthesize, if somewhat sweepingly, the mainstream Western perspective[17] – the current Western perspective, since axioms and perspectives change over time – is based on the axiom that the world contains only what can be defined by natural law and what is, therefore, subject to the possibility of study: the world contains only that which can be studied (Feyerabend 1991, 88s). From this perspective, an ideal connection with the world depends fundamentally on knowledge that allows control of it. By contrast, the Enlhet perspective, which is part of a complex American Indigenous tradition, is based on the axiom that different levels of society, human and nonhuman, exist and interact, although not all are visible to the eye. From this perspective, an ideal connection with the world depends fundamentally on the construction of society between and within each of these levels through the balanced integration of diversity.

■■■

With the purpose of deepening the concept of perspective, let us consider the differences between Enlhet accounts and Mennonite documents regarding the complex processes involved in the immigration of one group into the territory of the other (Kalisch and Unruh 2014). As is to be expected, each side describes the event from a different

position: from Enlhet territory or from a journey toward it; from sur-
prise at the event or the firm decision to go ahead with it; from centuries of attachment to the land or from confusion after a flight marked
by terror and arrival in a totally unfamiliar place; from the place of the
vanquished or the victor, etc. Additionally, in their respective narratives, what has been discussed above can clearly be seen: that, during
the encounter – or clash – between the two parties, the Enlhet were
guided by a practice of sharing that was oriented toward the construction of a common, balanced social space (pages 119–23), while the
Mennonites were guided by a logic that sought control of the other
with relation to their own ends (Kalisch 2014b). These orientations
toward control and toward equilibrium, each founded on different
axioms, go far beyond simple discrepancy between objectives and
values that might define a preferred form of action toward the other.
They determine what is expected of the other; that is, they manifest
a framework according to which the actions and expressions of the
other are read.

To appreciate how far-reaching a framework such as this is – one
that facilitates and discards readings – and to see at the same time
the nature of the type of perspective under discussion here, let us turn
to the account by Haakok Maaset of two Mennonites who were able to
put an end to the lethal threat of smallpox (pages 83–5). Haakok
Maaset states these Mennonites' actions in a way that the Mennonites'
own account of the situation would not have (we do not have such
an account, but its categories are familiar). There is a dilemma here
whose cause is not simply the typical disparity between descriptions
by the agent, the observer, and the affected person of the intentions
of a particular action. Rather, Haakok Maaset explains how the two
Mennonites did something that, in fact, they could not do because
the reality they inhabit does not allow them even to imagine doing
such a thing. Thus, from the hegemonic position, which includes the
Mennonite position, it is easy to assume that the Enlhet reading of
the action described is incorrect.[18] However, even supposing that Haakok Maaset's particular interpretation does not apply to the actors' intentions, such a failure does not allow us to disqualify as unrealistic
and inappropriate – though it is disqualified by some – the Enlhet
position from which he reads the Mennonites' actions, and which is

reflected, for example, in account 23 by Kam'aatkok Ketsek of the invisible dimensions of society (pages 142–3, 160). As has been argued above, the differences between the Enlhet and Mennonite descriptions do not rely on a particular way of speaking about what is seen. That is, they are not different representations of the same reality – if they were, comparison of the two expressions would be possible on the basis of how accurately they represent that reality.[19] Rather, they refer to what is seen and reflect what is not seen (Viveiros de Castro 1998, 478). The two descriptions present us with realities that are constituted differently, and it is logical that what Haakok Maaset sees from his position cannot adequately describe what the two Mennonites saw from theirs.

I refer here to positions that are defined by the concrete composition of a particular reality. In parallel to this, the perspective of Kam'aatkok Ketsek and Haakok Maaset, as well as being a specific perspective in space and time (page 158), is what might be called an ontological perspective (Descola 2014, 437; in Tola 2016, 131).[20] This type of ontological perspective reveals aspects of the phenomenological world that from other positions, created from other axioms, cannot be seen (it is for this reason that they facilitate and invalidate readings). They thus open different possibilities for action and, at the same time, interaction with these phenomena produces its own consequences: it produces its own phenomenologies. It is in this sense that, although Enlhet and Mennonite narratives of the immigration of the Mennonites into Enlhet territory refer to events that are related insofar as they occurred at the same time, in the same space, and even had the same protagonists, each group describes the events on the basis of different configurations of reality and, at the same time, using categories and logics that are incompatible, just as two sets of axioms are not compatible. The events are rooted in different worlds. The diversity between the worlds thus revealed is the precursor to the diversity between discourses, representations, cosmovisions, and cultures, and in great part determines them.

▪▪▪

Different representations of the same reality could perhaps be compared in relation to the accuracy of these regarding that reality.

However, if we take as a starting point the idea that reality is not a single reality, the question of which of the available perspectives – each related to a specific representation – best reflects a reality that would exist independently of humans becomes irrelevant. Indeed, this preoccupation with reality reflects the criteria of a Western perspective that seeks to understand the phenomenological world – the experienced world – with the aim of dominating and controlling it. However, beyond a particular preference for an instrumental logic that seeks to subjugate and manipulate the world, the perspectives of all societies are constructed on the phenomenological world in which they live; otherwise, their life would not be possible. In parallel to this, every perspective opens up its own specific potentialities for an interaction particularly suited to certain phenomenological facets of our planet, facets that form part of a wide range of phenomena interacting in complex and even contradictory ways.[21] However, to speak of reality or the phenomenological world, reference to the potentialities that all particular traditions have in their relationships with the world is not sufficient to demonstrate the inadequacy of the question as to which perspective is the best in dealing with the phenomenological world with which one interacts but is not unique.

By their nature, axioms cannot be proven to be true or false. They are postulations of the world that are subject to change over time but are not in themselves negotiable. If, by their nature, axioms are neither negotiable nor compatible with other sets of axioms, then every perspective – and thus each one of the realities corresponding to those perspectives – can be evaluated only on the basis of its own axioms. The same is true of representations of those perspectives. By contrast, if different perspectives were compared and judged by the axioms of one particular perspective, the perspective by whose axioms all the others were measured would automatically prevail over the others and impose itself as the assumed truth – as does the Western perspective. That is, there is no way of identifying which is the best or the correct perspective, nor which is the correct description of an event. We must simply accept the existence of different, incompatible realities; of different worlds.[22] The implications of this incompatibility should not be underestimated. It means that it is not possible to express one world using the categories or words of another; the two cannot merely be integrated and neither is possible to "cherry-pick" the best parts of several different worlds.[23] It is for this reason that the difference between perspectives is considered radical.

▪▪▪

The radical difference that emerges between incompatible axioms greatly complicates communication between people of different perspectives.[24] It might be argued that this cannot be the case, because there are continual acts of communication between, for example, the Enlhet and the Mennonites. The question in reply is: where is the communication that includes the Enlhet perspective; communication that is more than the adaptation of the Enlhet to the categories and channels of the intruders? Kam'aatkok Ketsek died in 2016 (see accounts 17, 23, 27). Who listened to what she communicated, in her words and her attitudes, while she was alive (page 143)? And of those who did perhaps listen, who among them understood it? Who at least considered it a valid proposal for life and shared living within Enlhet territory? Who took it seriously? Questions such as these surround my profound concern for communication between groups with barely compatible viewpoints (page 7). It is these questions, and not an interest in theoretical or philosophical discussion, that define my unease at presenting these reflections. What Kam'aatkok Ketsek said, what Kaymaap-Takhaalhet continues to say, appears as irrelevant as a dusty museum exhibit. However, their grandchildren follow in their footsteps: the need for communication does not disappear on the death of their Elders.

▪▪▪

Nobody can understand the shape of realities different from their own. However, the enormous limitation of today's Western perspective is that its protagonists cannot even imagine the possibility of worlds totally different from, but no less coherent than, their own, and even less that those worlds might have their own potentialities, potentialities different from those of the West. Although they do glimpse the existence of other perspectives, they cannot understand them, nor can they accept or admit them, and they continue to believe that theirs is the most truthful, valid, and effective.[25] For although they understand that there is wealth that is not of the material kind, from their perspective material concerns predominate absolutely, and on this basis they judge the constructions of others. They lose a great deal by this perspective. They will not easily overcome their poverty; no society can renounce its perspective in a moment. But by basing themselves in a Western perspective they oblige others to do so. It is a perspective of great violence.

Worlds, Accounts, and Bridges to Communication

It has been argued above that reality is not absolute but always the reality of someone or of some society; it is reality in relation to a specific perspective (in this sense, it is relative). The fact that all reality is constructed on certain axioms in no way relativizes its absolute significance for the respective society. For experiences are made in a concrete world and to live in the world it is essential to maintain continuous connection with it. It follows from this connection that one's own reality – and, therefore, truth itself – is the history of a relationship with the world. This means that a society has ideas about the world and acts in accordance with them, and the world simultaneously responds to those actions, thereby confirming or challenging the ideas that motivate them. The reality created is, therefore, in no way an arbitrary construction (in this sense, it is not relative). Consequently, once again, the fact that different realities and worlds exist does not mean that all societies other than one's own have become disconnected from reality and inhabit a mistaken or unreal world. Quite the opposite: all societies, including one's own society, have invented their world, but by giving the phenomenological world its necessary importance, each inhabits a very real world. However, a society comes to live in an unreal world from the moment the categories of another world are superimposed on its own; from the moment the categories of another reality dominate its own, as occurs in the context of colonial oppression.

In the Enlhet accounts, the description of precise details is notable. The importance the relators give to detail reflects the prominence of the aforementioned link with the phenomenological or experienced world in Enlhet memory. It should be stressed that this connection is not limited to knowledge of, for example, animals and plants, or physical things generally. It necessarily includes knowledge of the past, which is vital, as lived experiences continue to generate repercussions in different actors and so persist through time:[26] I need to know what happened yesterday in the village, the country or the world in order to be able to act appropriately today.

■■■

We have before us a radical difference between perspectives that makes the expression of the world in the categories and words of the other impossible, so making communication between people of different perspectives enormously difficult. How, then, can a reduction in the distance between such worlds be imagined? Experiences are produced within the experienced world. For this reason, although the experience of different peoples means that an event is never a unique event, there are equivalencies in those experiences observed from different perspectives. These equivalencies constitute possible bridges between perspectives; experiences might serve as a path toward processes of communication between perspectives marked by radical difference. They could serve as starting points for articulation and, through it, produce a reduction of distance. Speeches made by people who do not work toward seeking these equivalencies end instead in attempts to persuade and convert the other.

A reduction in the distance between the intruders and the Enlhet using the aforementioned equivalences as its starting point will not occur automatically. As has been seen, for example, the similar anxieties experienced by the Enlhet and the Mennonites did not become a shared axis on which the Mennonites sought a balanced relationship (pages 140–1). In reality, if we consider the unequal and deep-rooted power relationships obstructing, to a large degree, an acceptance that one vision is neither better than the other nor unique, it seems highly unlikely that such a reduction in distance might occur. However, where experiences intersect in the lived world, the Enlhet accounts could serve as a mirror for the societies that have dispossessed them so utterly (pages 6, 8). They could bring the dominant society, seeing itself reflected in the accounts, to understand something about itself through the eyes of the Enlhet. Through the accounts, the relators invite Paraguayan society – and simultaneously all colonizing societies – to share with the Indigenous population the construction of new channels of communication and to enter on the process of articulation that is indispensable for any future interaction in equilibrium.

■■■

The Enlhet are still seen as "an unknown people" (pages 4, 6). This said, to be known or not is a question of perspective; it depends on the place of the person applying the label. The Enlhet accounts were given from a perspective very different from that of the reader. By redefining what is within and what is marginal, they challenge the reader's notion of his or her own centre. They open up an interplay of centrality and marginality between different perspectives that generates a variety of constellations in tension. They are tensions between the ability to imagine and not, between the ability to understand and not, between the ability to act and not. The reader's entering into these tensions – which brings flexibility to the conviction that a single valid perspective exists – is necessary (though not sufficient) in order to be able to think about the beginning of communication between societies as different as the Enlhet and the Paraguayan, and between all the Indigenous Peoples of the Americas and the societies of their present-day states. For only if all participants begin from their own perspectives does articulation between them become possible.[27]

Details and the Accounts

In account 2, Malhkee·tko-Ngkoyoy' explains in a way typical for the Enlhet how the phenomenological world and the perspective of her people combine. She evokes images of shared living with the Bolivians that come from her own perception. At the same time she makes clear that these images were explained to her by her parents[28] (page 34). That is, in the things she says, for example about Bolivians, there is a meeting of her own perception and what her society maintains.

In addition, in the readings she gives to her experiences she herself performs acts of signification that she crystallizes throughout the series of images she recreates in the account: she makes the images speak.[29] In account 32, Yamasma'ay' illustrates, with his description of the haircut, this way of signifying experience: on the one hand, the description is a report of concrete experience; on the other, it serves as a metaphor for the subordination of the people (page 151). In the testimony of Haakok Maaset (account 21) we see something similar in relation to smallpox and the process of subjugation of the Enlhet (page 138). These are not interpretations of the accounts given by me from our position today; they are significations of experience that have always circulated within the Enlhet community itself.

This illustrates that synthesis, evaluation, and judgement do not manifest themselves in abstract reflections; they are expressed through the combination and recombination of detailed images that describe the experiences related, whether these are the relator's own experiences or not. With this practice of reflection bound to images, it is unlikely that Enlhet Elders might become fanciful in their reflections. The same cannot be said of reflections in the Western tradition, however, with their marked orientation toward the abstract.

■■■

The relators make their images speak, and in order to do so, they employ details in their accounts. Indeed, the care they take over such details when giving their accounts is remarkable. For example, Haakok Maaset (account 21) mentions the species of tree under which the boy was killed by his desperate father. This detail is irrelevant to the point of the account, but is crucial when we understand it as part of a strategy of signification that employs images to sketch, explain, evaluate, and broaden the world; images that help maintain a necessary connection with the lived world.[30]

The care taken over details fulfils another important function related to the construction itself of the accounts by their respective relators: the details create a skeleton that lend a structure to the accounts that keeps them very stable over time. Thus, although memory of the past is reconstructed from the present (pages 11, 159), use is made of accounts that come from the past – from "inherited raw material" (Izquierdo Martín 2008, 181). In this way, a dual dynamic is produced: memory lends sense to events, and communication of the experience and its sense re-signifies memory. There is another dual dynamic: a constant from the past – the re-memorization of experiences, images, and details – meets a variable in the present – the selection and composition of these to present conclusions and evaluations. Concurrently, a certain friction is produced between the way the Enlhet memorize their past and the expressions within which they recognize themselves in the present. It is these frictions that make memory speak.[31] We will return to this question later (page 188).

Memory: Structures

The memory of a people is among the vital resources with which it constructs its reality, in a process during which it re-signifies, and at the same time reconstructs, that memory. Therefore, the statement that one's own reality is not arbitrary means that memory is also not arbitrary. In order to see that this assessment includes the process of constructing the past from the present, let us look briefly at the functioning of an activated memory, a memory through which what a people says and is circulates.

Although the accounts are full of historical details, they are wholly different from inventories or records of facts constructed to ensure that these facts are accessible to future readings (pages 11, 123). Rather, through the concretization of details in circulation, images are composed that have the potential to refer to a complex system of meanings and knowledge and thus support communication of them in Enlhet society. Having said this, Enlhet society has always maintained its memory in an exclusively oral form and knows no resource by which to set down the word, such as, for example, writing.[32] So, in order to guarantee the communicative circulation of knowledge and senses in accounts, it supports its accounts with staged representations (for example, during ceremonies), in enacted practices, and in the territories through which its people pass constantly, among other things (Kalisch 2009h; Santos-Granero 2004). It is these *concrete*

Figure 4.3 ▪ "Society supports its accounts with staged representations." *Savaalak*, figures from the female initiation ritual called *yaanmaan*. The ritual ceased to be celebrated among the Enlhet in the 1950s. This photo is from a Toba-Enenlhet community where it continues to be celebrated sporadically.

actions around images, practices, and places that open up reference to that complex system of senses in circulation we call memory. They activate it and simultaneously cause the expressions that reflect it to circulate; they incentivize re-memorization and so prompt dialogue. Although memory is, therefore, not understood as an absolute discourse such as scientific, historiographic discourse claims to be, both the references contained within the images, practices, and places and the aforementioned skeleton of the accounts in the form of details provide memory with a structure to contribute to its constancy.

▪▪▪

All relators construct and reconstruct their accounts in such a way that, with time, those accounts acquire stable lines on the basis of which they then mould them in the moment of the telling in the form of an accidental version. This process, which lasts the relator's entire lifetime, takes place in the context of continuous articulation with interlocutors within the society. In parallel to this, relators are always very conscious of the inevitable judgement of a large and diverse audience whose composition varies constantly. In this way, as long as it has evolved within a framework of current orality, every account is approved by those in whose presence it has been formed; it is endorsed by society. It is both reliable and representative.

Although it is possible that an event might not have happened in spite of the fact that a relator states that it did, the fact that he or she can count on the audience's acceptance of its expression is "as revealing as the simple occurrence of an event, which is, after all, related to chance ... The important thing is that the reception of the ... [account] is possible for contemporaries because the person who produced it believed it to be so. From this point of view, the concept of false is not relevant" (Todorov 2010, 66). It follows that the concept of true is not applicable either. Rather, memory describes in a *reasonable* way the connection of a people with the past and its protagonists (page 124). Consequently, the multiplicity and polyphony of perspectives it opens up (and which may even be contradictory) is not problematic. On the contrary, it allows different people and groups to recognize themselves in the narrative and makes that narrative much less prone to serve as a vehicle for ideologization, as is the case for any linear narrative that can be employed in the service of an interested truth, whatever that truth may be.

Disconnections and Silences

No people's reality is arbitrary – although the opposite is so readily presumed from the dominant perspective – because it is connected with the lived world. Neither is memory arbitrary as long as it maintains this connection. However, not every reading of the present draws on experience in the same way. In the case of the Enlhet, for example, there has been continual fading of memory, channelled and enabled by multiple pressures placed on their society by the invaders and compounded and manifested by the fact that attention to accounts of the past has fallen out of use. Therefore, although many accounts are still related in private spaces, they lack an attentive audience and many references both to concrete experience and to knowledge, logics, and meanings have been lost forever. The result is progressive amnesia, the effect of which continues to corrode Enlhet memory.

In place of what circulated in the memory that has been exposed to this growing amnesia, those statements have been implanted, and continue to be implanted, that create the fewest contradictions in the context of subjugation and subordination; that is, contradictions with the state of siege under which the people live. A new set of strands has crystallized in the narrative of the Enlhet that has gradually replaced the original set, which included, among other things, experiences lived during the process leading to defeat (page 141). In spite of this displacement, the original set of strands did not, and does not, cease to interfere with the more recent and now dominant set; it questions and challenges it. The more recent set of narrative strands thus appears more coherent the more awareness of the original set is lost and with it, by extension, the experiences that constituted memory. With the same intention, namely of avoiding challenges to the new set of narrative strands, perceptions of the present are accepted only selectively and current experiences that serve to make clear the state of siege are silenced. That is, we are left with a narrative reconfigured on non-communication both about the past and about crucial aspects of the present. It is a narrative simultaneously without a past and partially disconnected from experiences as they continue to be made. This partial disconnection of the new set of narrative strands from experience has clear formal consequences for the modes in which these strands are expressed: there is a marked tendency for the *description* of detailed experiences to be substituted by the *declaration* of qualification and opinion.

As has been discussed, memory is narrative placed in circulation. It is the social consciousness of the narrative, and it is polyphonic communication (pages 11–12). The two sets of strands of the narrative of the Enlhet people, which simultaneously imply two versions of its memory, are part of this polyphony. Nevertheless, although the two sets can coexist not only within the group but also within a single person, they do so on an unequal footing: the new set dominates and continues its ascendency while the original is clearly in decline (Kalisch 2013; 2014c; 2014d; 2015). Thus, however much of the original set (still) presents challenges to the more recent one, this new set, in turn, creates clear interferences with the original, which become ever stronger as the original set is reproduced by persons no longer brought up in the categories that support it. (We will return to these persons later, page 183).

In accounts reflecting the original narrative strands, these interferences manifest themselves, for example, in the appearance of declarations of generic qualification – themselves characteristic of expressions belonging to the new set of narrative strands – oriented to the criteria of the new set. For example, the relators frequently close an account by *stating* that "Today we live well; before, we lived badly." However, the details they have just shared do not support this assessment; on the contrary, they *demonstrate* a clear, concrete notion of good living in the past (Kalisch and Unruh 2014, 299, 397, 412, 418–19, 461). That is to say, an explicit statement that has not been argued, but which the dominant discourse sees as credible, sits in opposition to a tacit evaluation that is argued but which, by not being made explicit, is easily overlooked, even more so because it is often dismissed by the dominant discourse as non-credible or even false. This opposition appears constantly in accounts reflecting the traditional strands of the Enlhet narrative. For example, much of what the

Enlhet, in line with Mennonite discourse, *state in the abstract* about their supposed salvation by the Mennonites has no basis in the experience they themselves *describe in concrete terms* in their accounts. Moreover, their accounts *contradict* it (for extensive examples of this, see Kalisch and Unruh 2014). Thus a process is reaffirmed within which communication about *detailed experiences* lived from the Enlhet's own protagonism is increasingly overlaid with discourses that take up often hostile *generic hypotheses* that the victors have made regarding the Enlhet past (page 9). Concomitantly, there is a disconnection between expression and experience, between narrative and life, and the result is that the Enlhet inhabit a surreal world (page 168).

■■■

The weakening of the link between expression and experience describes a complex process that varies depending upon the generation and individual people. However, although it has many gradations within the current population, it has lent a clear direction to the development of society as a whole. For as the strands of narrative without a past have been reaffirmed, the Enlhet have become increasingly incapacitated to work on the consequences of the past in the present (page 126).[33] As a consequence, people have come to see themselves as the object of processes that do not depend on them. Thus, there is a relationship between the absence of history and transformation into object. This manifests itself in, for example, official commemorations of the establishment of the so-called Enlhet "missions," the predecessors of today's *comunidades*, "communities." Here we see, on the one hand, an absence of references to Enlhet history previous to their establishment and, on the other, continual exposure to what the missionaries designed and decided for the people in order to then instruct them in accordance with it.[34] Thus we see that the aforementioned turn from description to declaration or statement is much more than a simply formal question. The turn also reflects the fact that with the abandonment of their own history, the Enlhet have begun to align themselves with the consumption of external initiatives oriented not toward action by the Enlhet themselves – the condition of actor – but to the claims of ideas and actions from without.

Figure 4.4 ▪ "We see an absence of references to Enlhet history." Presentation of Paraguayan dance by young Enlhet people during the fiftieth anniversary of their community. Several decades ago, the holding of traditional Enlhet celebrations and dances was prohibited by the missionaries, and to this day it is stigmatized as diabolical among the Enlhet themselves. However, presentations of Paraguayan dance are permitted at public events and in schools.

■■■

Through the Enlhet reconfiguration of their own narrative, the invaders have succeeded not only in occupying and usurping the history of the people – something that colonizers always attempt to do with the past of the colonized – but have at the same time occupied and usurped their present. For when a subjugated society no longer has a history and is incapacitated to work on the consequences of the past; when it ignores at the same time a certain kind of experience of the present; when it finally transfers the taking of initiative to the society of the victor, all arguments and all argumentation inside that subjugated society become useful to the victor's society. Its members, the subjugated, find themselves continually reduced to their condition of subordinates and cannot break free of it. Then, without a past, and in addition without a present of its own, society is left with no option but to project itself also onto a future of others that again relies on alien initiatives, thus causing time to stop and the present to become eternal.[35] In short, a narrative without a past creates a yawning lacuna, a black hole from which no word can escape; once again, it produces only silences and encourages silence.

■ ■ ■

With the weakening of the connection between expression and experience, expressions of experiences have become increasingly overlain by statements of hypothesis and conjectures about the world. An environment has been created in which many of the ideas circulating among the people are no longer exposed to constant contrast – articulation – with events and observations of the past and the present. Such isolation of ideas leads to their appearing more important than events and observations. Through colonial ideology, the colonized have been ideologized. This ideologization favours a state of agitation that is crystallized in, for example, the fervour with which Enlhet people devote themselves to the church and other external impositions. By their activism, they attempt to silence any perception of the black hole. In reality, however, only more silence is produced, silence hidden by vain chatter (page 126). It is a noisy silence.

■ ■ ■

With the usurpation of the Enlhet narrative, the history of the people has been colonized. In parallel, the people have projected themselves onto models of submission and subordination: their vision has been colonized. By this plundering of their past and future, they are condemned to silence: their pain has been colonized. However, the history, the vision, and the pain have not disappeared. They are still there, silenced. Although amnesia gradually corrodes the possibility to talk about them, they persist among overlapping silences. In parallel, many fragments of the original narrative remain but are hidden. They wait, in the mortuary, to be buried forever, victims of amnesia, of the physical deaths of those who circulated them. They wait, standing by to serve when the Enlhet People resolves to reconstruct itself on its own protagonism, which it can only do from the starting point of what remains within it, be that potential or wounds. In summary, in the two sets of strands of memory not only are two different pasts traced but two presents and two possible futures projected.

■■■

Kaymaap-Takhaalhet (in account 17) states that the horror of their experiences brought to tears the people who bore witness to them. It made their words tremble, but it did not stop them from speaking. The silences discussed here were not caused by the depth of the trauma (although there were cases of this also; see page 117). They are silences subsequent to the suffering and include not only historical experiences, but extend to speech around an entire way of life. They are silences directly related to a proposal for peace understood as the unobstructed functioning of the status quo (page 144). It is a peace obtained and conserved at the cost of the silence of the defeated and subjugated party. This proposal for peace has its basis in an idea of reconciliation that is despicable because the price of the restoration of supposed harmony is again paid by those who suffered all of the damage in the foregoing conflict (pages 143–4).

Despite the perversity of such a proposal for a sterile, frozen, chilling peace, when the pact of capitulation was sealed by mass baptisms toward the end of the 1950s (pages 141, 151–2), the Enlhet accepted it. They accepted that, in order to fulfil the pact and maintain the appearance of harmony, they must be silent. They took ownership of the idea that to find possibilities for protagonism under these conditions, they, the vanquished, must imitate as far as possible the victors and orient themselves to their discourses, activities, and proposals. The victors, on the other hand, define the willingness of the other – of the vanquished – based on his or her readiness to enter their discourse (less important is his or her capacity to put it into practice), to pretend that

Figure 4.5 ▪ "Promiscuity toward the victors foments the abandonment of the self." Enlhet wedding feast. It is usual for places at the newlyweds' table to be given to Mennonite guests, normally the employers of the couple's families.

there is no other relevant discourse. From this predisposition, the victors draw the dedication they give to their relationship with the vanquished, which in turn defines the degree of delusion the vanquished has to participate in the world of the victors. This extortionist practice has generated a promiscuity of the vanquished toward the victors that differs completely from articulation between them.[36] Instead, the discourses, activities, and proposals of the victors, developed from their perspective and oriented to their objectives and interests, are superimposed on those of the vanquished and displace and crush them.

Thus, imitation of the victors by the Enlhet does not have the potential it appears to have of opening the way for active participation as protagonists in the victors' world. On the contrary, it manifests itself as another form of silence. In parallel to this, promiscuity toward the

victors, although appearing to show unity provokes silence and subsequent forgetting; it foments the abandonment of the self. Both imitation and promiscuity are opposed, therefore, to the creation of new
possibilities for Enlhet protagonism. Further, they aid in the victors'
maintenance of subjugation over time. For this reason, it cannot be
overstated that all those members of the victors' society who define
their way of relating to the other, the vanquished, on the basis of his
willingness to enter their discourse are complicit in the subjugation
that began almost a hundred years ago under the historical conditions
examined closely in this book. Not only those who actively reject the
memory of the other, but also those who ignore it are the co-authors
of his silencing (Piedras Monroy 2012). This deliberate ignorance,
which makes articulation between the vanquished and the victor impossible, leads the vanquished to see promiscuity as the only solution
to the dilemmas of the present while, in reality, it aggravates them.

Hidden Memory: Collections

With the disarticulation of oral dynamics within Enlhet society, the
sharing of accounts has become limited to a few people. The original
strands of memory of the Enlhet people have faded and possibilities
for resistance to the kind of ideologization that promotes subjugation
have diminished dramatically. In the face of this situation of amnesia,
the question arises as to the contribution of the accounts collected in
this book. Before broaching this question, however, it is necessary to
describe some characteristics of the accounts.

The accounts in the present book are manifestations of the Enlhet
Oral Tradition, firstly recorded as audio and then written down, in
the original language, Enlhet. However, on being recorded they were
taken out of circulation; thus they lost their (implicit) reference to
a specific situation and context and an accidental version has been
made absolute. That is, at the moment of recording, even in an audio
format, the accounts ceased to form part of an oral dynamic and instead become testimonies of it. This implies an important change in
the characteristics of the accounts. Nevertheless, in order to understand the inevitability of this change, it is important to examine the

historical constellation through which the Enlhet people passed in the moment of recording.

For several decades, the practice of social communication by which the narrative of the people was transmitted and passed into the memory of those following behind had been weakening with increasing rapidity. In addition, the period since the beginning of the new millennium has seen the passing of the last people to still have a strong hold on Enlhet memory in its original strands and who retained relative independence from colonial logic due to the fact that they were already adults when their people accepted defeat (page 141). Today, they are dead. The generation following them has internalized the categories of submission to a much higher degree, and its accounts are qualitatively different to those of the previous generation: the opposition of native categories to those of the recently arrived world has become obscured. With the death of the Elders and their accounts, the memory of the qualitative features of the original Enlhet world was doomed to be lost forever and, with it, the possibility of understanding many of the contradictions of the Enlhet world today.

For example, the Enlhet concept of *nengelaasekhammalhkoo* – socially constructed peace – referred originally to one's own initiative for constructing peace, but has suffered a re-signification, now implying the expectation of the initiative from the other for its constant reconstruction (Kalisch 2011b; for further examples of similar inversions of readings, see Kalisch 2014b; 2020). Without the voices of the generation whose accounts are relatively independent of submissive thinking, it would not have been possible to detect this qualitative change that now paralyzes the life of the people. Neither would it have been possible to develop an awareness that disarticulated reconfigurations of the current world are not appropriate to discussion of the past. That is, without these accounts, the incoherencies, paralysis, and innumerable obstacles of the present take on an eternal quality and what the subjugators say appears true: that they are part of the essence of Enlhet being. Again, in parallel to this, with the loss of access to their own past, the Enlhet are entirely vulnerable to external discourses and it is extremely difficult for them to imagine models other than those of submission and subordination. In a narrative without a past, they cannot apply, and can no longer even imagine, other options for resolving the many difficulties they experience as the subjugated than those proposed and imposed by the subjugators (page 177). Rather, in a de-historicized narrative that draws constantly on the same logic and argumentation used to reinforce their submission, they invest their potential for construction to a large extent in the building and refinement of their own cage (Kalisch 2013; 2014c; 2014d; 2015). In sum, as they resort unavoidably to the practices and concepts through which their subjugation is actively advanced, they gradually succumb to the trauma of the subjugated.

▪▪▪

In these conditions, in order to avoid, in the disappearance of accounts from circulation, a loss of the potential for resistance and reconstruction latent in the memory of a different past oriented to Enlhet categories, the setting down of these accounts was unavoidable. It is in this light that the motivation for our devoting ourselves for many years to the collection of accounts from a wide variety of Enlhet relators should be understood; it is a collection that reflects to the greatest degree possible the original polyphony of the Enlhet Oral Tradition while it was still current. Again: these relators are now almost all dead.

In collecting the Enlhet accounts, it was very clear to us as the editors of this book that the task was not one of storing memories. Neither was it the creation of a canon of authentically Enlhet voices. For we understood neither narrative nor history as an end in itself. Rather, we assumed that both of these things have a precise function in the reconstruction of society and its life (for this reason, the translation of the accounts into Spanish or English was never a principal concern for us). In addition, we knew that the accounts can only realize their potential for resistance and contribute to the people's fight for freedom if the people activate modes of communication that place their accounts back into circulation, albeit in ways that are different from those of former times, so that the accounts can reintroduce meanings guaranteed by tradition and historical trajectory to the processes of communication within Enlhet society that creates memory.

These strategies for activation, however, are not the focus here (see Kalisch 2010a).

■ ■ ■

The limitations of a fixed account as compared to one in communicative circulation in society are considerable. On the one hand, it no longer receives the quasi-automatic attention of members of society who must invest initiative and personal effort in noticing and listening to it. On the other, in the original context of orality, the representation of an experience occurred in parallel to its projection on other, current, experiences; that is, the expression of the account simultaneously constituted an act of interpretation. In the case of a fixed account, however, interpretation occurs only from the moment of reception. That is, it has become independent of the act of sharing. It can thus be protagonized by all, independently of their understanding of the account and its world, and as a result becomes more prone to improper readings.

Despite these disadvantages, which are considerable, the accounts are essential for today's generations, who know no life other than that of the prison of the communities. These generations no longer have the possibility to live for themselves those diverse experiences so radically in contrast to the discourse of the intruders who have subordinated them. For them, it is *normal* to live as the deprived and dispossessed (page 125). Therefore, in the absence of experiences that would enable reflection and expression, a different perception and emotions, much ambition for freedom relies on the importance of an Enlhet narrative that speaks from beyond the impositions that currently subdue the people. Although presented in the fragmented form of recorded testimonies, such a narrative has decisive potential. For in view of the enormous distance between the other, dominant, narrative in circulation today within Enlhet society, the usurped narrative, and the world the Elders describe, the accounts clearly contradict attitudes of submission. They are firmly opposed to those statements that produced and continue to produce the fewest contradictions in a context of submission and subordination. They, therefore, have the potential to challenge:

Figure 4.6 ▪ "They know no life other than that of the prison of the communities." Around 1980, a small number of Enlhet still had their place of residence in the vicinity of a Mennonite village. Pa'aymong Apyaap, for example, lived with his second wife, who appears in this photo, in a grasshouse in Poy'seskeya, Hohenau. Only after she died in about 1980 did he move to the Enlhet mission of Lhaapangkalvok, Filadelfia.

Accounts dressed up in certainty and forever eager to show us
a bearable image of our past in which we can recognize ourselves and be content. That image ... does not seek description
or comprehension, but rather the construction of a memory
superimposed on our own memory, promoting the worst kind
of amnesia and thus constructing a new, changeling identity as
tame and docile as it is hollow, manipulated and false. (Piedras
Monroy 2012, 56)

Under these circumstances, the accounts are an annoyance, because
they challenge the pact of reconciliation. They are a genuine annoyance; they are even an annoyance to many Enlhet though it is they
who pay the price for the farcical peace that has been put in place
(pages 143–4, 180). Therefore, to bring out of hiding accounts that
constitute the original strands of their memory and to place them into
circulation once again implies an act of courage. It is of the greatest
importance that there be people who have the courage to challenge
the present with their accounts. By their attitudes, Enlhet society
keeps alive the possibility of recovering a silenced past and proposing
a different possible future: in their being spoken, the accounts are reason for hope. Although they are still spoken clandestinely,[37] they are
vital for the people to see perhaps, one day, the black hole that produces only silences. For this reason, to speak of the past is a political act.

The oppressors – to borrow the term from the national anthem –
are clearly conscious of the enormous political potential that all independent, active memory has to propose and support a way of being,
a proven model of a life in liberty opposed to the slavery of currently
imposed models. For very good reason, they make it their business
to destroy any image that might serve as a stimulus to the original
strands of memory, whether by its elimination or its domestication
as a recollection – its folklorization. Indeed, they have institutions
tasked with carrying out this very destruction, for example, the missionary work of the Mennonites and the educational work of the
State. For, from their perspective as victors, they consider that the disappearance of the tentacles of the past would mean the disappearance
of a crucial block to what they call the development of the Indigenous

Peoples and to what they think of as the functioning of the status quo that has placed them on the winning side.

The Past Is Not So Dead

For the purposes of clarity of expression, I have used the term *the Enlhet*. However, the internal complexity of their society, small though it is, cannot be reduced to unilinear syntheses. I have stated that in their memory they weave threads that are varied and at times even contradictory, just as the current life of their society and of individual people is in contradiction between resistance and surrender, between the underpinning of their own protagonism and their investing in that of the other, between a strong statement of self-identity and shame at what they are (Kalisch 2013; 2014c; 2014d; 2015). These contradictions reflect interferences between different ways of looking and of identifying oneself that in turn point to the coexistence of the legacy of their past with dynamics alien to it.

By containing different strands, memory is enabled to support different dynamics in Enlhet society, whether these occur simultaneously or at different historical moments. The present juncture gives clear preference to the set of strands corresponding to submission, with all the silences it implies and the amnesia it causes; it contains strands of memory characterized by the construction of a changeling identity whose promiscuity facilitates manipulation. It is a set of strands through which the context of submission and subordination is assumed; in parallel to this, with it the Enlhet attempt to hide the contradictions that have been and continue to be produced within that context (page 175). As this set of strands has come to dominate, the aforementioned function of memory in creating friction between speech about the past and speech from the present (page 172) has decreased greatly. However, as long as the accounts exist, there remains the possibility – though it may be hidden in the obscured polyphony of a shrouded memory – of shedding light once more on a history buried under multiple layers of forgetting. This light does not change what happened, but it can create frictions once again and so contribute to seeing the past in a different way (González de Oleaga 2008,

167) in order to attempt to change some of its consequences in the present. Again, to speak of the past is a political act.

■ ■ ■

Why this concern for the accounts, if they are of the past, either to suppress them or make use of them? Why not leave dead things to the dead? Because the past is not as dead as it seems. The past does not disappear simply because it is denied and silenced, for, as I have argued, its consequences are in the present. Accounts of lived experiences contribute to seeing the consequences of the past in the present and to understanding them as something out of the ordinary. They facilitate understanding of the world of the present in the light of one's own historical trajectory and tradition and not as an immobile and unmovable configuration. As has been mentioned, they question, for example – implicitly but very strongly – the dominant hypothesis that the Mennonites saved the Enlhet from extinction. They thus question the parallel discourse that life since salvation is better than life prior to it; that for this reason, life in the present must be qualified as absolutely good despite the fact that it is not experienced as such. To take another example, the relators' clear decision to avoid presenting themselves as victims (page 122) is in tension with the strong investment in external protagonism in the current life of the Enlhet. To the extent that such tensions, which might be considered collisions, are perceived, past experiences and the images that describe them create contrasts in light and shade that give shape to the present (page 125) and thus allow differentiation. They challenge all normality.

It is thus understood that the information in the accounts is important not because it fills in blank spaces on the map of knowledge of the past or because it safeguards parts of an abstract "common heritage of humanity" (Article 1, UNESCO Universal Declaration on Cultural Diversity 2001). Rather, after the rupture caused by the capitulation of the Enlhet people, a renewed attention to the accounts – their existence alone produces nothing – can generate new awareness of the Enlhet's own past that enables them to *use* it again. The accounts show that there is a problem with the present, and their orientation toward freedom opens the possibility of imagining new horizons. They have the potential to reorient the prevailing preference for the strands of submission; to encourage a search for routes out of the condition of submission. They make possible readings of the present that enable the people to face up to the narrative that is instrumental to those who dominate everything; to those who abhor the Enlhet. In this way, they enable awareness of the black hole that causes the silences. In short, they place the people in a position where they can re-establish a connection, in renewed awareness of their own history, between their experiences, expressions, and desires.

▪▪▪

The past is not as dead as many would wish it to be. It has consequences for the present. In addition, many of the values, logics, attitudes, hopes, and concerns reflected in the accounts of the past, despite having been to a greater or lesser extent transfigured, remain important in the Enlhet present. In the same way, much traditional knowledge, despite being fairly fragmented, and a vague awareness of their own historical experiences, persist. All of these continuities of what is rooted in the tradition of the people exist in spite of the fact that the Enlhet must manage all differences between themselves and others in conditions of continual repression and a parallel obscuring of the original strands of their memory. They remain relevant in daily life despite having been buried under the profound silences through which challenges to the aforementioned pact of reconciliation are avoided (pages 144, 180, 187).

The multiple continuities relating to the life of the Enlhet, however unconscious or invisible they may be, guarantee a strong affinity between the accounts of the past and life in the present. Therefore, if the people were inclined at any moment to the other set of strands of their memory, the strands that had been hidden – that of a life sustained by protagonism under its own terms – the accounts of past experiences would take on their real importance, well beyond authorizing a manner of viewing that challenges the normality of the present. Such an inclination would offer a clear profile of what is still alive and thus aid in its renewed use.[38] For the vast amount of concrete information contained in the accounts has the potential to guide actions and reflections; to orient projections and visions. If this potential is exploited, the accounts can enable the marking out and realization of paths away from the dominant routes, which appear safe as, having been marked out by the victors, the victors themselves ensure they are not altered. These new paths in turn are as uncertain as any future but enable the taking of realistic steps because they are connected with Enlhet reality. In proven practices, observations, reflections, and conclusions they offer thorough-going expressions that authorize the people to overcome the silences within their society (page 125). With speech about the life of the people recovered, the Enlhet can employ it once again as part of constant communication that enables them to reconstruct it permanently from their own perspective.

The importance of the communicative *circulation* of all things relative to the life of the people, of the *activation* of the original strands of its memory, should not be underestimated: it is the reflexive processes that take place in society through constant discussion of concrete practices and attitudes, and not academic reflections, that make the life of a society. Therefore, if the people are enabled to say what they do – if they are able and if they are allowed – they can do what they do in another way and, in addition, assume it positively. In reality, the accounts have never ceased to have the effect of authorizing reflection and action. Their use as a resource for shaping concrete life, though it manifests itself only sporadically and in reduced spaces, is the reason why the accounts have not been abandoned altogether. Only when the possibility of connecting them to life disappears is it probable that the accounts themselves will cease to exist.

■■■

I have argued that the accounts create and recreate history and establish contrasts that challenge the present. In addition, they allow the reconnection of the present with the past that nourishes it, offer criteria for shaping it, and help Indigenous society rediscover words for that which it no longer expresses. This potential to facilitate the word brings us back to another crucial function of the accounts. I have mentioned that many accounts of concrete experiences have been eaten away by amnesia; other accounts continue to be spoken, but no one pays them attention. In both cases, what is lost are the images of the experiences; however, the confused feelings produced by the experiences persist. For example, concrete knowledge of suffering at the hands of the Paraguayans disappears, but the fear of them does not (pages 124–5). Once again, the past, whose consequences do not disappear simply because it is no longer spoken of, is not so dead as might be imagined. On the contrary, experiences, "[when] transformed into forgetting and not into past, nevertheless continue to wander aimlessly as the present, haunting our ambition and frustrating our expectations" (Piedras Monroy 2012, 256). Pain itself, though seeming not to exist for its having been repressed and hidden, remains counterintuitively active and an obstacle to life. This happens not only in the life of those who experienced it in person. In addition to conditioning those people's self-perception, the memory of their experiences – however shrouded in silence – contributes to determining the identity of those around them and who come after them in time, despite the fact that the latter can no longer have access to the memory, as it is no longer an active memory of the people (Piedras Monroy 2012, 132).

It is here that the ability for expression becomes crucial. As the people recover words for their own past, they will be enabled to speak of their losses, fears, and wounds. When words for the past become words for the present, the Enlhet will be able to open themselves to the pain of their suffering and face all the grief they have suppressed for decades and hidden behind profound silences and vain chatter (pages 126, 179). Therefore, once wounds are assumed as part of a concrete past they can be addressed and, although not forgotten, put aside (Todorov 2000, 24). For this reason, the return to memory is not, as many believe it to be, a return to the past. It grants freedom to face the present.

■■■

Among all the contradictions, and as much as deep-rooted memory may be hidden alongside usurped memory, the strands of resistance remain active, especially among the oldest members of society. These individuals anchor in a radical otherness and their insistence in a different world are clear manifestations of these strands, whose currency shows that they continue to consider and present themselves as actors: their anchor has saved them from becoming, in their self-perception, victims (pages 122–3). In parallel, they do not devote themselves to insistently seeking parties culpable for their present condition or project themselves passively onto demands for reparations for the immense and multiple injustices they have suffered (page 143).

However, things are changing, and there is energy in the change. As has been mentioned, through silences that prompt forgetting, the Enlhet are rapidly losing access to their past and thus the possibility of understanding the present on the basis of their own historical trajectory. These silences leave them without a history and lead them to see themselves as the object of processes that are independent of them. In such circumstances, the danger that the Enlhet might come to understand themselves as victims is not only latent but growing: victims of dispossession and marginalization, they themselves would say; victims of their own ignorance, they are made also to say by the intruders. To oppose the option of understanding oneself as a victim and of thus becoming de facto a victim – a person or a society does not become a victim solely because of what other people and societies make of them or it – is to resist the temptation to rely, as the victim, on a moral power that bestows the right to reparation (pages 122–3). Such resistance does not mean denial and suppression of one's own past suffering, nor a renouncement of reparations. It means assuming one's suffering in order to free oneself from it; it means fighting for reparations under one's own terms. In order to be enabled to do this, the accounts are crucial.

■■■

A return to the accounts and to memory would open many doors. The accounts would constitute an antidote to the ideologization, related to the adoption of the colonizers' terms, that favours submission; they would provide the Enlhet people with ways to understand themselves from their own history and thus from their own protagonism. They would support self-initiative and in this way counter the fallacious illusion that the unbearable present might be resolved by apportioning historical blame. They would prevent the fundamentalism so often generated when the vanquished discover that the fervent activism accompanying promiscuity toward the victors does not help overcome the contempt the victors demonstrate toward them; when dazzled admiration of the dominant society turns to blindness motivated by repulsion by it. Fundamentalism of this kind manifests itself as an ideology fascinated with the traditional and uses discourse about the past, of which in reality it is unaware, as a vehicle for violence caused by disappointment with the victors (Hassoun 1996). Although firmness is necessary in order to readjust the constellations of power, violence generated by a fundamentalism *without history* includes no propositional element; it can only end in self-destructive frustration or even bloodshed. The original strands of memory, however, would enable the Enlhet to see themselves as actors *with history* and thus to articulate an "inside" and an "outside"; that is, to both identify themselves and place themselves in a network with other actors without behaving promiscuously toward them.[39] In this way, it opens up new proposals for interaction, as demonstrated by Kam'aatkok Ketsek's proposal regarding assumed responsibility (page 144). On this point, we turn to the necessary communication between the Enlhet and the intruders.

Bridges: The Narration of History

In order to facilitate an approach to an Enlhet history of the Chaco War, this book has provided a selection of manifestations of the multiple and polyphonic communication we call memory. There are other possibilities for mediating – for conveying (Hassoun 1996) – the perspective of the Enlhet in a way that might serve as a bridge between different worlds and aid in the construction of new channels for communication. One of these possibilities would be to narrate Enlhet history by integrating the different accounts in a way that neither sacrifices the polyphony they demonstrate nor betrays the perspective from which they were spoken. For various reasons, an integration such as this of the various accounts would be a complex undertaking.

■■■

The account is not a genre, but a receptacle for a variety of content; the accounts that constitute Enlhet memory belong to genres as different as, for example, report, description, narration, and myth. In parallel to this, each relator has his or her own preferences for specific themes and, given that the content of each account influences its formal characteristics, references to the environment and things, habits, conventions for shared living, convictions, ideas, attitudes, and historical events differ from each other in their formal realizations. In addition, some relators report constellations, events, and processes with great precision and much detail[40] while others prefer to highlight connections between different experiences or emphasize the novelistic effect of the retelling. All of the accounts, no matter their form, would serve as input for a bridging narrative integrating them under the concepts, logics, and readings facilitated by the native voices themselves.

Not all the accounts are equal with regard to their coherence with other Enlhet accounts, and Enlhet society itself expresses opinions about them. The emphasis on native concepts and logics, therefore, does not run contrary to the need for a critical view of individual accounts in order to determine their respective reliability and representativeness. For this purpose, coherence between accounts should not be confused with the congruency of what they express. One of the conclusions from the extended period of work with these accounts is that, in the great majority of cases, contradictions between different accounts are not due to error or a lack of precision in one or other of them; the contradictions do not occur by chance. Rather, such contradiction produces, within the polyphonic memory, a new sense that must be examined: in order to reach a better understanding of Enlhet history, what differs between the various accounts is as valuable as what is common to them. Another conclusion has been that what we might initially have considered an imperfection in a given account was often the result of a gap in the editors' knowledge; as our understanding of the traditional Enlhet world increased, many such presumed imperfections vanished. In this sense, the critical view of this book combines with a broad methodological respect for the Enlhet accounts.[41]

■■■

In integrating the accounts into a bridging narrative, further challenges arise. The prismatic fragmentation inherent in the original Enlhet narrative combines with the multiple ruptures and suppressions it has suffered.[42] This situation often demands quasi-archaeological work in order to decipher the history of the people.[43] It requires a constant alternation of a panoramic perspective on the accounts with contrast between particular accounts. In parallel to this, comparison and contrast of the Enlhet narrative with those of neighbouring groups allows the posing of new questions to the Enlhet relators and discovery and development of new readings that give a better understanding of the position of the Enlhet within the process that has formed current society in the Central Chaco.

External sources referring to the Enlhet world can support or endorse the Enlhet accounts, but cannot contradict them. They speak from a perspective that is not compatible with the Enlhet perspective, making it impossible to determine whether a contradiction is related to the veracity of one of the two accounts and the falsity of the other or to the incompatibility of the respective positions. Additionally, external statements about the Enlhet say little or nothing about the motivations and perspectives of Enlhet people; worse, they are often incorrect and even highly distorted, and so serve little or not at all for learning anything about the Enlhet.[44] By contrast, they do allow much insight into their foreign authors; it is worth remembering, in this sense, the conjectures of Anonymous (1933) regarding the origins of the smallpox (page 139).

This said, contrast with external narratives and the information they provide does not have as its purpose to judge or correct the Enlhet narrative. It serves another function: to allow a genuine bridging narrative to act as precisely that. All bridges need pillars on both sides of the river and, thus, this narrative, while totally rooted in the native perspective, must in some degree respond to the ways of seeing and reasoning of the other; to their ways of expressing and orienting themselves. To take a simple example, the Enlhet narrative does not contain references to the Western calendar. The establishment of correlations between the Western calendar and temporal references in the accounts helps the audience to better position itself within the Enlhet narrative from its non-Enlhet perspective. However, in making any contrasts, care must be taken not to overwrite the Enlhet perspective with alien perspectives, as occurs easily if the accounts are read with predefined expectations. In descriptions, for example, of the history of the mission by a missionary, or of education by a teacher, it occurs typically that phenomena, events, and processes are included or ignored, made or unmade, according to how they fit the pre-established categories of the corresponding viewpoint.

Who Represents Whom?

At this point, we come to an important complication, one that could even result in the bridging narrative – as a way in which the Enlhet can share their memory with the intruders on the basis of newly constructed channels of communication between the two parties – turning out to be no more than a nice idea. I have proposed the bridging narrative as a form of mediation intended to underpin communication between different worlds. Thus, it needs a mediator, but in that figure arises the question of who represents whom. Is it possible that the Enlhet themselves can realize such a bridging narrative, or that they cannot because it would imply a proposal from outside and would thus be linked to an alien methodology? Why would they realize it if they have their own modes of relating? If someone from outside created it, would they not be speaking *in place of* the Enlhet, just as the colonialists always have? Who gives them the right to do so? And how much would the results of their enterprise have to do with the Enlhet? What would the Enlhet's real protagonism look like in this case? What effects would it have for the construction of equilibrium between the two societies? Furthermore, if a member of the Enlhet people took on the role of mediator of their memory, how would things be different? If they were rooted in external discourses in the way that Enlhet teachers, for example, usually are, what implications would that have for their representativeness? And if they were not, how would they make themself heard, their discourse being so completely different to that of the Paraguayans, of the people of the dominant Western world?

In the end, the idea of a bridging narrative comes back to the centre of the complicated questions of how a colonized people – that is, one whose capacity for managing autonomous discourses and representing itself has largely disarticulated – can express itself. Moreover, the doubt arises of whether it can actually speak (Spivak 1994), since to be able to speak means also to be heard. The two must be differentiated. The relators demonstrate clearly that the Enlhet can express themselves or, less optimistically, that they used to be able to do so, as the authors of the accounts in this book are almost all now dead. However, although the Enlhet can express themselves, it may be impossible for them to speak *to* the intruders because the intruders do not understand or wish to listen to them. But can they speak *with* the intruders then? Perhaps the only way to do so is through the originary manifestations of their memory, through sharing desires, anxieties, joys, projections, and doubts with the images they paint, as they have done in this book. Still, in order for the intruders to be able to understand this speech – those of them who wished to listen – it would again need to be accompanied by mediation and translation, and thus the circle closes.[45]

■■■

The answers to these interrogatives are not simple. Additionally, we must differentiate between a desired theory and a possible practice of small steps, situated in a context where enormous silences have resulted not only in forgetting: speaking and also listening have both been unlearned. In such a context, every word spoken could be understood as a cry against the silence and thus as a cry announcing life. However, there are also cries that precede death and, in the same way, words that suffocate, words with which graves are dug. I cannot discuss these complex questions here, and much less propose answers. I will suggest only that an interrogation is not always resolved with new answers; sometimes new questions must be framed in order to open possibilities for travelling different paths. On these paths, the things one perceives are reconfigured. They are paths that enable an escape, at least to a small degree, from the ties of normality, an advance of one or two steps toward the recovery of greater freedom, from there to frame new questions, reframe some of the existing ones and leave others aside.

Articulations

The discussion thus far has been of silences, amnesia, imbalances, and of longing for lost freedom. These words describe the consequences of the settling of alien people – intruders – in Enlhet territory. The military occupied it by force of arms and, at the same moment, the Mennonites played their part with the plough in a process that, to this day, they call peaceful.[46] If they really had been peaceful, if they had been people who valued the hospitality of the Enlhet and acted with respect toward the original occupiers of the region, it would not be possible to qualify them as intruders as I have done thus far. However, their firm decision to take ownership of the territory harmonized perfectly with the intruders on the other front, the military; the two formed an alliance based on shared interests and quickly shattered the life of Enlhet society. As a manifestation of this, sharing – the symbol of equilibrium in action – soon became impossible (pages 114–15, 119–21). Whether they arrived, therefore, with swords or with ploughs, the military and the Mennonites are intruders; and they are more than this. To this day, they continue to deny the Enlhet the possibility, and even the right, to live under their own terms and logics, a fact that identifies them as the "oppressors" of whom the national anthem speaks. They thus demonstrate that the independence of Paraguayan society from the Spanish crown was never complemented by independence from the logic of dominion and oppression that Spain represented (pages 148, 157). Instead, structural violence continues to reign within it and makes a life of dignity impossible for many, not only for Indigenous Peoples but also for the majority of Paraguayans, who are excluded in their own country. Independence has remained incomplete.

Independence from the Spanish crown was established suddenly with the breaking of a "sceptre," as the national anthem says. The conclusion of this unfinished independence, though, will require painstaking processes of reorientation of the whole of society and the people who comprise it. Indeed, in the two hundred years since independence – and even since the conquest itself – there have been innumerable individuals who have fought to overcome the dominance of the logic of exclusion and destruction in their society, for the defence or re-conquest of freedoms, for another possible reality. They have had their successes, but the need to continue the battle for greater equilibrium has not diminished.

■■■

In order to construct and maintain equilibrium between the different societies within Paraguay, processes of articulation between them are required. Articulation is more than a communication that moves messages from one place to another and may or may not be answered with messages in return. That form of interaction, which in the interethnic context is sufficient in order to be qualified as intercultural, makes it easy to ignore the differentness of the person to whom one is directing oneself or, depending on one's specific position within the prevailing constellations of power, leads to denial of his or her uniqueness (page 167). This is a deceptive interculturality through which the established norms of exclusion and submission are reiterated and reaffirmed. Articulation instead refers to a type of interaction that nourishes itself equally from both sides with a focus on the condition of the other as a protagonist acting from their own cultural space.[47] That is, it is oriented to communication and interaction during which each protagonist assumes their own space and at the same time recognizes that the other "exists and has the right to be who they are and to occupy their place" (Esteva 1998, 330). It is for this reason that to aspire to articulation between two parties is to invoke equilibrium between them. Further, it is to commit to the construction and continued functioning of equilibrium.

Commitment to equilibrium implies that processes of articulation are clearly different from the type of uni- or bi-directional communication through which the interlocutors move static content. It is oriented to a constant recreation of the conditions of the communication itself – a communication both of, and through, practices, memories, and reflections – and motivates the shared generation of patterns for interaction in equilibrium and of mutually intelligible expressions. In this way, a new space for communication and interaction can be constructed using language and symbols both particular to this space and shared in common, which are highly interdependent with the spaces of the respective sides while being identical to neither. This common space enables the establishment of dialogue from positions that often are not, and do not become, compatible or intelligible. Such a dialogue, which implies taking up the challenge of respecting both one's own difference and that of the other, facilitates the generation, by the participants in the articulation, of a type of mutual understanding very different from the acquisition of knowledge about the other and their world through analysis and study. Although this knowledge is commonly considered an absolute precondition for successful communication, in reality, it does not lead to comprehension of a way of life different from one's own – to understand that, it must be learned as one learns another language (Feyerabend 1991, 75). This knowledge could, therefore, serve as a route toward the other but, without an understanding of him or her, the other cannot be valued in the condition of a protagonist (page 6). Thus, such knowledge would permit better handling of the process of relating – and better management of the other – but runs contrary to articulation with them. In this way, insistence on a necessity for this type of knowledge of the other – knowledge that comes from analysis and study – is both a manifestation and a tool of disequilibrium. Knowledge of the other constructed through dialogue in spaces of articulation, by contrast, creates connections with the other. It thus permits a sympathetic approach and ceases to become a mechanism for control: from dialogue, possibilities are created and recreated for shared living in a minimally balanced way, for assuming the difference of the other.

In reclaiming their concrete historical experience, the elder Enlhet generations emphasize the key necessity of dialogue for shared living in equilibrium. As Savhongvay' points out, "they lived in constant dialogue" (in Kalisch and Unruh 2014, 242–3), a dialogue simultaneously reflecting and forming the basis of *nengelaasekhaamalhkoo*, that equilibrium in continuous reconstruction, that peace in action (Kalisch 2011b), that attitude of hospitality (Esteva 1998) that makes possible articulation with the other on the basis of one's own needs, possibilities, potentialities, and solutions without imposing them on the other but giving them the right to do the same. The Enlhet have built this attitude of hospitality on the foundation of their philosophy of relating in which marked openness toward the other combines with a clear determination to maintain one's own freedom (Kalisch

2004). It is this combination that provides the two points of tension that enable the ongoing creation of equilibrium during articulation with others.

▪▪▪

The discussion thus far has been of processes of articulation between very diverse societies finding themselves obliged to live together within boundaries – for them, arbitrary – created, maintained, and defended by a nation-state that has never taken those societies seriously. This circumstance poses a fundamental question related to possible processes of articulation. As has been mentioned, articulation orients to the construction of equilibrium. However, at the same time, it needs equilibrium in order to be possible: there must be a certain equilibrium between markedly different societies in order for them to be able to construct and consolidate possibilities of articulation. That means that the new space for communication and interaction mentioned above, constructed through processes of articulation and with its own language and symbols, cannot be imagined as independent of the negotiation of currently accepted power relations.

This reference to negotiation is a reminder, on the one hand, that articulation with the other is not initiated in the expectation of favourable conditions; it does not happen automatically. Given that articulation implies beginning from one's own difference, there is no possibility of movement while those who are trapped in a system of domination do not distance themselves from it at least a little. Also, given that articulation means respect for the other and giving them their place, there is no possibility of a shift while those who entrap the other do not cease to do so at least a little, as a start. Therefore, if favourable conditions for articulation are not obtained automatically, their emergence must be nurtured. For this purpose, we should not disqualify in our haste a reorientation that begins with small steps. In fact, we cannot undervalue small steps, because the pace is set by the societies in articulation, each for itself. To suggest anything else would be to fall prey once again to the tentacles of colonial logic.

There is no reason to underestimate the pace of small steps. For, however much changes in configurations of the present may have infinitely small effects at any one time, the perspective varies with each step and new constellations with new contrasts are created (pages 125–6, 189). In this way, the landscape – the normality of an obvious present – ceases to be frozen or sterile and opportunities open up for new steps that, in the long term, will combine to become a path toward ever-greater adjustment. During a process of reconfiguration of this kind, therefore, constellations can emerge to favour the green shoots of communication between societies that enable the advance of construction and consolidation of modes of interaction in equilibrium. It is important to repeat, however, that even in favourable constellations these green shoots will not appear or develop automatically. Seeds must be planted, and although no shoot can be pushed or pulled to make it grow more quickly, nutrients can be provided: opportunities for the initiation and consolidation of unprecedented articulation must be sought and then exploited decisively.[48] If not, there is a danger that the energy released by transformation will be lost, or will translate into violence to the detriment of all (pages 193–4).

The reference to a necessary negotiation of power relations is a reminder, on the other hand, that the route to new freedom does not pass through the occupation of strategic positions of power by one's own people. Rather, it orients to a reconstruction of the very structures that create such positions. For their dynamics do not depend in the first place on who is in power, but emerge fundamentally from the very nature of the power system of the nation-state, founded as it is on domination and control (Esteva 2014). Additionally, this state was constructed from the cultural tradition of others and belongs as a result to a society that is not the Enlhet's own; the occupation of strategic positions of power within it, therefore, does not have the potential to create new spaces. In sum, from whichever angle it is viewed, to maintain current positions of power would be to remain trapped within the colonial model – indeed, within colonial logic – and to limit imagination to the concepts of that model.

The processes of reconstruction of constellations of power, "which will produce another way of doing politics and another kind of politics" (Subcomandante Marcos, in EZLN 1996, 69), will have a variety of protagonists – some more or less in opposition, others more or less allied – occupying different and very unequal positions in the current power landscape and having at times antagonistic interests as a result. Thus they will be processes that uncover existing tensions and frictions in the country instead of continuing to veil them in silence. However, if they are at the same time processes of articulation between the different societies and their actors, there exists the option that these tensions and frictions can be reworked and transformed in pursuit of the reconstruction of an equilibrium that makes them manageable and tolerable for all social actors.

■■■

One of the elements necessary for the creation of conditions favourable to articulation between the co-existent societies in Paraguay is the drafting of laws that, by defining rights and obligations, aid in redressing the inequality that marks life in the country; this inequality leads to a defence of individual advantage, thus running contrary to all articulation. However, the most immediate obstacles to the next steps in the advancement of constructing a more balanced society do not come from existing laws in Paraguay, which do guarantee some space for action.[49] The most serious impediments come from prevailing attitudes and convictions in the country that are, in addition, constantly reaffirmed by the very people against whom they are directed, be they from among the Indigenous Peoples or Paraguayan Guaraní- and Spanish-speaking society itself. As I have mentioned, the subjugated peoples themselves think and act in a way that reasserts their condition of subordination (pages 177, 184) so that they remain trapped within the reduction of their freedoms.

It is a complex and complicated task to find a way out of this vicious circle because, again, no action can be undertaken on the behalf of the subjugated without reinforcing the disastrous colonial dynamic instead of undermining it. Any way out depends on the disarticulated and paralyzed society taking the initiative; on its resolve and dedication to employing the potential that lies within it. This does not mean, however, that the dominant society is freed of its responsibility *in* the process – quite the contrary; but it can no longer claim responsibility *for* the process. That is to say, instead of attempting to influence the subjugated society and its processes, it must give space to the society

Figure 4.7 ▪ "No action can be undertaken on the behalf of the subjugated." Woman weaving a bag from *tamam'a* fibres. These bags are in constant use among the Enlhet to this day, although increasingly they are woven from fibres recycled from plastic bags.

of the other and communicate with its members in a way that is respectful, open, and critical, not self-interested. This is no small task, for it demands much. It implies the dominant society's beginning to reassess itself. In the end, any possible way out depends also on how the society of the oppressor approaches its relationship with the societies it oppresses.

■■■

In the aim of supporting articulation between the dominant society and the displaced societies, and thus the reconstruction of equilibrium, the present work contributes merely a grain of sand toward enabling a glimpse of Indigenous protagonism, the potential it holds, and the space it requires. With a view to the empowerment of Indigenous societies, I have argued in this sense for the legitimacy of a markedly different viewpoint from the one that dominates (in) Paraguayan society and Western society in general. I have insisted upon the unavoidable necessity that a society begin from its own viewpoint in seeking to recover protagonism on its own terms and overcome colonial ties. The space to see and act from one's own perspective is non-negotiable if the right to life is understood to be not a simple concession of survival, as colonial ideology proposes, but the guarantee of a dignified life (Kalisch 2012b; Kalisch 2014b). As long as this right is not guaranteed and colonial ideology continues to ignore and erase viewpoints, logics, and concepts different from its own, every act of viewing from a particular perspective is an act of insurrection that contributes one small step toward reconfiguring normality and orienting to overcoming colonial practices.

I have only outlined a possible path, along which no one might ever pass but which lies as a real possibility in the daily life of the people and may, like a seed, one day germinate. Therefore, and despite the fact that no one might ever travel it, its categories should be sketched out in order to clarify the horizon of possibilities so that, in due course, it might be taken more easily. In highlighting some of the outlines of this possible path it is my intention to convey what I have learned from participating in Enlhet social reality and listening to the accounts of the Elders, which reflect long historical experience of

shared living in conditions of equality and equilibrium. This foundation in an orientation toward equilibrium at once historical and every
day can enable the Enlhet, and Indigenous Peoples in general, when
the moment arises – it may arise; let us hope it does – to contribute
much, probably the greater part, to the design and concrete construction of collectivity within the arbitrary frontiers of what we call Paraguay, based on real articulation between the parties. It is they who can
contribute key elements to the construction of bespoke channels and
practices for communication that will enable each to look from their
own perspective and express themselves from their own position. For
the moment, these channels are practically non-existent in Paraguay
but are crucial in order to arrive at fairer shared living in the country.

Communication, Knowledges, and their Protagonists

Returning to the theme of memory – to the experiences and knowledges circulated communicatively by the people – I would like to
look at a particular aspect of current ideas on the interaction between national society and extremely diverse minority societies: the
management of knowledge and its protagonists. This aspect demonstrates paradigmatically the place where native memory – and with it
the life of the people – has been relegated in processes of communication with national society (page 167).

For the dominant society, there exists a body clearly responsible
for the creation and management of knowledge of itself and others:
academia. As any activity related to Indigenous societies becomes increasingly formalized, the conviction that it should be designed, or at
least endorsed, by academia grows. For example, with regard to the
use by Indigenous Peoples of their own languages and to processes
of learning, there is a belief that there must be a written grammar to
strengthen a native language and that there must be anthropological
or historical analysis to draw up Indigenous curricula. While those
who use and are familiar with these languages and cultures can serve
as informants they are not perceived as legitimate protagonists in
the construction and management of knowledge with regard to their
world through a native epistemology. Therefore, although the contribution of modern science to concrete processes is rarely significant,

the word of those who consider themselves representatives of academia, whether they are recognized by it or not, has great power to reject proposals and discard possibilities, and thus great potential for the creation of doubt.[50] As a consequence of this situation, clarity is needed as to what contribution science, from its privileged position, can genuinely make to Indigenous life in general, and in particular to the activation of an awareness of the people's own history that might allow them to reconnect current life with their past, which is the subject in question here.

■■■

Academia perceives itself as the only possible space for the construction of knowledge, and, therefore, rejects the idea that circles of knowledge with other objectives, methodologies, and contents, might exist outside its own. It confers upon itself a monopoly on what is valid knowledge and which knowledge is valid. This means, in practice, that a thing becomes knowledge only when academia represents it.[51] At the same time, just as for Western discourse in general, for academia the world is what it sees from its own perspective (page 163). As a result, the inclusion of academia in any model of communication produces a dual exclusion of Indigenous society: that of its perspective and that of the knowledges built from that perspective (and of how they have been built).[52] By this dual exclusion, the possibility of protagonism on its own terms for Indigenous societies is discarded right from the theoretical level, even in relation to what pertains to their own life. As a consequence, the proposal of an external protagonism becomes inevitable, which means the proposal of colonial practice.[53]

As Sousa Santos (2010; 2011) has pointed out, this colonial character is inherent to modernity, which is characterized by an abyssal divide between metropolitan and colonial societies. Concomitantly, Western epistemology is committed to what he calls "abyssal thinking," from which, he emphasizes, not even the most critical schools of the social sciences diverge. It is a way of thinking that defines what exists and, at the same time, that which does not exist because it does not fall within the expected coordinates for describing the world and its social realities. It creates a separation between the acceptable and the unacceptable that is reflected in practices of inclusion and exclusion that, in the end, determine the right that one has, or does not have, to protagonism under one's own terms (page 144).

It is commonly maintained that to question the role of academia implies the renouncement of quality – to use its own word, rigour – and thus of the possibility of access to reliable knowledge. In reality, however, it means only the renouncement of exclusivity of methodologies and academic concepts and opens up an option for native society to define what it considers to be high-quality and reliable knowledge based on its own methodology and from its own perspective and practice (Kalisch 2006; 2007; 2012b). To question the role of academia, therefore, does not mean the renouncement of rationality or a declaration that anything and everything is of equal value. But it does mean that there is far more that is of value than what academia imagines. It is to recognize that rationality does not necessarily lead down the road academia has taken in its reasoning and which, in combination with models of development, has brought the planet to the verge of collapse. It is to understand that what is said, done, and experienced in the present is deduced, *by its own logic*, from that which was said, done, and experienced previously: every society defines what is of value from its particular historical process (which also means: from its precise history of interaction with the world of phenomena; page 166).

■■■

It is no trivial matter for any society finding itself on the other side of the abyssal divide to give the corresponding space to its own perspective, and much less so for a society as small as the Enlhet. The colonial process has erased not only native knowledges, but their very methodologies and epistemologies; it has eliminated the spaces in which knowledge was produced and managed; it has caused an enormous vacuum with regard to possibilities for managing and applying knowledge; in general, it has created a world of greatly reduced possibilities for protagonism. This said, the insistence on native protagonism is not a reason to disqualify out of hand all knowledge academia may have built or contributions it may be able to make.[54] Rather, it requires the realization that its knowledge exists alongside other knowledges and not above them; that its knowledge is merely one part of a plurality of traditions for the creation and management of knowledge, that is to say, of very diverse concepts of what knowledge is, of modes, no less diverse, of creating it and of criteria for its validation: of an epistemological plurality coinciding with the immense cognitive and critical potential offered by different linguistic systems, category constructions, and symbolic universes. Insistence on native protagonism thus supposes the placing in doubt of the fundamental bases of prevailing epistemology (and even the rethinking of ontologies) in order to give space to this diversity – the assuming of which is an act of insurrection since it challenges the hegemonic model. It supposes an insistence on a necessary connection between knowledges and one's own context; knowledges, moreover, that require commitment to that context.

Space does not allow thorough discussion here of the complex theme of the giving of the necessary space to one's own perspective.[55] It should merely be remembered that it implies paths and spaces the Enlhet must construct and reaffirm for themselves, though at the same time they cannot do this alone. They must find others with whom they share the condition of being on the same side of the abyssal divide, subjugated by the suffocating ideologies and practices that prevail over, surround, and penetrate their societies. At the same time, although these are paths and spaces constructed within and from society, this excludes neither the need nor the possibility for them to be supported from a panoramic viewpoint that, in relating them, facilitates sight of native potentials, for example, but also of adversities and the tentacles of the logic of subjugation acting from both inside and outside native society (Kalisch 2013; 2014c; 2014d; 2015). Such support, oriented toward a dialogue with social actors – and not (only) to an exchange with and within academia – thus supports societal discussion of the processes and dynamics of which the society is the subject and to which it is subject. However, the question of accompaniment from a panoramic viewpoint in support of an understanding of processes and dynamics brings us to another complex, perhaps thorny, theme, one upon which it is important to dwell for a moment since it is directly related to the discussion of communication and articulation.

It is a complex theme because the act of understanding is protagon-ized from many sides and for many ends: processes of understanding have very different actors who, in addition, relate in different ways to each other. It is a thorny theme, for however well-intended the real-ization of accompaniment from a panoramic viewpoint, there exists a serious risk that it continues to draw on the abyssal thinking that causes exclusion to be repeated and makes impossible any sharing worthy of the name. No one escapes easily and suddenly from the hegemonic thinking that penetrates everything and everyone, as it cannot be overcome by generating alternatives still derived from ex-isting terms. Instead, "it requires alternative thinking of alternatives" (Sousa Santos 2010, 47) that is only conceivable at a theoretical and epistemological distance from the Western tradition and its abyssal thinking. In order to acquire this *distance* and to advance in the state-ment of different thinking – of an alternative epistemology – it is vital to examine prevailing and emerging social realities and acknow-ledge them. For it is in polyphonic social practices that we find those "latent tendencies that, however inchoate and fragmented, do point to new constellations of meaning as regards both the understanding and the transformation of the world" (Sousa Santos 2010, 47). Only through *closeness* to the diverse existing realities is it possible to take ownership of those alternatives to modern Western forms of thinking and acting that orient to equilibrium and help, at the same time, to gradually escape the abyssal thinking that motivates them.[56]

■ ■ ■

The following focuses on possible actors in a panoramic accompani-ment for native processes; those who examine and describe concrete social and political processes that are not framed in the dominant logic. It should be remembered that the question of knowledge is directly linked to that of possibilities for protagonism, which has been the reason for highlighting the importance of the connection between knowledge, context, and commitment to that context. If the aim is to prevent as far as possible a colonial attack on native modes of knowing, then attention to this interface is non-negotiable. It cor-responds to the link, attention to which is equally indispensable, be-tween speech, specific reality – social, political, cultural, linguistic, historical – and commitment to that reality. The recognition of this link orients to understanding and accepting that speech about society is not independent of the position of the speaker in relation to that society and that, at the same time, it influences society in one way or another.[57] Therefore, although accompaniment from a panoramic viewpoint can be carried out both by members of society and externals, there are two indispensable requirements, technical and ethical at the same time, for both groups that define what I understand as a commitment to the context and to the actors that constitute that context.

Both those outside and those inside must adopt strategies that enable them to become aware of abyssal thinking and free themselves from it. Again, those inside also, for hegemonic thinking has penetrated everything and everyone. Additionally, both must be suitably placed so as to see with the eyes of those inside – some of those inside, having passed through educational processes that abhor nativeness, have unlearned this. Beyond this limitation, however, those who live what is inside, such as the Enlhet relators in this book, are immeasurably better placed than someone from outside to carry out panoramic accompaniment. At the same time, their being better placed to carry it out nevertheless goes hand-in-hand with the fact that their expressions collate less well with dominant discourses. This is the reason why they are not seen – or are not preferably assumed – to be active, relevant thinkers; in consequence, as I have argued at length, they try less and less to make themselves heard, often even among their own people. In this way, we return to the observation that both inability and unwillingness to see and hear the other create silences that render him or her, de facto, invisible (page 182). Accompaniment in native processes should be such that it supports those who accompany from within in re-establishing themselves as actors of knowledge.

On the subject of the actors in panoramic accompaniment of concrete social and political processes, reference to their origin inside or outside the respective society is not sufficient. A difference must also be drawn between whether they direct themselves to the native or the dominant society (the idea that they can direct themselves to both at the same time is, perhaps, just another manifestation of abyssal thinking, as it implies a unification of positions that are radically different, which is possible only if one of the two parties imposes itself; page 158). The following focuses only on the case of a person who is external to the native society but is aware that what he or she says is heard inside it (and who fulfils, of course, the two requirements stated above). Such a person knows that in their expression they enter into communication in some way with this society and that their words have an effect on it. However, they will not try to avoid the responsibility this implies on the pretext of neutrality in relation to the context they describe. By avoiding any claim to an independence they know not to exist they will cease to present their interpretations of processes and dynamics as the expression of a truth beyond the context to which these belong. Knowing, in addition, that expressions resting on the concepts of truth and universality make the negotiation of any type of equilibrium impossible, they will cease to aspire to the formulation of abstract universal theories that generalize their observations *from a particular perspective*. In the same way, they will not feel tempted to claim an invented prescriptive capacity within processes or false intellectual leadership that would grant them management of such universal theories. For they know that such theories demonstrate a practice of denial of diversity and thus disenable useful speech about a world that is not a single world (pages 163, 165).

The responsibility such a person assumes instead presents itself in a variety of ways. They do not advocate for the creation of knowledge but understand that they are merely highlighting knowledge. At the same time, they are interested in learning from the people who constitute and shape the context they describe, and not only in describing it. For example, they will be interested in learning from the Enlhet Elders their way of relating through the employment of images rather than formulas (page 171).[58] Although this person does not renounce synthesis, they will not be motivated by knowledge for the sake of knowledge (page 201), but by knowledge that is linked to society – a collectivity of actors – and has the potential to support any and all areas of its life. Always alert to the interference of complex and contradictory dynamics – which develop amid multiple silences – they will examine "forgotten themes, lost alliances, unacknowledged mistakes, unfulfilled promises ... disguised betrayals" and the pain hidden within society (Sousa Santos 2011, 21). They will assume at the same time that it is crucial to speak in terms of concepts managed by the respective society and within its tradition. For only in this way can they include the wealth and the freedom for reflection offered by those concepts in its language and which have not been subsumed or destructed by abyssal thinking – or less so, at any rate. Only thus can they see and highlight the historical and present potentials of the different society (pages 165–8). Only by this means will their expressions be intelligible – and therefore useful – to that society, so that it will be able to receive and reconstruct, or reject, them. In short, they assume their responsibility in a way that allows them to support clarification of the horizon of possibilities and aid in the imagining of new horizons.

When the person who interrogates and describes addresses the dominant society, fulfilling the first requirement, they will not speak in place of the other, representing them illegitimately (page 197), and neither will they judge the veracity of the other's description from the hegemonic viewpoint. Instead, they will understand themselves as part of a process of articulation between radically different social actors that is oriented to equilibrium (page 200). By fulfilling the second requirement, they will be enabled to facilitate, in this sense, access to the voices and viewpoints of the people, making them heard and providing ways to understand their symbolic and categorical backgrounds. They will be a person who conveys these from one world to another, a "conveyor" of voices and manners of viewing (Hassoun 1996). The knowledges produced by this process can be more than knowledge about the other. They have the potential to become knowledge that enables sharing with the other (page 201).

■■■

This book does not discuss every kind of knowledge, only historical knowledge. It presents accounts that refer to an important moment in the history of Paraguay, but whose hitherto unknown viewpoint is in clear conflict with that of Paraguayan historiography. In many places, the two narratives are not in conflict; they cross without meeting. For although they speak of the same region and time, the Enlhet relators paint a totally different world from the one understood from the historians' perspective, as we have seen, for example, in relation to smallpox (pages 141–3). To take another example, the usual narrative of historians in Paraguay is from the nation-state viewpoint, whether to legitimize or delegitimize it; the prevailing narrative of the Chaco War follows this line. In the Enlhet accounts, however, we find a narrative that neither comes from nor moves toward the nation-state and is neither relegated to such a notion nor projects itself onto it. It speaks from another paradigm, whose total incomprehension from outside has been manifested, for example, in the description of Enlhet territory as a desert (page 155).

The book presents incompatible and mutually incomprehensible differences that cannot be negotiated or agreed upon and can only be managed either through processes of articulation that create a new space of metaphor and signification or acts of exclusion and ignorance. Nothing has been contributed by historiography to the articulation of different perspectives. On the contrary, its very methodological and epistemological procedures lead to unawareness of such an option, for they orient it to discerning between the plausible and the non-plausible *from its perspective* and thus between the correct and the incorrect; the true and the false. That is, they orient to the disjunction between inclusion and exclusion that constitutes abyssal thinking. Under these circumstances, in order to differentiate possibilities for protagonism offered to Indigenous Peoples by the academic historiography that manages the history of Paraguay on the one hand and their own memory on the other, in order to understand where the former ends and discern the potential in the latter, it is useful to clarify the differences between the two.

The Accounts and Historiography

Both memory and historiography create narratives, although they do so with different methodologies and with distinct objectives. Through historiography, a group of specialists – historians – seek to represent the past in the clearest way possible in order to know and understand it. Memory, however, is society's communication of how it has lived history and how it is reflected in its history, and thus orients also to how its future is imagined. These purposes legitimize the respective modes of narrating history and, at the same time, imply different ways of understanding what is true. What for memory is the endorsement of society (page 174), for historiography is the objectivity derived from the methodological rigour historians must observe when deducing or reconstructing their narrative from what they call primary sources – fixed, conserved facts such as those found in archives in the form of texts, images, and sounds. They must select and interpret these sources in a way that makes it possible to discuss the plausibility of the argumentation that constitutes their narrative. Such a methodology is not inherent to speech about the past. It is a construction in time, a historical construction, and as a result, reflects a particular perspective.

Historiography reflects the perspective of the societies within which it was developed as an academic discipline. From this perspective, an increase in knowledge is of value in itself and responds to anxiety to control processes through the understanding of cause and effect between events (page 166). Concurrently, one of the objectives of historiography is to increase knowledge and understanding of the past in order to learn from it so as to behave more appropriately in the future.[59] In general terms, the concept of scientific knowledge is strongly influenced by the natural sciences; it is knowledge acquired through discrimination between the false and the correct and is thus connected with a concept of objectivity and truth, of a true nature of things (pages 208, 215), or, in the case of mainstream historiography, with an essential meaning of the past (Izquierdo Martín 2008, 184). In order to find this meaning and express it as clearly as possible, contemporary historiography takes account of the idea that humans have access to the course of the events we call *history* only through the *representations* we make of it based on recollections, evidence, and data. It also understands that all human activity has a specific perspective, for example, a precise way of relating a fact or expression to a time and place, because it is situated in a particular moment and space. In this sense, it understands the epistemological and methodological importance of recognizing that there are always different possible perspectives for representing events in the past.

■■■

I have argued above that the crossing point of events and their perception is mediated through readings circulated by the respective society
so that facts do not have a meaning inherent to them (pages 161–2).
This means that it is not sufficient to acknowledge a perspectivism
linked to a place in time and space or to specific interests and objectives. If the differences between the Enlhet and Paraguayan narratives
were solely of this order, a single, true history could be deduced from
the two in the same way that it is possible to reconstruct the shape of
a house from descriptions of its different sides. In order to see that
it is not so simple, it should be remembered that the respective narratives of Mennonite immigration do not paint a single world from
different sides, but paint different worlds (pages 163–4). That is to
say, the differences between the two narratives cannot be reduced to a
question of representation of things and events, but derive from what
these things and events are for the person who represents them. Thus
emerges what we might call an ontological perspective, which results
in the narratives being incompatible despite coinciding in their reference to the same phenomenological context – indeed, to the same
time and space (page 165). This mutual incompatibility makes impossible the identification of essences – universal meanings – of the past
and it is impossible to make a single reconstruction of it. That is to
say, just as the same fact is never a single fact (page 163), the same
course of events is never a single course of events. There are different
histories. Again, this does not mean that "anything and everything is
valid, but simply that it is not one thing alone that is valid" (González
de Oleaga 2014, 25). This is a strong claim: it means that the idea of
a "modern utopia of potentially unprejudiced knowledge" is vain (Izquierdo Martín 2008, 192).

Historiography that is unaware of, or rejects, observations leading
us to formulate the idea of an ontological perspectivism is trapped
within the idea that what it calls "essence," "the universal" and "reality"
are most accurately reflected from its own perspective and axioms. In
consequence, it says that smallpox is a biological process with precise
causes and effects; but is not payment for inattention to equilibrium
(pages 160–3). What we have here is much worse than uninformed

opinion, for, in addition to being unaware of the different perspective, it denies out of hand – as an article of faith – the fact that we are dealing with expressions that come from perspectives of equal condition with regard to their role as a historical construction responding to concrete purposes (although they are not equal in relation to their right to exist in the current world). Therefore, by treating the other perspective as non-existent, irrelevant, or mistaken, such historiography's concept of perspectives is limited to the differences between those with the same ontological viewpoint: the diversity one is willing to perceive falls within what one's perspective allows one to imagine. Such a severe reduction – a manifestation of the aforementioned abyssal thinking (page 208) – is comfortable because from the hypothesis of a single reality come essential truths which, as such, are universal truths: the historical discourse of academia is constructed as universal.

■■■

A good example of the universalization of a particular viewpoint is the way in which historians treat time. For them, it is linear, as recorded by chronometers and calendars, although there are other forms of experiencing it (even within their own society) and, thus, of defining it. In the Enlhet accounts, time corresponds, for example, to the intensity of experiences, expanding during moments of more energy and contracting in moments of less activity. The accounts also acknowledge cyclical time. In the form in which the Enlhet present themselves in their own society today, a resetting of historical time can be seen that is connected to the capitulation toward the end of the 1950s (pages 141, 151–2). This reset is visible when they commemorate Enlhet history during community festivals. Here, they do not speak of the origins of the members of the community or remember the people's territory and a world lost. Instead, history begins with the first instruction from the missionary at their respective mission stations (page 177).

The role of time in Enlhet memory warrants separate analysis that cannot be undertaken here. Suffice it to say that it is not a question of determining which way of representing time is the best, but of recognizing that differences correspond to different ends.[60] They thus have different potentialities and should not be substituted one for the other; they should articulate.

■ ■ ■

I do not offer these reflections in the interests of theoretical discussion; they are motivated by the need to construct new channels of communication between the societies co-present in Paraguay. It is important to make very clear that in general, when historiography forgets that it reflects a certain perspective and is, as a result, relative to other possible perspectives, it easily produces and promotes ideologies. In particular, when it forgets the existence of different ontological perspectives, it promotes the ideology of colonialism, which proceeds to impose readings and thus unify the meanings of events. It practices colonialism as long as it does not accept that there are other ways as valid as its own of creating and managing knowledge, even if it is unable to access them. There is a subtle but firm connection between colonialism and the historiography that legitimizes it, albeit an unconscious one. The connection warrants examination.

Decolonizing History

Both memory and historiography manage knowledge that finds its truth in the criteria for validation they themselves establish. In the Western tradition, that which is true is related to that which is invariable. Consequently, information that might be contained in an Oral Tradition with no resource to fix the word appears to be of doubtful value because its circulatory nature opens the way for arbitrariness and might result in imprecise, diffuse, or blurred information. This argument could be refuted by saying that it is true that information in the oral accounts so carefully remembered by their relators is obscured by a certain noise originating in the multiplicity of voices and perspectives, temporal distance, the translation of concrete experience to related expression, the step from one's own experience to that related by another, etc. However, the information in written expressions (and recorded, or filmed, expressions) with their immutable,

Figure 4.8 • "From their multiple distances they are incomprehensible, and it follows that what they say is unacceptable." Temporary houses built by the Enlhet when travelling, 1930s.

frozen words, are not themselves free of noise.[61] The noise can be caused by the fact that the author has a particular perspective or by the temporal distance between the event and its recording (for it is not the writing that makes the difference, but the immediacy writing allows), among other reasons. That is to say, written text is not in itself a true statement, given that the author themself may be mistaken and may even lie; indeed, it is much easier to lie than it would be in the oral context, where proximity to the audience is immediate. In general terms, therefore, if historians wish to use the Enlhet accounts to deduce from them information for historiographical purposes, they find themselves with challenges similar to those they face when they approach any other text: they are obligated to make a critical study of their sources. In the end, the incompatibility between historiography and memory is not the result of the quality of the data that is or is not available. Rather, the problem is that, since facts do not exist in an absolute form, much of the information contained in the accounts cannot be read outside the perspective that memorizes it.

Academic historiography, therefore, if it reads the accounts, does so from a marginal perspective and takes the information it understands to use in the narrative it creates. By this use of information taken from the Enlhet world, it appears to include that world but, in reality, its narrative remains entirely detached from that representing the course of lived experiences in the past from the Enlhet perspective. In spite of the inclusion of information about the Enlhet, the historiographical narrative thus produced is very different from the bridging narrative discussed above (page 196) and, simultaneously, contributes little or nothing to what has become a preoccupation of some currency in modern historiography: the decolonizing of history. By representing the history of the other on their behalf using concepts that are alien to them and readings that do not correspond to their perspective – including their information, perhaps, but excluding their perspectives – it is implied that the other has no legitimacy to self-represent or, by extension, on a more subtle level, to think and express themselves. At these multiple distances – they are distant from academia and from dominant logic in general and thus from the respective concepts and discourses – for academia they are incomprehensible and it follows that what they say is unacceptable. However, academia blames them and their world for its own limitation, disqualifying them, supposedly objectively, as "illiterate," "uneducated," "ignorant," "provincial," "underdeveloped," or "obsolete,"[62] or with direct contempt (although the line between objectivity and contempt is not easy to draw) as "non-contemporary," "backward," "inferior," or "superstitious." In sum, old colonial mechanisms are reapplied.

■ ■ ■

Decolonizing history is more than using information from and about the colonized in the narrative produced. It is also more than training Indigenous historians to represent the voice of their people outside their society and under concepts that do not correspond to them, as though the end recipient of all history were the victors. There is no way around it: if we wish to overcome colonial mechanisms there is no approach to the history of the Enlhet that does not take in the polyphonic narrative held by them. Decolonization of history should begin, therefore, by listening to other perspectives; by seeing what others narrate and how they do it. It would mean admitting readings generated by the Enlhet from their particular logics (like the accounts themselves, these are – where they have not been erased – unknown and discounted). It would require the acceptance of these different narratives as the equals of one's own, for neither is it a question of seeing history from the other person's side, from the other side; that would be inverted colonization. In the end, the decolonization of history should be a practice of recognizing that history is not a single history, of thinking of the past from many perspectives, as history with multiple perspectives.

A multiple history, different histories, do not exist in a vacuum but circulate within their respective societies. To recognize the past as a history with multiple perspectives, therefore, impedes the extraction of history from one society to dissect it in a sterile space in which it would lose its reason for being. Rather, it orients to the realization that acts of relating history have many actors, just as they are protagonized by many receptors. It is difficult for colonizing society to recognize that history is related by many, but more difficult still for it to think of processes of listening to it as having multiple protagonists. The colonizers can hardly bear that those who speak are many and diverse, but it is extraordinarily difficult for them to accept that there are important acts of communication in which they themselves are not participants. The fact that the colonizers' society might not be the purpose of all expression means that there are worlds different from their own and circles of power, however insignificant, that it does not control. It rejects this possibility and represses it.

Again, to open oneself to the Enlhet perspective – not to convert oneself to it, but to accept it as valid alongside others – is provocative: it challenges the belief in a stable, essential past with its own meaning. It challenges belief in absolute truth and clearly defined protagonists. It challenges some of the pillars of the modern world. However, it is necessary to take up this challenge, because the majority of the people living today do not live in that modern world.

■■■

The colonial dynamic is propagated on the basis of the logic of a unique representation, which makes it inherently elitist, creating a stratification that lays the foundations for moves toward domination and hegemonic imposition. Therefore, in order to see and think of the other – and of shared living itself – within a paradigm not linked to the colony, the turn from the protagonism of an elite to that of differentiated collectivities is an indispensable step (it is a change that comes back once more to the aforementioned question of who represents whom; pages 197, 214). In parallel to this, the decolonization of history cannot be an act carried out by a group of specialists more interested than others in the voices of the colonized. Rather, it refers to a mode of communication between the societies living together in Paraguay – or any other state – in which it is assumed that each lives according to a different narrative, where the possibility to do so is guaranteed, and where articulation is enabled on the basis of their respective particularities, among them their narratives of history.

However, the narratives of Enlhet and Paraguayan society have both been colonized. It is easy, therefore, for acts of concrete communication coming from the different narratives to meet in a shared colonial logic clearly supported by current constellations of power and set a course whose end is identical to its own beginning. To break out of this vicious circle, which impedes the construction of a new equilibrium, requires input from, for example, the accounts in this book and people with vision and firm roots – without roots there can be no vision – whose words have the potential to change our ways of viewing (though not in order to become our leaders). It requires people who recognize this input and it requires, within and between societies, processes of communication through which the input is taken up; processes that open the way for the small steps that slowly reconfigure things as they are perceived and enable a gradual breaking free from the impositions of the present to advance toward new forms of shared living (pages 202, 206).

■■■

The turn from the protagonism of an elite to that of differentiated collectivities does not imply a renouncement of the need for experts (page 210). Rather, it supposes a review of the role of specialists in relation to society and of the patterns of interaction between the two parties. In this way, a wide range of complex and challenging questions opens up around the generation and management of knowledges and meaning. Although these cannot be discussed in the present work, it is important to repeat they must be viewed from current practices in the different societies and from their potential for imagination (pages 213–14). In general, this turn in protagonism presupposes acknowledgement that there are historically proven solutions among societies with diverse traditions that far outreach what the hegemonic model allows to be imagined. It means a redefinition of the place from which solutions are expected to come, an understanding that there is not one single solution, only mutually constructed alternatives (Panikkar 1993). Or, as Sousa Santos (2011, 28) states: "we face modern problems for which there are no modern solutions."

The people who mediate in this context between different histories – whether in time or in space, whether between generations or between different societies – do not decide which of the perspectives or narratives is the truest; their key function is to *convey* existing narratives from one side to the other (page 214). They know that truth is not inherent to the facts themselves in any way that could allow them to reach it by words that reproduce the past mimetically; they renounce the idea of a canon describing the correct form of doing and seeing things. In this way, they cease to circle around the correct and incorrect and can no longer use as an excuse the argument that the decisions they take reflect a commitment to truth, on which they, however, do not have an influence, claiming, for example, that "I am just saying how things are." They cannot rely on the supposition that the accuracy of their statements with regard to facts frees them from the consequences of what they say. Rather, they know that when they speak they must make decisions that will have consequences for which they must assume responsibility (page 213). In this way, the truth of the past – the supposition that things were as one says they were – gives way to the responsibility of actors in the present, to the awareness that one sees things in a certain way and must respond to this (González de Oleaga 2014, 25). The result is a turn from the idea of truth to a practice of responsibility (González de Oleaga, 2008, 174).

Decisions

The Enlhet voices here invite us to break out of a familiar, ready-made narrative, with all the concomitant risk that the notions it implies may fall down. As a result, they oblige a decision as to whether to accept these voices as a crucial contribution to the decolonization of the narrative of Paraguay (and perhaps that of the nations of the Americas more generally) or to announce, on the contrary, the total defeat of the Indigenous world and declare that the native world is nothing more than a small appendix to the country, kept in a drawer with interesting exotic stories, discourses on injustice and necessary inclusion, intercultural education and folklore, and in many other cages in which the unfolding of their potential for the construction of lives is constrained.

▪▪▪

The Enlhet accounts open new horizons. For the Enlhet themselves, who have been subjugated by the State through a wide range of actors, the accounts enable the rediscovery that the world is not so limited as it appears today, that it is much larger than it seems. This discovery is crucial for them, for it is indispensable in order to begin the search for a dignified life. However, it is no less crucial for Guaraní- and Spanish-speaking Paraguayans themselves. The great majority of them live restricted to the limited spaces the State has established and that it organizes through authoritarian power based on the anachronistic idea of a homogenous, abstract nation at the service of elites. They are dispossessed within a society that dispossesses the Indigenous. This contradiction means that the Indigenous, unknown, ignored, and often belittled, are on the same side as the majority of Paraguayans, for they all have in common the severe reduction of their freedom. That is why Enlhet voices can be a mirror that poses questions (pages 6, 8) and encourages initial acts of articulation with the Enlhet that lead, in the long term, to rethinking the customary position taken with regard to them. If, as a consequence, new images of the dispossessed Indigenous are constructed, the process will have repercussions in the society of the dispossessors itself. For when Indigenous people cease to be considered as mere consumers of ready-made proposals and actions and become peers, co-constructors of Paraguay, it is not only they who will have more freedom and live with more dignity. The same goes for all social actors: these new images orient to a country of spaces particular to each collective that are autonomous, diversified, and at the same time interlinked. They are a call to a common project that does not homogenize and enable new steps toward a Paraguay of freedom and dignity for all.

▪▪▪

Don't cry. Be quiet. Bear it. This remains an important formula for the present-day coexistence of the Enlhet with the Paraguayans. The Paraguayans need to know the histories that make up the Enlhet narrative if they wish to be more than dispossessors and to prevent the potential for violence implicit in a hidden history of dispossession. Given the dark dynamics that describe the past and present, therefore, if the Enlhet voice obliges them to rethink their position relative to the other, there is an ethical decision to be taken. It is the decision as to what kind of country they want. They must make it knowing that no reconstruction of shared living comes free, but requires a commitment to long, sustained effort. There will be a good number of people who say they do not want the Indigenous Peoples as peers. But I place my hope in the others, for I know that there are many who long for a different Paraguay.

APPENDIX
THE NAMES OF THE FORTS

The following list contains the names of the forts shown on map 1.3, "Positions of the Paraguayan and Bolivian armies at the beginning of 1932." The assignment of the different forts on the map to one or other of the armies does not necessarily indicate the flag under which they were founded or the army occupying them at the time of the declaration of war in September 1932 (according to Barreto 1969; Bejarano 1979; Joy 1992). Even before this there had been minor clashes between the warring nations and the occupying forces at several of the forts had changed.

Name used on map	Other names	Enlhet name
Alihuatá (Bolivia)	Today: Teniente Ruperto Zenteno	Loom-Popyet
Arce (Bolivia)	Today : Gaspar Rodríguez de Francia	Yaatektama-Yelhem
Bolívar (Bolivia)	Today: Teniente Jara Troche	
Boquerón (Paraguay)		Yelhvayvoo-Pyettek
Cabeza de Tigre (Paraguay)		Tomaklha-Pook-Maama
Camacho (Bolivia)	Today: Mariscal Estigarribia	Kamatso
Campo Jordán (Paraguay)	Today: Campo Aceval	Lha'akme-Yaamelket
Carayá (Paraguay)	Bolivian name: Huijay Today: Coronel Hermosa	Veejay
Carlos Antonio López (Paraguay)	Pitiantuta	probably Namaalhek
Casanillo (Paraguay)		Konomaktollolaq
Coronel Martínez (Paraguay)		Maso-Sanga
Corrales (Paraguay)		
Cuatro Vientos (Bolivia)		

Name used on map	Other names	Enlhet name
Esteros (Bolivia)		
Falcón (Bolivia)	Bolivian name: Rojas Silva	Kenma'lha
Fernández (Bolivia)	Today: Luis Alberto de Herrera	Nataayet
Figari (Paraguay)		Maapelhkep
Gondra (Paraguay)		
Isla Po'i (Paraguay)	Previously: Villa Militar, Cacique Ramón	Nahangvet
Jayucubas (Bolivia)	Today: Capitán Serebriakof	
La China (Bolivia)	Today: Capitán Mazzei	
Loa (Bolivia)	Today: Teniente Aristigueta	
Muñoz (Bolivia)	Today: General Díaz	Ayvompeen-Saanga
Nanawa (Paraguay)	Today: Eligio Ayala	Nanaava'a
Orihuela (Paraguay)		Na'tee-Kho'
Platanillos (Bolivia)	Today: Teniente Acosta	Ya'kal'a
Pozo Azul (Paraguay)		Kemha-Pomlhek
Pozo Colorado (Paraguay)		Yelhvaseem-Yaamelket
Pozo Favorito (Paraguay)		
Rancho Ocho (Paraguay)		Maskamaklha-Pomaap
Rancho Quemado (Paraguay)		Lhepasko'
Saavedra (Bolivia)	Today: Ávalos Sánchez	Na'tee-Ptelhla-Maaset
Samaclay/Masamaclay (Bolivia)	Bolivian name: Aguarrica Today: Comandante Giménez	Maskamaklha-Toolhay
Toledo (Paraguay)		Hovko'
Trébol (Paraguay)		Ya'tempehek
Yucra (Bolivia)	Today: Capitán Ortellado	Savaayaamelket

GLOSSARY

The following table lists all the non-English words in the accounts and observations, with translations (except in the case of some of the interjections). In the case of words that do not come from Enlhet, their origin is given. For Enlhet terms for fauna and flora, in addition to the corresponding scientific name, the common name in Spanish/ Guaraní is generally provided. It should be noted that Enlhet terms for flora refer to both the plant and its fruit.[1]

In the Enlhet alphabet, the letter ' comes before the letter *a*.

'Yeenes'ay'	Friday (proper name, from the Spanish *viernes* and -*'ay'* indicating a proper name).
Aa'ey	The Pilagá, an Indigenous people of the Guaycurú linguistic family whose territory extends to the River Pilcomayo.
Aalha	Escalante, also known by the names Fischat (in Nivaclé) and San Leonardo (the name of the parish). Place name; see maps.
Aateng'ay'	Duckweed (from *aateng*, duckweed, and -*'ay'* indicating a proper name).
Aayat	Enlhet form of the Low German version of the Mennonite family name Eckert (proper name).
akpehek	Jacaranda tree (*Jacaranda mimosifolia*).
Akta'haklhee'	Expression of farewell; lit.: I leave/I leave you.
aktam	Capparis speciosa tree (*Capparis speciosa*). In Spanish, *naranja de monte, payaguá naranja*.
Akva'ak ko'o!	I have arrived! (Enlhet greeting).
Akyeeka'a ye'!	Greeting in passing; lit.: I pass you without stopping.
Alhkahayaam'	North Wind (proper name; as in all proper names, the word also denotes the object or idea – here, the north wind itself).
alhpong	Pisonia zapallo tree (*Pisonia zapallo*). In Spanish, *caspi zapallo*.

Alhvat	Guajhó; Paraguayan encampment to the west of Filadelfia (place name).
Alkeete'	Place near → *Hovko'*, Fort Toledo (place name).
alvaata'	Dry river bed; Enlhet word from which the Bolivian Fort Alihuatá took its name.
Alyav'atee-Pmankok	His Feet Are Short; Enlhet name for Mennonite missionary Abram Unger.
Angaité	Indigenous people, eastern neighbours of the Enlhet, whose language is related to Enlhet. Term of unknown origin.
apaava	Fabric, clothing, clothes, item of clothing.
Apva'at	Place name; see maps.
apveske'	Person with authority; leader. In Enlhet, the term refers to a person who naturally assumes responsibility; however, it was also used to denote Enlhet individuals selected or designated by the intruders to act as their guide, translator, informant, etc. (masculine form). → *cacique*.
apyoholhma'	Wise person with powerful knowledge, Elder with power (masculine form).
Av'aava'ay'	Long Grass/Tall Grass (proper name, from the plant *Imperata brasiliensis* and -'ay' indicating a proper name).
Ay'ay	Proper name with no specific meaning.
aveske'	Feminine form of → *apveske'*.
aykaaha	Algarrobo negro tree (*Prosopis nigra*).
Ayvompeen-Saanga	Fort Muñoz, General Díaz (place name; see maps).
cacique	Term employed by the creoles; in English, chief. The colonizers used the word *cacique* to denote Indigenous persons who served them as mediators in relating with local populations. In parallel to this, the term refers frequently to a person the intruders perceived as being in authority, despite the fact that this person may not have held an important position within his or her own society beyond the function of mediator. (In the current imaginary also, *caciques* are remembered as important leaders).
Cacique Kalape'e	→ *Kalape'e*.

Cacique Mita'i	Spanish: Cacique Niño (proper name, from the Guaraní word *mitã'i,* child).
Cacique Mitapuku	Cacique Niño Alto (proper name, from the Guaraní words *mitã'i,* child, and *puku,* tall).
Cacique Vaaso	→ *Vaaso.*
Chamacoco	Two Indigenous Peoples of the area northeast of the Enlhet territory, today known as the Tomáráho and the Yshir (the term Chamacoco is used traditionally in Paraguay).
comunidad	Spanish term; lit.: community. An area reserved under Paraguayan law for occupation by Indigenous families, usually of the same ethnic group; similar to the concept of a reserve/reservation in Canada/the US. These communities may be extremely small in physical extension, such as the suburban neighbourhoods of the Mennonite settlements. In addition, there are still a considerable number of communities in Paraguay that do not hold the title deeds to their land; that is, the inhabitants have no legal right to occupy the place in which they live. All of the villages founded as missions within the framework of the missionary project are today called communities.
Eehe, nengko'o	Reply to the greeting → *Kellbeep nak lha*!; lit.: Yes, it is us.
elle	Generic term for English people, from the Spanish *inglés,* Englishman.
engmook	Relative, fellow man/woman, ally.
Enlhet	Enlhet, human being, Indigenous, man.
Enlhet-neeten	Beings inhabiting the space above humans, that is, the non-earthly sphere; lit.: person from above.
Énxet	Neighbours of the Enlhet to the southeast, originally referred to as Lengua Sur, whose language is related to Enlhet; the term comes from the Énxet language.
Guaná	Indigenous people who inhabited the lands around Puerto Sastre and who spoke a language related to Enlhet. Term of unknown origin.
haakok	Orphan (masculine); used as an appellative or as part of a name.

Haakok Maaset	Orphaned By A Quebracho (→ *Maaset*) (proper name).
Haakok Melketna'ay'	Orphan Who Did Not Know (proper name).
Haakok Toolhay	Macá Orphan (proper name).
Haakok Yenmongaam	Orphaned By A Rifle (proper name).
Haalhama-Teves	Kilómetro 145, Puntarriel; terminus of the train from Puerto Casado (place name; see maps).
Haanmon	Enlhet form of the German name Herrmann.
Haatkok'ay' Sevhen	Nivaclé Orphan (proper name). The word *baatkok'ay'* is the feminine form of "orphan" and is used as an appellative or as part of a name.
hang	*Bromelia bieronymi*. The bromeliad family (*Bromeliaceae*), to which the pineapple also belongs, are plants with long leaves set in a spiral around a short stem. The species of the Chaco have barbs along the edges of the leaves. The Enlhet occasionally used the fibres of the *bang* for weaving. The plants known in Guaraní as *karaguata* are Bromeliads.
Heeva'ay'	Spear (proper name, from *heeva'*, spear, and -'ay' indicating a proper name).
Heey'	Yes, Good, Okay, Alright.
Hemaklha-Maaset	Neuanlage, Mennonite village in Colonia Menno (place name; see maps).
Hovaypo	Kilómetro 180 (place name; see maps).
Hovko'	Fort Toledo (place name; see maps).
Kaa'aok	Place northeast of → *Hovko'*, Fort Toledo (place name).
kaaya	a) Calabash with long fruits (*Lagenaria siceraria*). b) Latexplant, strangler vine (*Morrenia odorata*). c) Festivity, celebration.
Kalape'e	Proper name, from the Guaraní word *karape*, short in height, and the Guaraní suffix *i*, small; son of.
kam'aatkok	Orphan (feminine form); used as an appellative or as part of a name.
Kam'aatkok Ketsek	Small Orphan (proper name).
Kam'aatkok Tengkat	Orphan of Tengkat (proper name) → *Tengkat*
Kam'aatko-Kvaanyam'	Big Orphan (proper name).

Kapetaan Loope	Capitán López (proper name; Spanish, Captain López).
Kaymaan	Place name; see maps.
Kaymaap-Takhaalhet	His Brothers and Sisters Often Died (proper name).
Kellheep nak!	→ *Kellheep nak lha!*
Kellheep nak lha!	It is you! (greeting to more than one person; *kel* is a plural marker in Enlhet).
Kelyelhvayvoo-Pyettek	→ *Yelhvayvoo-Pyettek*
Kemhaklha-Yaanava	Straßberg; Mennonite village in Colonia Menno (place name; see maps).
Kemha-Maaneng	Lichtenau; Mennonite village in Colonia Neuland (place name; see maps).
Kemha-Paapeyav	Place within the present-day Ya'alve-Saanga mission (place name). → *Ya'alve-Saanga*
Kemha-Paatelh	Kleefeld; Mennonite village in Colonia Fernheim (place name; see maps).
Kemha-Pomlhek	Pozo Azul (place name; see maps).
Kemhaytaava-Amyep	Schönwiese; Mennonite village in Colonia Fernheim (place name; see maps).
kenaateng	Charata (*Ortalis canicollis*), bird species similar to the partridge.
Kenma'lha	Fort Falcón (place name; see maps).
Kenmaa-Paapen'	Lindenau; Mennonite village in Colonia Menno (place name; see maps).
Kenma-Navsa	Place to the west of Filadelfia (place name).
Kenmekpeyem	Ayoreo; Indigenous people of the area to the north of the Enlhet. The word *Ayoreo* comes from the Ayoreo language itself.
Kenmekpeyem sentekpongaam	Ayoreo; lit.: the Ayoreo who hit us.
Kenmekpeyem yenmongaam apmeeya'aok	Tomárãho Indigenous ethnic group; lit.: the Ayoreo with rifles in their hands. → *Chamacoco*
Kenteem	Broken Leg (proper name).
kentem'	*Bromelia serra.* The bromeliad family (*Bromeliaceae*), to which the pineapple also belongs, are plants with long leaves set in a spiral around a short stem. The species of the Chaco have barbs along the edges of the leaves. The Enlhet ate

the heart of the *kentem'*. To cook it, they collected a quantity of firewood, placed the *kentem'* whole, including the leaves, on the wood and lit it. When all the wood was burned the *kentem'* was ready to eat. (In Guaraní, it is a type of *karaguata*).

Kentem'-Pa'tek	*Kentem'* In His Eye (proper name). → *Kentem'*
ko'o	First person pronoun, I.
Konomaktollolaq	Casanillo; today the name of a Toba-Enenlhet community (place name; see maps). → *comunidad*
Kooneng-Pa'at	Under The Grass (proper name).
Laava-Pmenek	Nail In His Foot (proper name).
Lajkat	Sandorst; Mennonite village in Colonia Neuland (place name; see maps).
Lamas	Proper name, of Spanish origin.
Layve	Enlhet form of the Low German version of the Mennonite family name Löwen or Loewen (proper name).
Lengko	Mennonite, from the Spanish *gringo*.
Lengko pangkoo'	Mennonite of Colonia Menno; lit.: true Mennonite (the Mennonites of Colonia Menno were the first to arrive in Enlhet territory).
Lengko Peya	Enlhet nickname for one of the Mennonites; meaning unknown.
Lengua	Former name for the Enlhet and Énxet ethnic groups.
Lha'akma-Mpenek	Place to the south of Paratodo (place name).
Lha'akma-Phaymaka'aok	Place to the south of Paratodo (place name).
Lha'akme-Yaamelket	Campo Jordán (place name; see maps).
Lhaapangkalvok	Filadelfia, centre of Colonia Fernheim (place name; see maps).
Lhamhapmek	Rosenort; Mennonite village in Colonia Fernheim (place name; see maps).
Lhapo'o	Place to the south of → *Pongkat-Napoolbeng*, Campo Esperanza (place name).
Lhaptaana	Friedensfeld; Mennonite village in Colonia Fernheim (place name; see maps).
Lheetehepya'mehe'	Puerto Pinasco (place name; see maps).
Lheknemesma	Place within present-day → *Ya'alve-Saanga* (place name).

Lhengkatken	Tres Palmas; Mennonite settlement in Colonia Fernheim (place name; see maps).
Lhengva'alhva	Place within the present-day Sanapaná community of Anaconda (place name; see maps).
Lhepasko'	Rancho Quemado (place name; see maps).
Lheyaaho'pak	Place to the west of → *Lhepasko'*, Rancho Quemado (place name).
locro	Kernels of peeled maize.
Looma-Apyeseem	Angry Hair (proper name).
Loom-Popyet	Fort Alihuatá (place name; see maps).
Loope	Place name, from the Spanish *López*.
Loope'e	Son of → *Loope* (proper name using a version of the Guaraní suffix *i*, small; son of).
Lospata	Proper name of unidentified origin.
Loveinte	Teniente Montanía; from the Spanish Kilómetro 220 (place name; see maps).
Luz a los Indígenas	Light to the Indigenous; name of the missionary organization of the Mennonites of Colonia Fernheim, founded in 1935.
Maalhek	Tinfunque (place name; see maps).
maama	Generic name for several types of vulture.
maaneng	a) Capparis salicifolia bush (*Capparis salicifolia*); in Spanish, *sacha sandía, coca de cabra*. b) Traditional dance of the Indigenous peoples of the Chaco; also known as *choqueo*.
maaneng askok	Invisible being linked to → *maaneng* dance.
Maangvayaam'ay'	He Touched Her (proper name).
maapa'	Tuco-tuco, a small rodent (*Ctenomys minutus*).
Maapelhkep	Figari (place name; see maps).
maaset	Quebracho colorado tree (*Schinopsis balansae*).
Maaset-Yengman	Place name; see maps.
Maklha-Kenhek	Place to the west of Filadelfia (place name).
Maklha-Nempeena	Puerto Casado (place name; see maps).
Maklhavay	Principal station of the Anglican mission among the Énxet, founded in 1891 (place name; see maps).
Maklheyaat	Puerto Sastre (place name; see maps).
Malhkee·tkok	Name, used as an appellative or as part of the name of a woman whose brother or sister has died; lit.: she remained.

Malhkee-tko-Ngkoyoy'	Her Brother Died; She Is Not Tall (proper name); lit.: the small one who remained.
Manyeheme-Antamay'	Misión'i (place name; see maps).
Maskamaklha-Pomaap	Rancho Ocho (place name; see maps).
Maskamaklha-Toolhay	Samaclay, Masamakay (place name; see maps).
Maso-Sanga	Fort Coronel Martínez (place name; see maps).
Matna-Maaleng	Schönbrunn, Mennonite village in Colonia Fernheim (place name; see maps).
Matnamaklha'-Aa'ey	Place name mentioned incorrectly for → *Maskamaklha-Toolhay*.
meeme	Mama, my mother.
meemong	Palosanto tree (*Bulnesia sarmientoi*).
Meleklama-Pakanma	He Does Not Take Off His Hat (proper name).
Melteiongkasemmap	Toba-Enenlhet proper name.
Mennoblatt	Mennonite bi-weekly newspaper published in German in Filadelfia.
Metaykaok'ay'	He Does Not Notice (proper name).
Metyeeyam'	He Did Not Come Into The World Quickly (proper name).
Meyva-Saanga	Place name; see maps.
moktak	Ibis (*Theresticus caudatus*).
moktek	Algarrobillo, espinillo tree (*Prosopis affinis*).
Na'tamaaphek	Place to the west of → *Hemaklha-Maaset*, Neuanlage (place name).
Na'tee-Kho'	Orihuela (place name; see maps).
Na'teem-Saanga	Place to the east of → *Paskomkom-Amyep* (place name).
Na'tee-Ptelhla-Maaset	Fort Saavedra, today Ávalos Sánchez (place name; see maps).
naamok	Bottle tree (*Chorisia insignis*).
naava'	Quebracho blanco tree (*Aspidosperma quebracho-blanco*).
Nahangvet	Fort Isla Po'i (place name; see maps).
Nahapong	Faro Moro, first missionary station of the New Tribes Mission among the Ayoreo, founded in 1968 (place name; see maps).
Nalhpaateng	Halbstadt; Mennonite village in Colonia Menno (place name; see maps).

Namaalhek	Pitiantuta (place name; see maps).
Nanaava'a	a) Anglican mission among the Enlhet, Macá, and Nivaclé, founded in 1916; in 1925, it was occupied by the Paraguayan army and abandoned by the missionaries (place name; see maps). b) Place to the west of Filadelfia (place name).
Nanaavhak	Blumengart; Mennonite village in Colonia Menno (place name; see maps).
Nangkomelhne-Saanga	Name of the first mission in the area of → *Lhaptaana*, Friedensfeld (place name; see maps).
Nataayet	Fort Fernández (place name; see maps).
nempeena	Urunde'y tree (*Astronium fraxinifolium*); in Spanish, *gateado*.
nengelaasekhammalhkoo	Socially constructed peace; lit.: to respect one another mutually.
nengelyeetapaykam'	Smallpox (*Variola hemorrhagica*); lit.: we break.
nengyetepma	Smallpox (*Variola hemorrhagica*); lit.: we break; alternative name for → *nengelyeetapaykam'*.
nengyetyapma	→ *nengyetepma*
Nepolhnga'a	Heimstädt; Mennonite village in Colonia Neuland (place name; see maps).
Neyalvaata'	Chortitz; Mennonite village in Colonia Menno (place name; see maps).
nolte	A North American, from the Spanish *norte*, north.
Pa'aeklha'pe'	Loma Plata, centre of Colonia Menno (place name; see maps).
pa'ang	Carandilla, forest palm (*Trithrinax biflabellata*).
Pa'aymong Apyaap	Father of Armadillo (proper name)
Pa'ayvaeklha'ay'	He Shouts Again (proper name).
Pa'lhama-Amyep	Place within the Enlhet community of Campo Largo (place name; see maps).
pang	Toothpick cactus (*Stetsonia coryne*).
pangyeelo	Piece of cloth; from the Spanish *pañuelo*, handkerchief.
Panso	Proper name; from the Spanish name *Pancho*.
Pantaa'e	Proper name; from the Spanish family name Panta combined with the Guaraní suffix *i*, small; son of.

Paskomkom-Amyep	Laguna Verde (place name; see maps).
Pataam-Tata'a	He Carries Chickens (proper name).
Peesempo'o	Enlhet community in the vicinity of → *Pa'aeklha'pe'*, Loma Plata (place name; see maps).
Peetempok	Neu-Halbstadt, centre of Colonia Neuland (place name; see maps).
peeyem	A native stingless bee (*Tetragonisca angustula*); in Spanish, *jatei, rubito*.
pehen	Tusca, aromita bush (*Acacia aroma*).
Penseem-Pophehek	Short Finger; Enlhet name for Mennonite missionary Abram Ratzlaff.
peyem	Iguana (*Tupinambis rufescens*).
Plautdietsch	Language of the Mennonite immigrants; a variety of Low German (*Plattdeutsch* in standard High German).
Pongkat-Napoolheng	Campo Esperanza (place name; see maps).
popom	Honey wasp (*Polybia occidentalis scutellaris*).
Poy'-Aava-Ya'teepa	Place to the west of → *Lhepasko'*, Rancho Quemado (place name).
Poy'maalhek	Pozo Blanco (place name; see maps).
Poy'seskeya	Hohenau; Mennonite village in Colonia Fernheim (place name; see maps).
sa'kok	Girl; also used as an appellative or as part of a name.
Sa'kok-Nay'	Girl Who Came Here (proper name).
Samaklha-Ngya'alva	Place to the east of → *Kenmaa-Paapen'*, Lindenau (place name).
Sanapaná	Indigenous people, eastern neighbours of the Enlhet, whose language is related to Enlhet. Term of unknown origin.
savaalak	Costumed figures who play a particular symbolic role within the celebrations of → *yaanmaan*; see figure 4.3.
Savaayaamelket	Yucra (place name; see maps).
Savak'e	Lichtfelde; Mennonite village in Colonia Fernheim (place name; see maps).
Savhongvay'	He Has Experienced Everything (proper name).
seepe'	Boy; also used as an appellative or as part of a name.

Seepe-Pmommaap	Son of → *Haako'-Pmommaap* (proper name).
Seepe-Pta'heem-Pelhkapok	Boy With The Bent Shin (proper name).
Seepe-Pyoy'	Big Boy (proper name).
Selhta'ay'	Not Much (proper name).
semhengkok	Word spoken by an outsider that the Enlhet did not understand but sounds like an Enlhet word.
sengelpelhteetamoo	Soldier; lit.: he catches and ties us up.
Sengkenmelh	Place near → *Peetempok*, Neu-Halbstadt (place name).
seppo	Generic name for the different types of cassava (*Manibot esculenta*); in Spanish, *mandioca*.
Soopkaatek	Ugly Head (proper name).
Sooso'	Proper name with no specific meaning.
sooya'angka	Metal-tipped arrow.
sopkelloom	Paraguayan; lit.: furious, uncontrolled thing.
Ta'malmaa-Yman	Place to the south of → *Loom-Popyet*, Alihuatá (place name).
Ta'ne	Gnadenfeld; Mennonite village in Colonia Menno (place name; see maps).
Taalhe-Ktong	Fire On Her Arm (proper name).
Tahanmaklha-Paana'	Place within the Énxet community Sombrero Pirí (place name).
tamam'a	*Deinacanthon urbanianum*. A plant in the bromeliad family (*Bromeliaceae*), to which the pineapple also belongs. These are plants with long leaves set in a spiral around a short stem. The species of the Chaco have barbs along the edges of the leaves. Among the Enlhet, the fibres of the *tamam'a* leaf were the preferred raw material for weaving. (In Guaraní, *tamam'a* is a type of *karaguata*).
Tamocode	Ayoreo name for → *Nabapong*, Faro Moro (place name). → *Ayoreo*.
tamsava'	Species of small bush (*Croton lachnostachyus*).
Teejela'	Place name; see maps.
Teena'avhat	Place name; see maps.
Tekses-Saanga	Place to the south of → *Lha'akma-Phaymaka'aok* (place name).

teme'es	Unidentified insect.
Tengkat	Pozo Brillante (place name; see maps).
teves	Algarrobo tree (*Prosopis alba*).
Toba-enenlhet	Indigenous people, eastern neighbours of the Enlhet, whose language is related to Enlhet. Also called Toba-Maskoy or simply Toba.
Tomaklha-Pook-Maama	Cabeza de Tigre (place name; see maps).
Toopak	Place name; see maps.
Toopak-Amyep	Gnadenheim; Mennonite village in Colonia Fernheim (place name; see maps).
vaalha	Duraznillo tree (*Ruprechtia triflora*).
vaalha'a yetkook	A grove or group of *Ruprechtia triflora*. → *vaalha*
Vaaso	Big (proper name from the Guaraní word *guasu*, big/deer).
Vaetke-Ngkennavo'	Place to the south of Paratodo (place name).
valay	Soldier, Paraguayan, creole in general; from the Guaraní *volái*, man in uniform.
Vasee-Yaamelket	Pozo Colorado (place name; see maps). Present-day Pozo Colorado does not coincide with the traditional location of *Vasee-Yaamelket* (*Vasee-Yaamelket angkoo'*) where → *Yoyi Looma* established the centre of his ranch and that the Enlhet relators mention. It should be added that the Spanish name *Pozo Colorado* (Red Well) is itself a translation of the Enlhet place name.
vayke-neeten	Name of a traditional dance among Indigenous Peoples in the Chaco, also called *choqueo*, similar to → *maaneng*.
Vayna'	Wüstenfelde; Mennonite village in Colonia Fernheim (place name; see maps).
Veejay	Fort Carayá (place name; see maps).
Veenaamkolha-Na'ta'	Kilometre 152 of the railway line; in Spanish, Kilómetro 152 (place name; see maps).
Vellejey	Wiesenfeld; Mennonite village in Colonia Fernheim (place name; see maps).
ya'alva	Armadillo (*Tolypeutes matacus*); in Spanish, *tatú bolita, quirquincho bola*.
Ya'alve-Saanga	Name of the first missionary settlement among the Enlhet, founded in 1936 (place name; see maps).

Ya'hello'	Schöntal; Mennonite village in Colonia Fernheim (place name; see maps).
Ya'kal'a	Platanillos (place name; see maps).
Ya'tempehek	Fort Trébol (place name; see maps).
Ya'yeem-Paatelh	Place name; see maps.
Yaakap Apkekheem	Jacob the Hunchback (proper name); Yaakap is an Enlhet form of the German name Jakob.
yaam	Enlhet derivational prefix meaning similar to.
yaame'elle	North American; lit.: similar to an → *elle*.
Yaameklhenaamok	Place name; see maps.
yaamlengko	A Mennonite of Fernheim; lit.: similar to a → *lengko*.
yaamvalay	Bolivian; lit.: similar to a → *valay*.
yaamyavheene'	Honey bee (*Apis mellifera*); lit.: similar to a → *yavheene'*.
yaanmaan	Female initiation ceremony.
Yaanmaan-Tengma	Place within present-day → *Pa'aeklha'pe'*, Loma Plata, where the Mennonite cooperative supermarket is situated (place name).
Yaatektama-Yelhem	Fort Arce (place name; see maps).
yaatepvatahap	Small tree of the genus Jatropha (*Jatropha hieronymi*); in Spanish, *piñón, higuera del monte*.
yaayet	*Molle tree* (*Sideroxylon obtusifolium*).
Yamasma'ay'	They Left Him Behind (proper name).
Yatka	Proper name with no specific meaning.
Yav'aa-Na-Pma'aok,	Place within present-day → *Pa'aeklha'pe'*, Loma Plata (place name).
yavhan	A native stingless bee (*Scaptotrigona spp.*); in Spanish, *tapezuá, peluquerito*; also a generic term for honey from all bee species.
yavheene'	A native stingless forest bee (*Melipona favosa orbignyi*); in Spanish, *tumbypará, boca de barro*.
yengman	Natural clearing in a forested area.
Yelhvayvoo-Pyettek	Fort Boquerón (place name; see maps).
Yemha-Keta	Loma Pytá (place name; see maps).
yengman	Grassy, open, low-lying area where water collects during periods of rain.

Yepooma   Friedensruh; Mennonite village in Colonia Fernheim (place name; see maps).

yerba   Leaves of the Yerba mate bush (*Ilex paraguariensis*) dried and loosely ground to prepare a hot or cold beverage; Spanish term.

Yetna-Haapen'   Place to the east of → *Kenmaa-Paapen'*, Lindenau (place name).

Yohoon   Enlhet form of the Low German version of the German name Johann, John (proper name).

Yohoon Alhaaye'   Johann The Later (proper name). → *Yohoon*

Yohoon Kela   Enlhet form of the Low German version of the Mennonite name Johann Kehler (proper name).

Yoyi Looma   George Lohmann; North American owner of → *Vasee-Yaamelket* ranch (Pozo Colorado).

NOTES

PREFACE

1 According to Haakok Aamay (in Kalisch and Unruh 2014, 84; 2020, 84), Savhong-vay' (in Kalisch and Unruh 2014, 84–5; 2020, 85) and Metyeeyam' (unpublished).

2 See Kidd 1999, 44; Kalisch 2019, 302–3; Kalisch and Unruh 2014; 2020.

3 See Kalisch and Unruh 2014, 493; 2020, 493.

4 See Grubb 1911; 1993; 1914; Hunt 1932.

5 See Metyeeyam', in Kalisch and Unruh 2014, 212–16; 2020, 212–16. The Mennonites are an Anabaptist group that separated from the reforming movements of the sixteenth century and migrated toward eastern Europe. Some of them arrived in the Chaco via Canada; another group immigrated directly from Russia. The Mennonites of the Chaco speak one of the minority languages of Germany, *Plautdietsch* or *Plattdeutsch*, a variety of Low German, but, more than a German subgroup, they constitute a separate ethnic group (Klassen, 2001). During the first decades they managed their colonies entirely autonomously; only after the end of the Stroessner dictatorship in 1989 did state institutions begin to establish themselves in the region of the colonies.

6 See Unruh and Kalisch 2014, 317; 2020, 316.

7 The term *community* (in Spanish, *comunidad*) in this context refers to an area designated for occupation by a number of Indigenous families, similar to the concept of a reserve/reservation in Canada/the US, but consisting in many cases only of a few hectares in an urban neighbourhood. Map 1.2 shows the communities of different ethnicities that exist today within the traditional Enlhet territory. The communities are legal entities in Paraguay. However, they were neither established nor, in many cases, acquired, by the State, but by the Mennonite colonies, originally as "missions."

8 Asociación de Servicios de Cooperación Indígena Menonita (ASCIM).

9 To cite some examples at random, the war is described as a "glorious epic" (Ashwell 2012) during which the "national honour" was defended with "abounding heroism" (Quintana Villasboa 2016), to write "the most glorious page of our history" and "affirm [our] faith in a superior destiny" (UltimaHora Opinión 2011). The Enlhet view, on the other hand, remains entirely unknown, as was evidenced, for example, when the Spanish-language version of *Don't Cry* was presented to the president of the Republic of Paraguay on 29 September 2018 during the commemoration of Paraguayan victory at the battle of Boquerón, at the site of the former fort. An audiovisual recording of parts of the ceremony can be seen in Nengvaanemkeskama Nempayvaam Enlhet (2018).

10 The battle of Boquerón, from which the Paraguayan army emerged victorious, was the first major Paraguayan offensive of the war. The strategic and moral importance of this victory for the conflict has often been pointed out. To this day, 29 September, the date on which the Bolivian garrison surrendered, is a national holiday in Paraguay. The former fort, for its part, has been turned into a museum (none of the wartime forts retain a military function).

11 See also Palhkammaap'ay', in Unruh and Kalisch (2001, 34).

12 See www.enlhet.org.

PART ONE

1 The Énxet, or Énxet Sur, call themselves /eenłet/, while the Enlhet's own name for themselves is /enłet/. The phonological difference between the two terms consists in the former beginning with a long vowel and the latter with a short vowel. The differences in the written forms are explained by the fact that the lateral fricative /ł/, which is common in Enlhet-Enenlhet languages, is represented by *x* in Énxet spelling and by *lh* in Enlhet spelling. This graphic representation is the reason why Spanish speakers often pronounce them /enset/ and /enlet/ respectively. Although it is still common to see the term Énxet written as Enxet, in the spelling of the language itself, the lengthened vowel is expressed by the addition of the accent.

2 There are important exceptions, such as *Etnobotánica lengua-maskoy*, by Pastor Arenas (1981), which we would not wish to be without. In general, written output on all the Enlhet-Enenlhet peoples is minimal; only in recent years has the bibliography begun to expand (see the bibliography of the Enlhet-Enenlhet family in Fabre 2005, and an updated version in Fabre 2013). Glauser (2019) and Villagra (2014) are two more recent publications on the Angaité.

3 The term "Paraguayan" requires explanation. The Enlhet territory today is inhabited by Mennonites and members of the Spanish- and/or Guaraní-speaking collective. Both groups are of Paraguayan nationality but belong to different cultural and linguistic traditions and identify with their nationality in different ways. To reflect these differentiated constellations, in the present book, I use the term Mennonites on the one hand and Paraguayans or creoles on the other. This terminology is not satisfactory but is very common in the Chaco.

4 The (Spanish) names of these institutions are: Museo de Arte Indígena and Centro de Artes Visuales/Museo del Barro.

5 The accounts recorded in this book were given in the Enlhet language for an Enlhet audience. That is, the relators did not intend by the things they express to create any effect on the Paraguayans of whom they speak. Rather, they present them according to a perception authentically their own.

6 The Enlhet call Paraguayans *valay* and Bolivians *yaamvalay*, "like valay." Another sense of *valay*, however, is "soldier," and the relators frequently use the

word valay to refer to Bolivian soldiers where the context makes it clear that they are speaking of Bolivians and not Paraguayans.

7 Kooneng-Pa'at, in account 1; Sa'kok-Nay', in account 24.

8 For a somewhat more detailed description of relations between the Enlhet and Paraguayans in the decades after the war, see Redekop (1980, 43, 189ff).

9 The National Constitution of Paraguay of 1992 "recognizes the existence of indigenous peoples, defined as cultural groups pre-dating the formation and organization of the Paraguayan State" (Article 62). The term "people" and the recognition of the pre-existence of the Aboriginal Peoples implies an understanding of Indigenous societies as political entities within the State that have the right to propositional participation as protagonists on their own terms within this State. However, their recognition as political entities is obscured by the same article, which defines Indigenous Peoples as simply "cultural groups." In this same spirit, the Constitution employs the term *territory* only when speaking of the "national territory" or that of "the Republic." For the Indigenous Peoples, by contrast, it reserves the term *habitat* (Article 63 and others), which lacks any political connotation. In parallel to this constellation, the political dimension of the concept of "a people" has not yet been transferred adequately into jurisprudence or to the practice of concrete participation in society.

10 On the representation of this "civilization" of the "desert" in the consciousness of the national states involved, see Capdevila (2010b).

11 Until at least the end of the Stroessner dictatorship in 1989, Mennonite society was much more dominant in Enlhet territory than Paraguayan society, and to this day it continues to have a greater presence. For this reason, with regard to the Enlhet, it is necessary to talk about enveloping *societies* in the plural.

12 For example, P.P. Klassen (1983; 1999) describes the Chaco as a "space without time" and states that "there has been little change in the culture of the Chaco peoples for centuries and perhaps millennia; we might even speak of a static culture that satisfied the most primitive human needs, and was content with that" (1983, 127; 1999, 127).

13 For discussion of this subject, see Kalisch and Unruh (2014, 540ff; 2020, 546ff).

14 P.P. Klassen (1991, 60), for example, speaks of a great movement of Indigenous Chaco people towards the Mennonite colonies after 1935 (of a "großen Sternwanderung der Chacoindianer nach 1935"), motivated by "their curiosity and their impulse to migrate" (1991, 64). He supposes, controversially, that:

> The Ayoreo man did not stay in Cerro León out of heroism or attachment to his homeland. He is sitting elsewhere on a bicycle and buys powdered milk for his baby. The tribes of the Central Chaco did not retreat fighting in defence of their land; they [the Ayoreo] came out of the forest from curiosity, to taste bread, salt and sugar. (P.P. Klassen 1983, 137–8; 1999, 137–8)

With this statement – which reveals a line of thinking that dominates to this day in the Mennonite colonies – Klassen overlooks completely the intentions and actions of the Mennonites themselves, who desired and worked for the conversion of the Ayoreo (Canova 2011, 383–4; Hein 1990; Kalisch and Unruh 2014, 530; 2020, 536; Siemens 1948). He ignores also the fact that:

> The structural changes in the life of the Ayoreo in the last fifty years are closely related to the history of changing spatial reconfigurations [and] the logics of territorial power ... in the Paraguayan Chaco. (Canova 2011, 311)

These reconfigurations caused a range of specific pressures that the Ayoreo would not have resolved by retreating to spaces that were increasingly reduced and frequented by intruders and defending them. For his part, Klassen thinks from the point of view of a static opposition between a life "in the forest" and one in "the colonies" that leads him to state, for example, that:

> Despite the missionaries' efforts to secure the subsistence of the indigenous [Ayoreo] in the forest, whole groups of them would abandon the mission to seek money in the Mennonite colonies, money which they needed in order to access the articles of civilization they so desired. (P.P. Klassen 1991, 74)

In postulating this opposition – which does not correspond to that between life under the strong influence of external agents and one relatively free of it – Klassen suggests that the Ayoreo should have been content with what these external agents offered them in the forest; he does not perceive the possibility of nuanced encounters with "civilization." In parallel to this perspective, it is commonly maintained by the colonists that the problems arising from the appearance in the colonies of the Ayoreo – which made visible and continues to make visible "barbarity" in the midst of "civilization" (Canova 2011) – would be avoided if these barbaric people remained in their own world. The impacts of the Mennonite presence on the Ayoreo world, by contrast, although immensely greater than those of the Ayoreo presence in the colonies, are not seen as problematic by the Mennonites because they are not their problem. On the contrary, with the argument that, when the Ayoreo began to come "out of the forest," the Mennonites had not yet settled within their territory, they hide all reference to the pressure of Mennonite society on Indigenous society and at the same time are silent regarding their vigorous expansion into Ayoreo territory over recent decades. Instead, they maintain that the geographical approach of the Ayoreo to "civilization" was basically voluntary. They thus feel enabled to reproach them for it, for example with Klassen's aforementioned argument that they do not take responsibility for the defence of their own spaces and that all motivation on their part is limited to mere "curiosity" and interest in "the articles of civilization" and "powdered milk." This line of thinking is clearly hostile and coincides with the fact that there was no Mennonite approach to the Ayoreo beyond the interests of labour and proselytism. It should be pointed out that the Mennonites hold different discourses regarding the Enlhet and the Ayoreo, because they are very conscious that the beginning of their colonizing enterprise took place in the midst of Enlhet territory (P.P. Klassen 1991, 64–5). On the process leading to the capitulation of the Enlhet, see Kalisch and Unruh (2014); on that leading to the capitulation of the Ayoreo, see von Bremen (1991).

15 Several of the relators who appear in this book have personal memories of the war. Although these memories are based on childhood impressions, the relators have interpreted and refined them as they have listened to the accounts of others (Sa'kok-Nay', in account 1). By this insertion in the processes of sharing among the people, their recollections have been nourished from the common fund and become, in turn, a concrete image of it.

16 See, for example, Grubb (1911, 17ff); Baldus (1931, 72–3); Métraux (1946, 312ff; 1996, 172); Susnik (1972, 85).

17 G.B. Giesbrecht (1937); G. Giesbrecht (2000, 153); Hack (1960, 646); Loewen (1966, 31); Stoesz (2008, 110), and others.

18 Belaieff (1941, 19) says the Chamacoco (or Tomáráho) "remember well the places and circumstances of their centuries-old flight against the 'Guaná', under which denomination, with a degree of contempt, they include also the enemy tribes of their southern border: Lenguas [Enlhet], Sanapanás, Angaités – who previously reached the area beyond Pitiantuta." It should be stated in clarification, however, that only the Enlhet reached as far as Pitiantuta.

19 At the beginning of Mennonite immigration, the Enlhet did not yet know the name used by the Paraguayans to refer to the Ayoreo, "Moro," and when they referred in the language of the intruders to their two northern neighbours, they did not discriminate between them, calling them both Chamacoco: Tomáráho. They had learnt this word during their journeys to Puerto Sastre, where some Tomáráho lived. For this reason, Siemens (1948, 3) says after a deadly attack by a group of Ayoreo on Mennonite family that:

> [O]ur indigenous [the Enlhet] named only the Chamacoco [who live in the northeast of the Colony] as the culprits and said they were also their old enemies, while the military pointed to the tribe of the Moros, who are found further to the north west [of the Colony].

In their own language, although they used a single term for the Ayoreo and Tomáráho – kenmekpeyem – they distinguished clearly between the two groups. To refer to the Ayoreo and the Tomáráho, respectively, they spoke of the kenmekpeyem sentekpongaam – the kenmekpeyem who strike (with their clubs) – and the kenmekpeyem yenmongaam apmeeya'aok – the kenmekpeyem with firearms in their hand. The Tomárãho used firearms and wore clothes, while the Ayoreo used neither article from the white world.

20 The traditional term *Chamacoco* included the Yshir and the Tomárãho; the latter were neighbours of the Enlhet. Of the Tomárãho, Nicolás Richard (personal communication) states that having come from south of Pitiantuta their main regrouping point after the Chaco War was along the railway of the tannin factory at Puerto Sastre. Some of them returned to their own places in the interior, but most of them remained working in Puerto Sastre. When the factory closed towards the end of the 1950s they moved to the north and today live in Puerto María Elena.

21 Heeva'ay', in Unruh and Kalisch (2000, 141ff); Hein (1990).

22 The different actors gave different names to the forts; a comparative summary of these names is provided in the appendix.

23 Metyeeyam', in Kalisch and Unruh 2014, 212–18; 2020, 212–18; M. Friesen 1996; M. Friesen 1997, 80ff; 2016, 65ff.

24 The dates of the founding of some of the forts in the northern region of the Enlhet territory illustrate the advancing military presence there (Barreto 1969; Joy 1992; Richard 2007). The Bolivians founded Huijay (Carayá)/Veejay in 1928, Platanillos/Ya'kal'a in 1930 and Camacho (Mariscal Estigarribia) in 1931. The Paraguayans, meanwhile, established forts Coronel Martínez/Maso-Sanga, Isla Po'i/Nahangvet, and Toledo/Hovko' in 1927; and Trébol/Ya'tempehek, Corrales in the region of Toopak, and Boquerón/Yelhvayvoo-Pyettek in 1928.

25 Despite what the names given by the intruders to the Enlhet (Lengua Norte) and the Énxet (Lengua Sur) suggest, the southern part of the territory of the Enlhet (today also called Enlhet Norte) was not inhabited by the Énxet (today also called Énxet Sur). Rather, the Énxet lived to the east of the Enlhet (Unruh and Kalisch 2003).

26 U. Friesen (2013, 45–6) mentions the years 1910 and 1912 as possible dates for the arrival of Lohman in the Chaco. The establishment of the Pozo Colorado ranch would have occurred some time after this.

27 The name Nanawa comes from the Enlhet toponym Nanaava'a, which means "there are yellow quebracho trees (there)."

28 Many Enlhet in the region spent time in this mission, which was abandoned after the Paraguayans established Fort Presidente Ayala in the immediate vicinity in 1925.

29 The dates of the foundation of some of the forts in the southern region illustrate the advance of military operations there (Barreto 1969; Joy 1992; Richard 2007). The Bolivians founded Esteros in 1920, Muñoz (General Díaz)/Ayvompeen-Saanga and Saavedra (Ávalos Sanchez)/Na'tee-Ptelhla-Maaset in 1923, and Arce/Yaatektama-Yelhem in 1928. In parallel to this, the Paraguayans

established forts General Bruguez in 1919, Cabeza de Tigre/Tomaklha-Pook-Maama in 1923, Orihuela/Na'tee-Kho' in 1924, Nanawa/Nanaava'a in 1925 opposite the Anglican mission station of the same name, and Falcón/Kenma'lha, Gondra and Samaclay (Agua Rica)/Maskamaklha-Toolhay – not Matnamaklha'-Aa'ey, as Barreto (1969, 319) suggests – in 1928.

30 The eastern neighbours of the Enlhet did not come into contact with the battlefront; their experiences with respect to the Chaco War are situated in this rearguard space. On Toba-Enenlhet memory, see *Melietkesammap* (2007); on the Angaité, see Villagra (2014).

PART TWO

1 See the *Nengvaanemkeskama Nempayvaam Enlhet* website at www.enlhet.org.

2 It should be noted that the contributions presented in this book are fragments of much longer testimonies given by each speaker.

3 On the military and smallpox, see the account by Kam'aatkok Tengat in Kalisch and Unruh 2014, 203–10; 2020, 203–10. On battles, see Yaakap Apkekheem in Kalisch and Unruh 2014, 178–80; 181–2; 2020, 178–80; 181–2. On internal processes within the groups, see Taalhe-Ktong in Kalisch and Unruh 2014, 168–71; 2020, 168–71 and Kam'aatkok Tengat in Kalisch and Unruh 2014, 203–210; 2020, 203–10. On approaching the Mennonites as a response to violence, see Av'aava'ay', in Kalisch and Unruh 2014, 190–1; 2020, 190.

4 The accounts contain Enlhet terms whose pronunciation requires clarification. The majority of the letters in Enlhet are pronounced with a similar sound to that in Spanish. Letters differing in their pronunciation from Spanish, or which do not exist in Spanish, are:

    ' represents a glottal stop;

    lh represents an unvoiced lateral fricative, similar to a sibilant *l* (as in Welsh *ll*);

    h is read as in English.

    Ng represents a velar nasal, as in *walking*;

    y is read as in English *yes*;

    v is read as the *w* in English *water*.

    A double letter, whether a vowel or a consonant, is pronounced as a lengthened sound. The stress in an Enlhet word always falls on the final syllable. The Enlhet language can be heard in the video recordings of Kenteem (2008), Kam'aatkok Ketsek et al. (2010), Metyeeyam' et al. (2012), and Maangvayaam'ay' (2015), and in the audio-visual recordings of the *Biblioteca de la memoria hablada* (2021).

5 Sa'kok-Nay', Mica de Friessen, daughter of the head chief Cacique Vaaso, was from the area now called Loma Plata and died in 2015 in Peesempo'o (see also account 24). In the audiovisual material *Éramos nosotros, los que vivieron aquí*

(Metyeeyam' et al. 2011) she can be seen relating accounts. (In all footnotes referring the reader to audiovisual material the account there is not necessarily the
one given here.)

6   Enlhet place-names often bear no relation to Mennonite or Paraguayan geo-
    graphical systems. Where possible, approximate references are given for Enlhet
    place-names mentioned in the accounts, but in some cases no translation is pos-
    sible. The reader should also bear in mind that a non-Enlhet place-name fre-
    quently post-dates the time with which a particular account is concerned. For
    example, in account 1, the place-name Pa'aeklha'pe' is translated as Loma Plata,
    but the Mennonite community in that place was not founded until 1938 (H.
    Ratzlaff 2012, 79) and was only so named in 1960 (H. Ratzlaff 2012, 80), many
    years after the events described.

7   In August of 1927, the first immigrant group of Mennonites arrived in Loma
    Plata and built a temporary settlement that would eventually house sixty fam-
    ilies (H. Ratzlaff 2012, 73–4). It was abandoned within a year, however, as the
    colonizers settled in the villages they founded. It was only in 1938 that the fi-
    nancial centre of Colonia Menno was re-established in Loma Plata under the
    name Sommerfeld (H. Ratzlaff 2012, 79). The account of Sa'kok-Nay' makes no
    reference to this first Mennonite encampment in Loma Plata.

8   The Enlhet thought that the white men illuminated the area with their binocu-
    lars to see things that it was impossible to see with the naked eye, just as the
    knowledge of their own Elders, the apyoholhma', allowed them to see things that
    were invisible to ordinary people.

9   Malhkee·tko-Ngkoyoy', Rosita de González, was born in the region of Fort Ali-
    huatá, Loom-Popyet. She died in 2016 in the community of Campo Largo (see
    also accounts 8, 10, and 20).

10 The prefix yaam means "similar to" and is used to form new nouns. The
    name for the Bolivians, yaamvalay, therefore means "similar to the valay, the
    Paraguayans."

11 The idea that the Bolivian military brought their wives with them is corrobor-
    ated in, for example, Hoyos (1932).

12 Another version of this account can be found in Kalisch and Unruh (2014, 161–3;
    2020, 161–3).

13 Savhongvay', Abram Klassen, was born in the area around Neuland (see also
    accounts 13 and 14). He died in 2009 in Ya'alve-Saanga.

14 See also Palhkammaap'ay', in Unruh and Kalisch (2001, 33–7).

15 Enlhet greetings express the relationship between the speaker and interlocu-
    tor. The greeting Akva'ak ko'o means, literally, "I have arrived/I am now here."
    The person giving the greeting indicates that he now shares the space with the
    person he is greeting. Other greetings include, Akta'haklhee', "I leave/I leave you"
    and Akyeeka'a ye', "I pass you without stopping."

16 A slightly abbreviated version of this account can be found in Kalisch and Unruh (2014, 426–7; 2020, 426–7).

17 Ramón Ortiz was from the area of Teniente Montanía. He died in Peesempo'o in 2006 (see also account 11). In the audiovisual material *Apva'at* (Kaymaap-Maama et al. 2012) he can be seen relating accounts.

18 Seepe-Pyoy', Juan Antonio, the second son of Chief Antonio, is from the region of Paratodo. The Mennonites did not reach this region until 1948 (see also account 30). Seepe-Pyoy' relates accounts in different audiovisual editions in the *Biblioteca de la memoria hablada* (2021), for example in no. 2, Seepe-Pyoy' (2021).

19 Kenteem, Enrique Malvine, who died in Filadelfia in 2012, was from the area southeast of Mariscal Estigarribia (see also account 16). In the audiovisual material Kenteem (2008), Metyeeyam' et al. (2011), and Kaymaap-Maama et al. (2012) he can be seen relating accounts.

20 Camacho was the Bolivian name for the place Paraguayans call now Mariscal Estigarribia. There is no name for the place in Enlhet.

21 Haakok Maaset, Jacobo Maaset, was from Ya'alve-Saanga (see also account 21). He died there in 2015.

22 Malhkee·tko-Ngkoyoy', Rosita de González. See also accounts 2, 10, and 20.

23 Maangvayaam'ay', Ricardo Cangrejo, was born after the war but gives a rich account of it (see also accounts 26 and 31). In the audiovisual material *Maalhek* (Maangvayaam'ay' 2015), Maangvayaam'ay' can be seen relating accounts. Maangvayaam'ay' also relates accounts in different audiovisual editions in the *Biblioteca de la memoria hablada* (2021), for example in no. 40, Maangvayaam'ay' (2021). Maangvayaam'ay' died in 2020.

24 To understand Malhkee·tko-Ngkoyoy''s account (Rosita de Gonzalez; see also accounts 2, 8, and 20), it is necessary to understand certain aspects of the movements of the military in the area. Fort Saavedra, Na'tee-Ptelhla-Maaset, was founded by the Bolivians in 1923, and Fort Arce, Yaatektama-Yelhem, in 1928. The Paraguayan army took Arce on 23 October 1932 and Fort Alihuatá, Loom-Popyet, where Malhkee·tko-Ngkoyoy' lived, three days later. Alihuatá was retaken by the Bolivians on 13 March 1933, although their attempt to retake Arce in May 1933 was unsuccessful. On 8 December that year, Alihuatá was recaptured definitively by the Paraguayans. Fort Saavedra fell on 13 December 1933 and Fort Muñoz, Ayvompeen-Saanga, on 19 December of the same year (Joy 1992; see also Querejazu 1965). When the Paraguayans first took Alihuatá in October 1932, the Enlhet abandoned the area and retreated to a place unoccupied by the military (see also Maangvayaam'ay' in account 31). However, when news reached them that the Bolivians had returned to Alihuatá, Malhkee·tko-Ngkoyoy' and her group went back to live with them. Malhkee·tko-Ngkoyoy' gives a detailed account of this episode, which is not reproduced here. Instead, space is given, albeit limited, to her description of the time after her return to Alihuatá in March 1933.

25 From Canuto's account, which is not reproduced in this book, it is clear that the Enlhet who went to Bolivia lived there in camps as prisoners of war, in very harsh conditions. Canuto managed to escape. He returned to the Central Chaco after a long and difficult journey and lived in the same community as Malhkee‐tko-Ngkoyoy', Campo Largo, where he died in 2011.

26 See also account 4.

27 Compare this account with a Mennonite description of the event in Enns (1996, 111).

28 The Paraguayan Civil War (or Barefoot Revolution) of 1947, in which the government of Higinio Morínigo, with the support of the Colorado Party, defeated a rebellion led by Liberal Party alliance. Chaco infantry divisions, including ex-combatants from the Chaco War, formed part of the government forces.

29 Seepe-Pta'heem-Pelhkapok, Marco Lovera, died in 2014 in Peesempo'o. In the audiovisual material *Éramos nosotros, los que vivieron aquí* (Metyeeyam' et al. 2011) he can be seen relating accounts.

30 Another version of this account can be found in Kalisch and Unruh (2014, 246–8; 2020, 246–7).

31 Savhongvay', Abram Klassen. See also accounts 3 and 14.

32 The reference is to the Mennonites of Colonia Neuland, who arrived from 1947.

33 The Mennonites of Colonia Menno arrived from 1927.

34 The Mennonites of Colonia Fernheim arrived from 1930.

35 A shorter version of this account was published in Kalisch and Unruh (2014, 185–8; 2020, 185–7).

36 Savhongvay', Abram Klassen, was from the area of Neuland (see also accounts 3 and 13). The appearance of the military drove his group to move to the area of Filadelfia, where he lost his parents to smallpox and was left with his grandfather.

37 P.P. Klassen (2012, 6) describes this episode from the point of view of the Mennonite family mentioned:

> My wife remembers another event which happened in the village of Schönwiese. The Mennonite settlers knew that Central Command had given the order to shoot Lengua indians [Enlhet] because they were blamed for giving away the Paraguayan position to the enemy. One day an indigenous man arrived with his small son in the yard of my parents-in-law's house looking for work. My wife's mother told him that he could cut firewood. While he was getting on with the task, a truck carrying military personnel stopped in the road. The Mennonite woman understood the danger and signalled to the indian to hide in the kitchen, but he refused. At that moment the soldiers entered the yard, tied his hands and took him to the forest behind the crop field. Shortly after, a shot was heard, and then the soldiers returned. My wife's family, named Legiehn, never knew what they did with the body. As far as the

boy was concerned, they supposed he had run away back to the indian settlement.

38 There is some confusion over the location of Fort Trébol arising from the popularity of the so-called Trébol Rodeo in the area near Loma Plata. Some authors, including Joy (1992, 139), have maintained that this is the place corresponding to Fort Trébol. However, the fort was in fact near Filadelfia within the less well known Parque Trébol (Boschmann 2012, 101; H. Friesen 1996, 79s; Haakok Maaset, in account 21).

39 Anonymous (1933) reports that:

> Since the New Year the two colonies [Fernheim and Menno] have been baking 8000 kg of bread per colony weekly in accordance with their contract with the government. This work, and the transport of flour from the railway station [at Puntarriel] and of the bread to the forts, provides a small income for the settlers.

Voices within Mennonite society have stated on several occasions that in economic terms the immigrants benefited from the war (P.H. Klassen 2008, 93; G. Ratzlaff 1993, 31; 2015, 146–7).

40 The father of Metyeeyam' (Jacobo Paredes) was from Neuanlage (Hemaklha-Maaset), located on the eastern edge of Colonia Menno (which did not exist when Metyeeyam' was born). His mother was from Loma Plata, Pa'aeklha'pe' (see also account 22). Metyeeyam' died in 2012 in Peesempo'o. In the audiovisual material *Éramos nosotros, los que vivieron aquí* (Metyeeyam' et al. 2011), he can be seen relating accounts.

41 Kenteem, Enrique Malvine, refers here to the area to the west of Filadelfia (see also account 6).

42 According to Boschmann (2012, 102), this road was opened before the arrival of the Mennonites of Fernheim in the first half of 1930.

43 The famous Fort Nanawa, located at the southern edge of the Enlhet territory, had the same name in Enlhet, *Nanaava'a*, which means "There are *naava'* trees (there)."

44 Here Kaymaap-Takhaalhet, Aaron Ortiz, and Kam'aatkok Ketsek, Marta de Loewen (see also accounts 23 and 27), each describe the same event. Both are from the area where the centre of Colonia Neuland is today, that is, from Heimstädt, Nepolhnga'a, and Neu-Halbstadt, Peetempok. The mother of Kam'aatkok Ketsek died from smallpox when she was a baby (see account 23); she was brought up by her maternal aunt, the mother of her cousin Kaymaap-Takhaalhet. Images of both can be seen in the audiovisual material *¡Entalhnemkek valay apkenmopoy'!* (Kam'aatkok Ketsek et al. 2010) and in Kalisch and Unruh (2013). Kam'aatkok Ketsek died in 2016; Kaymaap-Takhaalhet in 2019.

45 The Enlhet practiced infanticide, that is, they killed children immediately after birth. This custom can be understood as a type of abortion. By contrast, it was extremely unusual to kill a child after it had been accepted by the group: an event such as the one described here was considered horrific by the Enlhet. In this regard, Haakok Maaset mentions in account 21 that a man who killed his son went mad.

46 In her account, Kooneng-Pa'at, Margarita de Benítez, daughter of Cacique Kalape'e, mentions the area to the east of Filadelfia (see also account 25). Keep in mind that the front did not pass through the Mennonite colonies, but remained to the west of them.

47 Based on a statement by Friesen from 1933, P.P. Klassen mentions a prolonged drought that resulted in "the wells in the villages of the Mennonite colonies becoming a strategic consideration for Paraguayan army chiefs during the Chaco war" (1996, 91–2).

48 Yamasma'ay', Isbrandt Dück, was from Teejela', about 25 km east of Mariscal Estigarribia; he died in Filadelfia in 2010 (see also account 32). In the audiovisual material *Apva'at* (Kaymaap-Maama et al. 2012) he can be seen relating accounts.

49 The most intense phase of the Chaco war in Enlhet territory was between the years 1932 and 1933. Thus, the Enlhet expression "after the war" does not refer to the official end of the war in 1935, but to the moving away of the front. The point in time when the front moved away from the area is different for the different parts of the Enlhet territory.

50 During the first years of her life, *Malhkee-tko-Ngkoyoy'*, Rosita de González (see also accounts 2, 8, and 10), lived in Fort Alihuatá, *Loom-Popyet*, with the Bolivians. As she mentions, the events she describes here occurred after the Bolivian recapture of Alihuatá in March 1933 (see account 10).

51 Haakok Maaset, Jacobo Maaset, was from the area that would later be known as Ya'alve-Saanga Mission (see account 7). He died there in 2015.

52 The Enlhet thought that the *seppo* (mandioca) was of the type that they were familiar with and which had to be cooked for a full day to remove its poison.

53 Metyeeyam', Jacobo Paredes. See also account 15.

54 The relationship between smallpox and the *maaneng* dance implied here is explained by Haakok Maaset in account 21. *Metyeeyam'* relates the end of the epidemic in similar terms to those of Haakok Maaset, although that part of his account is not reproduced in this book.

55 "Lengua" was the name applied by outsiders to both the Enlhet and Énxet. This mistake was not officially corrected until the 2002 National Census (DGEEC, 2003). In the popular non-Enlhet conscious, however, the name Lengua is still common.

56 The *kenaateng* is a bird similar to the partridge and under normal circumstances is commonly hunted by the Enlhet as a source of meat.

57 Kam'aatkok Ketsek, Marta de Loewen. See also accounts 17 and 27.

58 Similar accounts have also been given by Savhongvay' (in Kalisch and Unruh 2014, 185–8; 2020, 185–7), Metyeeyam' (in Kalisch and Unruh 2014, 165; 2020, 165) and 'Yeenes'ay' (in Kalisch and Unruh 2014, 173–4; 2020, 173–4).

59 Sa'kok-Nay', Mica de Friessen. See also account 1.

60 Kooneng-Pa'at, Margarita de Benítez. See also account 18.

61 Maangvayaam'ay', Ricardo Cangrejo. See also accounts 9 and 31.

62 In account 17 above, Kaymaap-Takhaalhet and Kam'aatkok Ketsek describe the massacre of a group of Enlhet. In the present account, Kam'aatkok Ketsek, Marta de Loewen, describes what happened after that massacre (see also account 23).

63 The parents of Sooso', Marta de Fernández, lived in Fort Arce, Yaatektama-Yelhem (see also account 29). Following the Bolivian retreat in October 1932, they made a decision different to that of Malhkee-tko-Ngkoyoy''s group (see account 10). While that group took refuge in an area relatively free of military (see also Maangvayaam'ay' in account 31) and later rejoined the Bolivians, the parents of Sooso' approached the Paraguayans in the area of Rancho Quemado, Lhepasko'. In reaction to the violence of the Paraguayan soldiers, however, they quickly returned to a region they had occupied traditionally, Poy'-Aava'-Ya'teepa, which lay outside the area of military movement. Sooso' relates accounts in different audiovisual editions in the *Biblioteca de la memoria hablada* (2021). A version of the account given here can be viewed in No. 20, Sooso' (2021). Sooso' died in 2017 in Comunidad Paz del Chaco.

64 When the front moved away, the parents of Sooso', Marta Fernández, settled in the region of Paratodo (see also account 28).

65 This is a variant of the most common exchange of Enlhet greetings, in which the person giving the greeting expresses recognition of the interlocutor by saying, literally, "It is you" (singular or plural); the reply means, "Yes, it is me/It is us."

66 Seepe-Pyoy', Juan Antonio. See also account 5.

67 Maangvayaam'ay', Ricardo Cangrejo. See also accounts 9 and 26.

68 See pages 250n15, 255n65.

69 Yamasma'ay', Isbrandt Dück. See also account 19.

PART THREE

1 In other publications I have presented a much broader interpretation of the role of the Chaco War as part of the colonial process: Unruh and Kalisch (2008); Kalisch (2009a; 2011a); Kalisch and Unruh (2014; 2020).

2 In Kalisch and Unruh 2014, 434; 2020, 434.

3 Barreto (1969, 37), for example, states even several years after the war that "The [Nivaclé] indians of the interior led a nomadic life similar to other tribes of inferior condition inhabiting the region." They are people who lack a "creative civilization" (Barreto 1969, 38).

4 See Kalisch (2011b; 2014b); Kalisch and Unruh (2014, 217–18; 2020, 217–18).

5 See Sa'kok-Nay', account 1; Kooneng-Pa'at, account 18; Haakok Maaset, account 21.

6 See Malhkee-tko-Ngkoyoy', account 8; Maangvayaam'ay', account 9; and Seepe-Pyoy', account 30.

7 The forming of a taboo indicates that the choice of this strategy for avoiding violence does not permit judgement on the sexual morals of Enlhet women, a judgement that has often been made. Instead, it reflects a need to adapt to the strategy of the military.

8 These notes are discussed at greater length in Richard (2007).

9 The Bolivians called Indigenous women "chinas" (literally, Chinese). The name of Fort La China (map 1.3) refers explicitly to the events described by doctor Hoyos in his diary.

10 On the function of gifts from the Enlhet perspective see also Metyeeyam' (in Kalisch and Unruh 2014, 212–16; 2020, 212–16 and Kalisch and Unruh 2014, 217, 310, 515; 2020, 217, 310, 519).

11 This "philosophy of relating" can be summarized as the clear decision to maintain one's own liberty combined with marked openness toward the other (Kalisch 2004). Openness toward the other and what is theirs, and the determination to maintain one's own liberty, create two extremes in tension that allow the possibility of managing equilibrium during articulation with others.

12 Fort Toledo was founded in 1927 by the Paraguayans. The Bolivians established Fort Camacho (Mariscal Estigarribia) in 1931. On 28 July 1932, Toledo was captured by the Bolivians, according to Barreto (1969) and Joy (1992).

13 An indirect reference to Bolivian exploration can be found in the adoption by the Bolivians of certain Enlhet place names. Huijai, for example, the Bolivian name for Fort Carayá, corresponds to the Enlhet toponym Veejay. The name of Fort Alihuatá, Loom-Popyet, which was built on a riverbed, corresponds to the Enlhet word for riverbed, *alvaata'*.

14 In this way, Richard's (2008) hypothesis in relation to Zamuco space, namely that the initial front reflected ethnic constellations pre-existing the arrival of the military, is confirmed *mutatis mutandis* for the Enlhet-Nivaclé space.

15 In Kalisch 2014a, 31.

16 At the outbreak of war in 1932, there was a sudden, massive influx of soldiers into the region. A few points illustrate this. Fort Isla Po'i (also called Villa Militar and Cacique Ramón), Nahangvet, the headquarters of the Paraguayan Central Command, was founded in 1927; in January 1929 one lieutenant and twenty infantrymen were stationed there (Barreto 1969, 144). On 7 September 1932, shortly after the official declaration of war, 7,500 soldiers were waiting at Isla Po'i to be taken to Fort Boquerón (Zook 1997, 92). This mass arrival of soldiers made the life of the Enlhet at the forts difficult and even impossible ('Yeenes'ay' in

Kalisch and Unruh 2014, 173–4; 2020, 173–4). Certain ways of relating had been established with the soldiers who had arrived previously, but now soldiers were arriving who had no connection with the region and its inhabitants. The Enlhet experience was that these soldiers were much more violent. In their words, they were people who "wanted to kill us" (Sa'kok-Nay', account 1; Kooneng-Pa'at, account 18; Metyeeyam' in Kalisch and Unruh 2014, 165; 2020, 165).

17 See Haakok Maaset, account 7; 'Yeenes'ay' in Kalisch and Unruh 2014, 173–4; 2020, 173–4.

18 See Ramón Ortiz, account 11; Seepe-Pta'heem-Pelhkapok, account 12.

19 See Malhkee-tko-Ngkoyoy', account 8; Haakok Maaset, account 7; Maangva-yaam'ay, account 9.

20 See Kenteem, accounts 6 and 16; Kooneng-Pa'at, account 18; Sooso' account 28, among others.

21 See Malhkee-tko-Ngkoyoy', account 2; Maangvayaam'ay', account 9; Seepe-Pta'heem-Pelhkapok, account 12.

22 See Ramón Ortiz, account 11; Kenteem, account 16.

23 In Kalisch and Unruh 2014, 248; 2020, 247.

24 See *Savhongvay'*, accounts 13 and 14; *Metyeeyam'*, account 15; *Kenteem*, account 16; *Kaymaap-Takhaalhet* and *Kam'aatkok Ketsek*, accounts 17 and 27; *Kooneng-Pa'at*, accounts 18 and 25; *Sa'kok-Nay'*, account 24; *Maangvayaam'ay'*, accounts 26 and 31; *Sooso'*, accounts 28 and 29; and *Seepe-Pyoy'*, account 30.

25 Named Fort Zenteno by the Paraguayans.

26 Called Fort General Díaz by the Paraguayans.

27 The Missionary Oblates of Immaculate Mary (in Spanish, *Oblatos de María Inmaculada*) were invited by the Bolivian government to work with the Niva-clé (Durán Estragó 2000, 20). They arrived in the Chaco in 1925 and founded the Mission of Escalante, Aalha, to the west of Fort Muñoz/General Díaz, Ayvompeen-Saanga, in 1928 (Durán Estragó 2000, 51).

28 Maangvayaam'ay' (in Kalisch 2021) describes the process of reduction of numerous Enlhet groups to the Campo Largo mission.

29 In Kalisch and Unruh 2014, 121; 2020, 121.

30 Kidd (1992) provides a summary of outbreaks of smallpox and other epidemics mentioned in the literature for the period 1884–1933 within the sphere of influence of the Anglican mission.

31 Smallpox was not the only disease afflicting the Enlhet at the beginning of the 1930s. Between 1927 and 1939, typhus took the lives of many of the recently arrived Mennonites (M. Friesen 1997, 305ff; 2016, 250ff; P.P. Klassen 2001, 112; Quiring 1936, 144ff). These and other diseases also claimed lives among the Enlhet, although it is difficult, if not impossible, to estimate the number of victims (Kalisch and Unruh 2014, 513–14; 2020, 517–18).

32 Further reference to smallpox among the Enlhet can be found in Seema Maalya (in Kalisch and Unruh 2014, 192–4; 2020, 192–4), Sa'kok Yemna'teem-Naa'at (in Kalisch and Unruh 2014, 196; 2020, 196), Yaakap Apkekheem (in Kalisch and Unruh 2014, 198–200; 2020, 198–200) and Kam'aatkok Tengkat (in Kalisch and Unruh 2014, 208; 2020, 208).

33 See Malhkee·tko-Ngkoyoy', account 20; Haakok Maaset, account 21; Metyeeyam', account 22; Kam'aatkok Ketsek, account 23.

34 See Yamasma'ay', account 19; Savhongvay', account 13.

35 See Savhongvay' (accounts 13 and 14). Among the Mennonites themselves some voices maintain that, during the war, "the Mennonites could have vouched more systematically and forcefully for the indigenous. However, this possibility seems not to have concerned them much" (R. Wiens 2015, 161). Perhaps the suspicion entertained by Savhongvay' is correct, that their main concern was to remain on good terms with the military (pages 57–8). Indeed, G. Ratzlaff (2015, 146) mentions that one of the effects of the war was "to establish the good relations between Paraguayans and Mennonites which continue to this day."

36 See Kooneng-Pa'at, accounts 18 and 25; Sa'kok-Nay', account 24.

37 In German, *Licht den Indianern*. The statute of *Licht den Indianern* is cited in H. Wiens (1989, 40–1).

38 In contrast to the smallpox epidemic, the evolution of relations with the Mennonites during and after the war is not a prominent theme in the accounts compiled in the present book. It is treated extensively in Kalisch and Unruh 2014; 2020.

39 The Mennonite group in Fernheim arrived from 1930 and soon proposed the beginning of missionary work among the Enlhet. The Chaco War delayed them somewhat, but in 1935 they founded the missionary organization *Licht den Indianern* (*Light to the Indigenous*) and built the first mission station at Nangkomelhne-Saanga, near Friedensfeld, to the south of Filadelfia. The administrator was Abram Ratzlaff, Penseem-Pophehek, one of the two men to whom Haakok Maaset refers in account 21. In August 1936, the mission station was moved to Ya'alve-Saanga and was inaugurated in October 1937 (H. Wiens 1989, 234). Abram Ratzlaff continued to work there (G. Ratzlaff 2004; H. Wiens 1989).

40 In Enlhet accounts, a motif revealing a general fear of missionaries appears repeatedly. A Mennonite missionary appears and someone warns, "The father of the sickness is coming!" At this warning everyone runs to hide. This name given to the Mennonite, "father of the sickness," and the reaction to his arrival, can be understood in relation to the aforementioned action of the missionaries regarding the smallpox.

41 I refer here to complex processes that cannot be reduced to a single factor. For example, resistance to missionary activity was also made difficult by the continuous reduction of Enlhet space and of the possibilities for protagonism remaining to them (Kalisch 2021). These two factors exacerbated one another, but

there were others. In general, within any complex process there are dynamics that reinforce each another mutually and others that oppose and attenuate.

42 Similar series of events have occurred elsewhere. For example, Grubb (1914, 142) states that in 1902 smallpox scourged the region, decimating entire Énxet villages. "But the Indians actually under the care of the mission escaped entirely ... and the popularity of the mission steadily grew."

43 Seepe-Pyoy' (2021), for example, mentions in an account not included in the present book that the smallpox was caused by an incident at the Nanawa mission where Enlhet, Nivaclé, and Macá lived together. During an absence of the English missionary some of them entered the mission store and took what was in it for themselves. On his return, the missionary was very angry and cursed the people of the mission: "You will pay for this. You will see, people will die everywhere."

44 In the words of Melteiongkasemmap (2016), Julián Medina:

> Before, there were a lot of people in these lands, but only a very few survived the sickness. All the villages used to be full of the laughter of celebrations, but when the sickness came, the laughter stopped. The sickness did away with joyful games. There are still very few Enenlhet in Casanillo to this day. There were a lot, but the sickness wiped them out; it left very few.
>
> The sickness came because one of the Enenlhet took something from a Paraguayan. The Paraguayan was angry and decided to kill the Enenlhet. But he didn't do it with rifles; he used the sickness, the smallpox epidemic. The Enenlhet alive today are the survivors of the epidemic; there are still only a few of them, even now.

45 The timing and conditions of defeat and subsequent capitulation are different for each Indigenous group in the Chaco. However, like the Enlhet (Unruh and Kalisch 2008; Kalisch 2011a; Kalisch and Unruh 2014; 2020), all of them lived the same experience, an experience that affected them profoundly and defined the terms of their acceptance of subordination and all the consequences these implied. Reflecting on defeat, the account of Melteiongkasemmap illustrates that the Toba-Enenlhet (just like the Enlhet) are conscious of the violence in assistance – manifested in this case in the offer of vaccination – which is not based on articulation and equilibrium, but on the specific interests of the agent.

46 At first sight, it is surprising that the epidemic has been so absent from Mennonite memory. For example, the Mennonite historian P.P. Klassen (personal communication) questioned whether smallpox and other diseases had caused a significant number of deaths among the Enlhet. However, this collective amnesia regarding smallpox serves as a useful support to the supposition that the Enlhet were saved by the opportune arrival of the immigrants.

47 It is worth quoting Redekop's argument at length, as it encapsulates an aspect of the notion of salvation still put forward to this day in Mennonite society:

> *The missions have enabled tribes to develop autonomy for survival in a modern world culture.* When the Mennonites came, the Lengua indians [Enlhet] were almost extinct ... [They] faced a dark future. But with the economic opportunities provided by the Mennonites in the Chaco, the future of these major groups ... seems assured. Though the documentation cannot be provided here, it is fairly certain that these Indian tribes would have been subjugated to the more powerful Paraguayan society and become a proletariat. It now seems fairly certain that these Indian tribes will become autonomous societies and eventually Paraguayan citizens with a proud heritage to protect. (Redekop 1973, 315–16)

For discussion of the disappearance of the Enlhet see also Eitzen (2002), G. Giesbrecht (2000, 150–3), H. Giesbrecht (2008, 255), Loewen (1964, 3; 1966, 31), Redekop (1980, 163), Siemens (no date, 5), Stoesz and Stackley (1999, 2), H. Wiens (1989, 32, 114) and others.

48 See G. Giesbrecht (2000, 36, 232); Kalisch and Unruh (2014, 521, 567; 2020, 525–6, 578–9); P.H. Klassen (2008, 40), among many others.

49 The immigrants were clearly aware of the terror that the Enlhet suffered at the hands of the military, as testified by the large number of written references to both military violence against the Enlhet and to the Mennonites' often vain attempts to save Enlhet individuals on specific occasions. See for example Kaethler (1996), Janz (1996, 146), P.H. Klassen (2008), and P.P. Klassen (2012).

50 I quote, without further comment, the minutes of meetings of Filadelfia educators (1933–35):

> The life of the indigenous people around our homes, and constant contact with them, awoke in some of the brothers in our Colony the idea that the moment had arrived to consider compensation for the hunting grounds of which they had robbed them. This would not be in the form of money, as the settlers do not have it. They believe that they should take the gospel to them, the Good News of our Saviour. (Protokollheft für Lehrerkonferenzen, 1933–35)

51 The immigrants did not question the fact of dispossession. They were conscious of it but understood their missionary work as a form of mitigation. For discussion of this see Kalisch and Unruh (2014, 529ff; 2020, 535ff).

52 For extensive discussion of this, see Kalisch and Unruh (2014, 567–8; 2020, 578–9).

53 Giesbrecht (2000, 36), for example, states that "the Mennonites arrived at the right time for the Enlhet, who were in danger of extinction. They received the immigrants as friends, as vital assistance and as a refuge." Stahl (1993, 37) adds that the work of the mission "awoke in the Chaco aboriginals a sense of dependency which in their own cultural terms signified something very natural and positive."

54 See Unruh and Kalisch (2008); Kalisch (2009a; 2011a); Kalisch and Unruh (2014; 2020).

55 It is a constant in the Mennonite narrative that the encounter was peaceful. For further discussion of this, see Kalisch and Unruh (2014, 519ff; 2020, 523ff).

56 Kalisch and Unruh 2014, 246; 2020, 246.

57 See Ramón Ortiz, accounts 4 and 11; Maangvayaam'ay', account 9; Kenteem, account 16.

58 For example, the execution of a girl is a double violation of the traditional ethical code of the colonizers, which establishes special protection for both adolescents and women.

59 It should be remembered that the mass deployment of troops who lacked any connection to the region and its inhabitants had the opposite effect (page 256n16). These troops were seen as "people who wanted to kill us" (Sa'kok-Nay', account 1).

60 Richard (2007) provides information in this regard based on military documents of the time.

61 In Kalisch and Unruh 2014, 168; 2020, 168.

62 See also Metyeeyam', in Kalisch and Unruh 2014, 165; 2020, 165.

63 See Sooso', account 29 and Kalisch 2012a.

64 The person with power has the option of acting violently and so representing a danger even to his own people. However, although this danger is frequently referred to by the Enlhet themselves, his daily task was the protection and healing of his people.

65 Metyeeyam', account 15; Sooso', account 29. Compare also Anonymous, in Kalisch and Unruh 2014, 183; 2020, 18; and Yaakap Apkekheem, in Kalisch and Unruh 2014, 181–2; 2020, 181–2.

66 See Sa'kok-Nay', accounts 1 and 24; Kam'aatkok Ketsek, account 27.

67 See Kalisch 2021; Kenteem, in Kalisch and Unruh 2014, 293–6; 2020, 293–6.

68 See Kalisch and Unruh 2014, 562, 567–8; 2020, 573, 578–9.

69 See Unruh and Kalisch 2008; Kalisch 2011a; Kalisch and Unruh 2014; 2020.

PART FOUR

1 Kaymaap-Takhaalhet died on 5 July 2019, after the publication of the original Spanish language version of this book.

2 On 23 May 2016, the following note was published by ABC *Digital*, the website of the national newspaper ABC:

> The Minister of Education, Enrique Riera, has confirmed that he and President Horacio Cartes have today decided to reinstate the obligatory singing of the National Anthem in the nation's schools ... At a press conference ... the Minister stated that the requirement to sing the Anthem "every morning in schools" is "so as not to forget history; to maintain our national identity." (ABC Digital 2016)

3 See map 1.2; see page 243n7.

4 Images of the former fort can be seen in the audiovisual material from the official commemoration of the Battle of Boquerón on 29 September 2018, when the Spanish-language version of this book was presented to the president of the Republic. (Nengvaanemkeskama Nempayvaam Enlhet 2018).

5 In the words of Barreto (1969, 105): "The land to the north of Fort Nanawa extends as a vast desert inhabited only by hostile indians – as far Bahía Negra ... with the two places separated by a distance of some 600 kilometres."

6 Neither of the two societies acknowledges this violence. In Mennonite society, it is common to hear that the State should assume responsibility for the dispossession of the Indigenous, since the immigrant Mennonites bought the land and occupy it legally. In Paraguayan society, on the other hand, the issue is frequently seen as a Mennonite problem as it is they who occupy the Enlhet territory. The two societies, however, have formed an alliance to subjugate the Enlhet, and for this reason both must be actively involved if they wish to find a solution to what is a very complicated situation.

7 In an account not included in this collection, Kooneng-Pa'at summarises this subtle distinction within the same violence as follows:

> The Paraguayans occupied Nahangvet, Fort Isla Po'i. They killed our ancestors (see 'Yeenes'ay', in Kalisch and Unruh 2014, 173) and took possession of their plantation. The Mennonites did the same thing; they took the people's fields. But they didn't shed any blood; they left us the edges to plant our crops.

8 Within Enlhet society, different independent political bodies existed simultaneously. In addition to its internal complexity, Enlhet society was also superimposed on others; that is, its territories were not exclusive (Kalisch 2021). The scope of the present book does not allow for exploration of this theme but it is important to note the marked difference between this and the construction of society and territory proposed by the Nation-State.

9 New categories such as *comunidad,* "Enlhet Community," and "Enlhet People" are expressions of this force for homogeneity, which has imposed organizational concepts that did not exist as such.

10 Unruh and Kalisch 2008; Kalisch 2011; Kalisch and Unruh 2014.

11 See, for example, G.B. Giesbrecht (1936; 1956, 66); P.H. Klassen (2008, 40); Krieg (1948, 230); Stoesz and Stackley (1999, 51); H. Wiens (1989, 28, 96).

12 For the immigrants, wealth was *produced* in, and extracted from, the lands they occupied. This perspective explains the devastation of the natural environment locally, visible in satellite images. Enlhet territory has been almost entirely de-forested (see map 1.4).

13 To dwellers of the hegemonic world of today, accustomed to washing machines, mobile phones, computers, and motor vehicles, much of what was perceived as abundance in the past is seen as scarcity. In the same way, much of what is called poverty in today's world is merely a projection of external categories on alter-nate realities. It is a dangerous projection because in the presence of prevailing power imbalances it results easily in the destruction of the different perspective.

14 This meaning of *metaphorical* is not the meaning of the term by which all human language is metaphorical, including that which manifests itself in the form of physical laws. That usage refers to the fact that the word does not engender the world but mediates human relationships with the world in a way that facilitates interaction with it.

15 Inevitably, communication that allows senses and meanings to circulate, despite speaking of the present, is fed by the past; by tradition. Indeed, when the Enlhet speak with their polyphonic memory of what they are, they show no specific interest in clearly separating out a historical element of memory based on past experiences from an ahistorical element focusing on present experiences. In-stead, past and present are in constant communication.

16 Illich (1998) offers some illustrations of axioms within the European tradition. He states that in the thirteenth century writing acquired a certain level of im-portance in European life outside the monasteries. At the same time, although it continued to be a skill practised by a few specialists, a logic of writing soon emerged and spread across society independently of the ability to read and write. This new logic manifested itself, for example, in the replacement in only a few decades of simply spoken contracts by written contracts. Thus emerged what Illich calls a "mental space"; that is, a specific way of perceiving, doing, and feeling that is unquestioned because it is completely invisible from within the corresponding tradition. This concept of mental space coincides closely with what is called here the construction of reality. Similarly, with the rapid spread of computers and related devices, the cybernetic logic being constructed in societies is received and applied even by people who do not use digital tools. For example, with the ability to remake, almost always, almost anything on a

computer, to "reset" it at any time, the concept of irreversible consequence loses clarity, even in areas of life that have nothing to do with information technology. This has, and will continue to have, important effects on the construction of the corresponding reality.

17 The term *Western* should be read with care. On the one hand, societies that might call themselves Western are quite diverse; on the other, within each of these societies there are many dynamics that, in addition, are often contradictory or self-critical. With these reservations, then, the adjective "Western" refers here to a set of characteristics and predominant projections that are repeated throughout the societies referred to. In this sense, even Paraguayan society can be subsumed under the term although in other ways it is perhaps not very "Western."

18 The fact that the actions were described by others in terms unfamiliar to the actors themselves has a parallel in the observation that the Enlhet read their employment in work by the immigrants as an action based on reciprocity while at the same time the intruders read the Enlhet wish to share as based on physical necessity, despite its corresponding to a need to relate (pages 119–20). There are different actors here acting with intentions that are not mutually intelligible. This mutual unintelligibility of intention might certainly lead to the easy assumption that the interpretation made by the other of one's own actions is erroneous. However, rather than its allowing such conclusions, unintelligibility in fact points to the need to begin processes of communication that allow one to approach the perspective of the other instead of attempting to understand him using one's own intentions as a guide.

19 It is important to repeat that, for this reason, it is also not legitimate to eliminate the challenge posed by the radical difference between the two descriptions by reducing the account of Haakok Maaset to a metaphor for subjugation (page 138), or Kam'aatkok Ketsek's reading of smallpox as a metaphor for total disaster (page 160).

20 Different ontological perspectives appear among societies rooted in different traditions but also at different moments in the historical development of a particular society.

21 The aspects that constitute the phenomenological world, the experienced world, are always linked to a specific place and time. For this reason, the Western preference for abstraction can be understood as a way of distancing oneself from reality. In this sense, it is not accidental that it should coincide with large-scale destruction of everything on the planet, be it in the physical, social, or spiritual realm.

22 Every perspective has its own potentialities. The Western world, which has no notion of what it has destroyed, boasts readily of its potentialities. It is certainly true that some activity carried out from that perspective has met with success; for example, the curbing of infectious diseases that cause widespread mortality.

However, the conviction that Western ideas and technologies can be applied without consideration of local contexts to produce supposed "development" has caused disaster on such a scale as to give the impression that they have brought much more destruction than aid. (Feyerabend 1991, 74)

23 To say that two worlds cannot be integrated or joined does not imply that there can be no articulation between them or that each cannot make elements of the other its own. Rather, it is emphasised here that a cultural system is an integrated whole from which isolated elements cannot be eliminated and others added *simply by decision*. It does not function as a buffet from which to serve oneself freely to select the best of what is on offer. For this reason, it makes no sense to speak of the good or the bad in one culture compared with others. Rather, what is good is not defined by, and does not exist independently of, what is bad within a culture (to maintain the exclusion-dependent dichotomy) and the two aspects can only be treated as interdependent. Despite this, among the Mennonites of the Chaco (and not only there), it is common to draw a distinction between positive and negative elements in traditional Indigenous culture (elements that reflect fairly closely what are, for the colonizers, the known and the unfamiliar, respectively) to maintain the former and eliminate the latter. This idea has been transmitted to Indigenous communities. The Community Statute of Peesempo'o (2010?), for example, written with outside assistance, contains the following:

4.f) We value the positive aspects of our ancient culture ... g) At the same time we declare our rejection of certain practices of our ancient religion, such as witchcraft and the initiation ceremony.

24 The radical difference experienced due to the fact that multiple worlds and multiple ontologies exist means that the respective parties see different things, including things that are related in different ways among themselves and things that create obligations and have consequences that are not the same. Communication between people speaking from such incommensurable worlds requires more than respect for diverse representations of the world, i.e., for culture. It requires acknowledgement of the differences between worlds; of the different ontological positions.

25 There are several historical reasons for this limitation that are not the subject of this discussion. For example, its orientation to a concept of absolute truth and its long colonial trajectory.

26 This raises an interesting point: that of shamanic journeys. As mentioned in relation to account 30 by Seepe-Pyoy', old people with powers act within a world that is invisible to the common people (page 149). They speak, therefore, of facts that others might not accept as being events occurring in the phenomenological

world. This has effects, both on memory and on the attitudes of non-Enlhet people in their relationship with the Enlhet, that are not the subject of discussion here. Suffice it to say, just as in the case of experiences in the visible world, the details of these journeys are usually related by their protagonists across the years without any kind of variation that would cause the experience they share through the account to become confused.

27 The experience of the present translator is interesting in this regard. Having entered, albeit to a limited extent, the Enlhet world in order to read the accounts from that perspective, his later re-watching of audiovisual recordings of Enlhet accounts proved rewarding in an unexpected way, despite unfamiliarity with the Enlhet language itself: the distance between the English- and Enlhet-speaking experience having been narrowed, the relators' tone, concentration, and gesture become eloquent; their voices are heard. The reader is invited to make the same experiment.

28 However, when she does not have this explanation for her images they are lost: of the prostitution of her mother before her father's own eyes she has no memory (page 117).

29 It would be worthwhile to analyse the function of dialogue in Enlhet accounts. It is employed as a strategy to express extremely complicated constellations in a few words.

30 As a reflection of the importance of this connection with the experienced world, there is a clear tendency among Enlhet relators to speak of events, situations, and contexts related to their personal memories. Those with which they do not have this relationship (but which we know of through other relators, or may suppose to have occurred or existed) appear little in their accounts.

31 For example, in the accounts of the first period of living with the Mennonites, the Enlhet speak of the concrete conflicts that accompanied their dispossession while at the same time highlighting the fact that the Mennonites were "people who respected us." What appears to be a contradiction is in reality due to the fact that they do not qualify the first Mennonites in absolute terms, but in comparison with those of today, who "no longer respect us" (Ramón Ortiz, in Kalisch and Unruh 2014, 430). That is to say, they criticize the Mennonites of today on the basis of a comparison with their parents, which allows the Enlhet to express criticism without understanding it as a renouncement of the highly-valued construction of community with their neighbours that they could not and cannot be without.

32 A memory – in the restricted sense of the communicated conscience of one's own history – is not necessarily unwritten. For example, the Paraguayan people's memory of Stroessner's dictatorship manifests itself as an interaction between personal experience, on the one hand and, on the other, analysis and discourse disseminated through a variety of media. This type of memory is in a kind of competition with historiography (Izquierdo Martín 2008). However, that is not

the subject of the present book; rather, what is important here is that Enlhet memory does not exist either alongside or in opposition to Paraguayan historiography. It is a native means of making and maintaining the narrative of the people.

33 Their relationship with their territory is an illustrative example of the loss of access to their own past. Those who were already in their youth when the immigrants arrived (and who are now no longer living) described in great detail the places that they were from and which had no connection to the newly-established colonies. However, when their children speak of their own origins, they cite the recently-founded Mennonite villages as geographical reference points. This generation is formed of people who are today around seventy-five years of age (although their age varies depending on the start of Mennonite settlement in their region). Many of them now have only vague memories of the region their parents were from, or know of it only by name. Their own children in turn usually define as their place of origin the community in which they have spent most of their life (all those under sixty years old today; sometimes more); often they do not even know the names of the places their grandparents occupied. This is clear evidence of a process of forgetting not only of information but also of a great deal of knowledge and of a way of situating oneself in the world, hand in hand with a loss of awareness of Enlhet territory that makes impossible a challenge to, and perhaps even questioning of, the reduced condition in which they live today.

34 Yamasma'ay', in Kalisch and Unruh 2014, 313–17; Maeklha'ay'-Pmayheem, in Kalisch and Unruh 2014, 339–42.

35 For example, in the "indigenous aspirations and 'projects for life'" cited by Stahl (2007, 389–92), there is a clear predomination of and orientation to models brought by the intruders. The problem, however, is not the orientation to external or alien models – each person has the right to orient himself to whatever he wants. The central issue is: on the premise of whose protagonism is the reality of this orientation to be realized?

36 This refers to a constellation in which access is gained to the minimum space necessary for survival at the price of the surrender of one's dignity. This constellation is the origin of an attitude of prostitution rooted in the minds of both the subjugators and the subjugated, although it naturally manifests itself differently in the two parties. It can be thought of here as structural prostitution (Unruh and Kalisch 2008, 121; Kalisch and Unruh 2014, 539).

37 In reference to the fact that this part of the people's memory survives only in hiding, Hassoun (1996) calls those who still circulate it "smugglers of memory" ("contrabandistas de la memoria").

38 The relators do not limit themselves to abstract statements, for example that the Enlhet used to live well, which in itself would be as precarious a statement as that they live better today than before. Instead, they argue the accuracy of

their assessments with concrete experiences of their own. That is, their descriptions demonstrate their assessments, just as the details they share in them provide concrete starting points for work on the problems of the present. They reveal concrete, proven forms of their own protagonism; they show the Enlhet being in the capacity of actor (pages 6, 122, 152).

39 Like memory itself, identification does not point to true origin; nor is it the result of internal homogeneity. Instead, through discursive practices of exclusion and participation, it is oriented to what one proposes to be (Hall 1996, 4).

40 Some relators even emphasize the sources of the information they give. The most obvious example is Metyeeyam' (c. 1922–2012), who held an extremely extensive repertoire of accounts characterized by their concision and by mention of their respective oral sources.

41 One of the reasons for this respect, for example, is the coherence of the accounts of a particular relator across the years. In the same way, the number of details related, even where these might be secondary, reflects the great care with which the accounts are transmitted (pages 168–9).

42 As events become more distant with the passage of time and their first-hand witnesses die, experiences are gradually synthesized into images no longer supported by an emphasis on historical detail, as happens, for example, in the case of expressions of a mythical nature. The present work is not the place to discuss the way knowledge of historical detail is dealt with in the oral dimension across generations. However, it should be noted that the Mennonite narrative is subject to processes similar to those of the Enlhet, for although supported by written documents, it relies in large part on the oral dimension. As a consequence, we find that very little is known about the concrete experiences of the immigrants during the time of the Chaco war.

43 In many cases, there is insufficient data to be able to reconstruct the course of events. However, such limitations do not oblige us to avoid speaking of our past. For narratives about the past are never an absolute representation of it but an approach, similar to what Borges (1960) described in his famous *On Exactitude in Science*: absolute representation of the landscape on a map results in the disappearance of geography because it eliminates geographers.

44 This is illustrated clearly in Kalisch and Unruh (2014, 64, 210–11, 231–2, 558–9) with regard to the supposed constant hunger suffered by the Enlhet.

45 A narration directed to the Enlhet themselves would be quite different from one for non-Enlhet, and even for an audience of Enlhet who have never participated in the Oral Tradition of their people. Despite the forgetting, the Enlhet remain connected to the perspective from which the accounts are expressed and would understand the information narrated much more easily then the intruders; above all, they would be receptive to its perspective. The form itself of the narrations would differ. While presumably a narration for a non-Enlhet audience would be based on a written text (although, in fact, the intruders too are

distancing themselves from the written word), the narration for the Enlhet, as well as being in their own language, would be realized orally so as not to impede its later dissemination. It is important to highlight the fact that the Enlhet narration would not substitute the dissemination of recorded accounts, but would work in tandem with it in order to generate, to the greatest extent possible, processes of autonomous re-appropriation.

46 The Mennonites acknowledge the peaceful attitude of the Enlhet as one of the main reasons for the fact that contact with them has been "peaceful and even friendly" (Klassen 1980, 64). At the same time, they take for granted that they, who define themselves as peaceful people, could not have been the cause of conflict, because it has never been their habit to consider what their immigration meant for the native people. From their viewpoint, therefore, "conflicts" and "problems" appear only when the actions of the Indigenous people challenge their own interests (Klassen 1980, 64), which allows the process of immigration to be qualified in the following terms, reflecting clearly the current Mennonite position: "[T]he arrival of the Mennonites did not cause conflicts with the Indians. In the 1920s and 1930s land in the Central Chaco was abundant, as there were only a few hundred Indians in the colonisation area ... Another important reason why problems did not arise was that the Indians became better off, since they found work in the newly established colonies" (Kleinpenning 2009, 15).

47 Articulation, which as such orients equilibrium, is necessarily intercultural if it occurs between different peoples. However, an intercultural process, that is, an interaction that crosses frontiers between two peoples, is not necessarily committed to equilibrium. It is for this reason that the term *intercultural* lends itself easily to misuse and is avoided here (Kalisch 2010), although it is impossible to prevent altogether the unfortunate fact that terms may be distorted.

48 Communication, which affects those who participate in it and changes them, is indispensable for the construction of equilibrium, but it is not sufficient in itself. In due course, there will be a need to take ethical decisions, be they for or against equilibrium. In parallel to this, the subjugated will need to create new positions of power outside the existing system to oblige those who have the advantage in the unequal system to move toward a new equilibrium.

49 The scope of the present book does not permit discussion of the importance of guaranteed rights or rights that need to be guaranteed in order to safeguard spaces for action, whether national – above all the National Constitution – or international, such as universal human rights or the rights of Indigenous Peoples. See, in this regard: the *Universal Declaration of Human Rights*; the *American Convention on Human Rights* (National Law 1/89 of Paraguay); International Labour Organization Convention No. 169, *Indigenous and Tribal Peoples Convention,* and National Law 234/93 of Paraguay; the *United Nations Declaration on the Rights of Indigenous Peoples*, and the *American Declaration on The Rights of Indigenous Peoples*, adopted by the Organization of American States in 2016.

50 In this sense, Panikkar (1993) identified modern science as one of the factors responsible for the profound inferiority complex among most present societies, expressed, for example, in the affirmation that they do not wish to "go backwards" but "to be modern in their own way." The term *modernity* encapsulates the way of life proposed by those who manage science. To desire to be modern, therefore, is to invest in the proposals of others; it follows that it is a self-deception to think that one could be modern in one's own way. For this reason, orientation to modernity results in modern science acting, in the words of Panikkar, as a virus corroding the vast majority of cultures from within.

51 The monopolization of knowledge by academia is linked to the origins of Western rationalism. As Feyerabend (1991, 113–14) points out:

> [It] destroyed this unity [of emotion, facts, and structures managed within society] and replaced it by a more abstract, more isolated, and much more narrow idea of knowledge. Thought and emotion, even thought and nature were separated, and kept apart by fiat ... One consequence which is clear to everyone who can read is that the language in which knowledge is expressed becomes impoverished, arid, formal. Another consequence is an actual drawing apart of man and nature. Of course, man eventually returns to nature, after much error he returns to nature but as her conqueror, as her enemy, not as her creature.

In parallel to this role of conqueror, the purpose of knowledge is control, and what motivates exploration of the unknown is an interest in exploitation. The semantics of this logic of conquest are demonstrated in an article selected at random from *ABC Digital* (EFE 2016) reporting the "discovery of two new species of frog in Ecuador": "It is important to conserve these species, as they have a large number of chemical compounds in their skin with antibiotic, antifungal and antibacterial properties that could be used in the manufacture of medicines." Here, the conservation – or protection – of life is legitimized not with regard to life itself but to its possible utilization. It is something that favours not the "protected," but the "protector." The verb "conserve" is a synonym of "take ownership for the purpose of exploitation."

The semantics within which this logic of conquest is presented reveal clearly the motivation for the increase of knowledge: greed. In the past, for example, America was discovered in order to be conquered, without the slightest respect for life, to appropriate its riches. Indeed, it was sought for this purpose. Today languages and cultures are not of interest as indispensable dimensions for real people to be able to be the protagonists of a dignified life but, culturally, as "the common heritage of humanity" (Article 1 of the UNESCO Universal Declaration on Cultural Diversity, 2001) and, linguistically, as "the cultural heritage of the Nation" (Article 140 of the National Constitution of Paraguay, 1992). When research into languages and cultures is proposed, therefore, it is not for the value they have for their speakers and bearers (for example, Article 42 of Paraguay's Law on Languages [*Ley de Lenguas*], which deals with the theme of research, makes no reference to them), but because they are considered the *capital* of humanity. In order to secure this capital, its real owners are declared members of a shared collectivity – humanity – so that what is theirs appears as belonging to all while they themselves continue to be undervalued: as "illiterate" and "backward," for example (adjectives that reinforce, each in the same way, the idea that these people are not functional for the modern world). Thus, a tried and tested mechanism of expropriation reappears; one we have already seen in relation to Indigenous territories and the new Paraguayan State (pages 127, 156).

52 This exclusion is serious, as:

> [T]here are lots of things they don't understand and few things they do understand. But instead of trying to learn they assert that the things they do understand are the only things that can be understood. For some reason they have convinced almost everyone else that they are right and so we have now the strange spectacle of people without sight teaching everyone else the most efficient way of becoming as blind as they are. (Feyerabend 1991, 88–9)

53 Ignorance of the different perspectives is far more serious than the fact that academic knowledge is managed in an elitist way. However, both defects have the same effect: the exclusion from native society of protagonist action.

54 In order for a contribution from academia to be useful outside it – there are many that never will – it must pass through processes of reconstruction and appropriation on new epistemological axes that take it outside western academic logic and allow its use non-hegemonically.

55 For a variety of reflections in this regard, see Kalisch (2006–15).

56 Escaping the idea that only science offers true solutions and recovering confidence in one's own potentialities requires recognition that academia does not allow the possibility that others might enter into communication with it because it declares different realities to be non-existent. Therefore, until one ceases to define oneself in relation to academia, one submits inevitably to its hegemony.

57 For this reason the term *accompaniment* is used rather than *research* or *analysis*. These two terms imply a non-existent neutrality and, additionally, make no reference to possible processes for communication.

58 To overcome abyssal thinking, the ways in which it has been cemented must be substituted by modes of thinking and speaking that do not transmit it.

59 The same logic underlies the common idea that more knowledge about the Enlhet would improve relations with them (page 201). However, detailed knowledge of the other does not alter the fact that the other is perceived as the object

(pages 6, 201). For this reason, an increase in knowledge about the other does not much influence attitudes of respect toward them – which require them to be accepted as a subject – and does not have the potential to improve ways of relating; on the contrary, it can aid in the destruction of the other (Todorov 2010). In the words of Mauricio Schvartzman (1983, 187), knowledge about the rain does not make it rain.

60 In this sense, an analysis of the concept of time in the European or western tradition would be very revealing. As González de Oleaga points out (2013, 302), "By the mid-19th century, the process of industrialization was bringing radical changes to the life of European people ... Little by little, time ceased to be associated with human events (harvests, the seasons ...) and began to depend heavily on the clock ... The clock allowed thought of a new, independent and quantifiable world." Mumford (1934, 14), for his part, suggests that "[T]he clock, not the steam-engine, is the key-machine of the modern industrial age." Murphy (2005, 70) maintains that "It was through the control of time, more than the announcement of a Judaeo-Christian god, that the process of missionization of others was begun by the West. Through displacement of multiple temporalities evolved by societies historically, an instrumentally ordering discourse of knowledge and world history was imposed."

61 In fact, the words are not so frozen, given that their sense and readings are in turn subject to changes that can even create considerable obstacles to their comprehension.

62 Although these labels are understood as describing absolute characteristics, in reality, they are relative to a specific system of references. For example, the existence of a lack of education or ignorance does not imply nothingness but rather the absence of a response to a certain expectation: that the other should be functional for the dominant world.

GLOSSARY

1 The scientific names facilitate research of the fauna and flora of the territory, which will serve to illustrate the accounts. In determining the names of plants, reference was made to Arenas (1981), V. Friesen (2004), and Ulmke and August (2004); additions and corrections based on these works were made under the direction of Verena Friesen, without whose assistance in many cases it would not have been possible to identify some of the plant names. She and Pastor Arenas have additionally assisted in identifying the common names of plants in Spanish. The identification of bee species was made with reference to Boggino (2011). It should be noted that, where a translation has been provided for a geographical name, in many cases this does not designate exactly the place referred to by the Enlhet place name but a nearby place named by the Mennonites or Paraguayans.

BIBLIOGRAPHY

ABC Digital. 2016. "MEC: Himno Nacional será obligatorio." *ABC Digital*, 23 May. https://www.abc.com.py/nacionales/mec-hara-obligatorio-canto-del-himno-1482550.html.

American Declaration on the Rights of Indigenous Peoples. 2016. http://www.oas.org/en/sla/docs/AG07239E03.pdf.

Anonymous. 1933. "Verschiedenes." *Mennoblatt* 4, no. 1: 6.

Arenas, Pastor. 1981. *Etnobotánica Lengua-Maskoy*. Buenos Aires: Fundación para la Educación, la Ciencia y la Cultura.

Ashwell, Washington. 2012. "Por un revisionismo de la historia patria." *ABC Digital*, 22 January. https://www.abc.com.py/edicion-impresa/suplementos/cultural/por-un-revisionismo-de-la-historia-patria-358323.html.

Ayala, Óscar. 2014. "El derecho al desagravio como forma del derecho a un espacio propio y autónomo." In *La tierra en el Paraguay: de la desigualdad al ejercicio de derechos*, edited by Patricio Dobrée, 63–77. Asunción: Programa Democratización y Construcción de la Paz.

Baldus, Herbert. 1931. *Indianerstudien im nordöstlichen Chaco*. Leipzig: Hirschfeld.

Barbosa, Pablo, and Nicolás Richard. 2010. "La danza del cautivo. Figuras niva-clés de la ocupación del Chaco." In *Los hombres transparentes. Indígenas y militares en la guerra del Chaco (1932–1935)*, edited by Luc Capdevila, Isabelle Combès, Nicolás Richard, and Pablo Barbosa, 121–75. Cochabamba: Instituto de Misionología.

Barreto, Sindulfo. 1969. *Por qué no pasaron. Revelaciones diplomáticas y militares*. N.p.

Bejarano, Ramón César. 1979. *Mapa del Chaco Boreal para el Estudio de la Guerra 1932–1935*. 3rd ed. Asunción: n.p.

Belaieff, Juan. 1941. "Los Indios del Chaco Paraguayo y su Tierra." *Revista de la Sociedad Científica Paraguaya* 5, no. 3: 1–47.

Biblioteca de la memoria hablada. 2021. Audio-visual recordings of Enlhet, Toba-enenlhet, and Guaná relators. Produced by Hannes Kalisch and Lanto'oy' Unruh. Ya'alve-Saanga: Nengvaanemkeskama Nempayvaam Enlhet. https://www.enlhet.org/memoria_hablada.

Boggino, Pedro Antonio. 2011. *Contribución al conocimiento de las Abejas Nativas del Paraguay*. Asunción: Arandurã.

Borges, Jorge Luis. 1998. "On Exactitude in Science." In Jorge Luis Borges, *Collected Fictions*, translated by Andrew Hurley. New York: Penguin.

Boschmann, Hans. 2012. "Trébol – eine historische Stätte in Fernheim." *Jahrbuch für Geschichte und Kultur der Mennoniten in Paraguay* 13: 101–26.

Canova, Paola. 2011. "Del monte a la ciudad: La producción cultural de los Ayoreode en los espacios urbanos del Chaco Central." *Suplemento Antropológico* 46, no. 2: 275–316.

Capdevila, Luc. 2010a. "La guerra del Chaco *Tierra adentro*. Desarticulando la representación de un conflicto internacional." In *Los hombres transparentes. Indígenas y militares en la guerra del Chaco (1932–1935)*, edited by Luc Capdevila, Isabelle Combès, Nicolás Richard, and Pablo Barbosa, 11–31. Cochabamba: Instituto de Misionología.

– 2010b. "Los fortines del 'desierto': ventanas abiertas sobre las relaciones indígenas/militares." In *Los hombres transparentes. Indígenas y militares en la guerra del Chaco (1932–1935)*, edited by Luc Capdevila, Isabelle Combès, Nicolás Richard, and Pablo Barbosa, 83–119. Cochabamba: Instituto de Misionología.

Capdevila, Luc, Isabelle Combès, and Nicolás Richard. 2008. "Los indígenas en la guerra del Chaco. Historia de una ausencia y antropología de un olvido." In *Mala guerra: los indígenas en la Guerra del Chaco (1932–35)*, edited by Nicolás Richard, 13–65. Asunción, Paris: Museo del Barro, ServiLibro, CoLibris.

Community Statute of Peesempo'o. [2010?]. Unpublished.

Dalla Corte, Gabriela. 2009. *Lealtades firmes. Redes de sociabilidad y empresas: la "Carlos Casado S.A." entre la Argentina y el Chaco paraguayo (1860–1940)*. Madrid: Consejo Superior de Investigaciones Científicas.

de la Cruz, Luis María. 1991. "La presencia nivakle (chulupí) en el territorio formoseño. Contribución de la etnohistoria de Formosa." *Hacia una nueva carta étnica del Gran Chaco* 2: 87–106.

de las Casas, Bartolomé. 1552. *Brevísima relación de la destrucción de las Indias*.

Dening, Greg. 2004. "Writing, Rewriting the Beach: An Essay." In *Experiments in Rethinking History*, edited by Alun Munslow and Robert A. Rosenstone, 30–55. New York: Routledge.

Descola, Philippe. 2014. *La composition des mondes. Entretiens avec Pierre Charbonnier*. Paris: Flammarion.

DGEEC (Dirección General de Estadística, Encuestas y Censos). 2003. *II Censo Nacional Indígena de Población y Viviendas 2002. Pueblos indígenas del Paraguay. Resultados finales*. Fernando de la Mora: DGEEC.

– 2014. *III Censo Nacional de Población y Viviendas para Pueblos Indígenas, Censo 2012. Pueblos Indígenas en el Paraguay. Resultados Finales*. Fernando de la Mora: DGEEC.

Durán Estragó, Margarita. 2000. *La misión del Pilcomayo, 1925–2000: Memoria viva*. Biblioteca paraguaya de antropología, vol. 35. Asunción: CEADUC.

EFE. 2016. "Estudiantes descubren dos nuevas especies de rana en Ecuador." *ABC Digital*, 4 Junc. https://www.abc.com.py/ciencia/estudiantes-descubren-dos-nuevas-especies-de-rana-en-ecuador-1486316.html.

Eitzen, Isaak. 2002. "Wie schön war es doch früher: Lesermeinung zur Serie von E. Unruh und H. Kalisch." *Mennoblatt* 73, no. 5: 5–6.

Enns, Peter. 1996. "Bombas sobre Fred Engen." In *Kaputi Mennonita. Arados y fusiles en la guerra del Chaco*, edited by Peter P. Klassen, 111–12. 3rd ed. Asunción: Imprenta Modela S.A.

Escobar, Ticio, and Lia Colombino. 2008. *Catálogo. Museo de Arte Indígena.* Asunción: Centro de Artes Visuales/Museo del Barro.

Esteva, Gustavo. 1998. "Autonomía y democracia radical: el tránsito de la tolerancia a la hospitalidad." In *Autonomías étnicas y Estados nacionales*, edited by Miguel Alberto Bartolomé and Alicia Barabas, 307–32. México: Instituto Nacional de Antropología e Historia (INAH).

– 2014. *Nuevas formas de revolución. Notas para aprender de las luchas del EZLN y de la APPO.* Oaxaca: Universidad de la Tierra/El Rebozo.

EZLN (Ejército Zapatista de Liberación Nacional). 1997. *Crónicas Intergalácticas EZLN: Primer Encuentro Intercontinental por la Humanidad y contra el Neoliberalismo.* Chiapas: Planeta Tierra.

Fabre, Alain. 2005. "Los pueblos del Gran Chaco y sus lenguas, primera parte: Los enlhet-enenlhet del Chaco Paraguayo." *Suplemento Antropológico* 40, 1: 503–69.

– 2013. "Los pueblos del Gran Chaco y sus lenguas, primera parte: Los enlhet-enenlhet del Chaco Paraguayo." https://www.academia.edu/3611583/Dic_Enlhet_Enenlhet.

Feyerabend, Paul K. 1991. *Three Dialogues on Knowledge.* Oxford: Blackwell.

Fischermann, Bernd. 2003. *Historia de Amotocodie.* Filadelfia, La Paz: Manuscrito.

Friesen, Heinrich. 1996. "Trébol se convierte en fortín militar." In *Kaputi Mennonita. Arados y fusiles en la guerra del Chaco*, edited by Peter P. Klassen, 79–81. 3rd ed. Asunción: Imprenta Modela S.A.

Friesen, Martin W. 1996. "El intrépido vikingo." In *Kaputi Mennonita. Arados y fusiles en la guerra del Chaco*, edited by Peter P. Klassen, 23–5. 3rd ed. Asunción: Imprenta Modela S.A.

– 1997. *Neue Heimat in der Chacowildnis.* 2nd ed. Loma Plata: Sociedad Cooperativa Colonizadora Chortitzer Komitee.

– 2016. *Nuevo hogar en el inhóspito Chaco.* Loma Plata: Comité de Historia de la Colonia Menno.

Friesen, Uwe. 2013. "Der Erschließungsprozess de Gran Chaco seit dem späten 19. Jahrhundert." *Jahrbuch für Geschichte und Kultur der Mennoniten in Paraguay* 14: 23–74.

Friesen, Verena. 2004. *Urundeʼy, Schlorrekaktus, Pehen. Ein Feldführer für Chacogehölze.* Herborn: Uniglobia.

Giesbrecht, Gerhard B. 1936. "Mission unter den Lengua-Indianern im Gran Chaco von Paraguay." *Mennoblatt* 7, no. 8: 3.

– 1937. "Indianermission im Chaco von Paraguay. Auf der anglikanischen Lenguamission." *Mennoblatt* 8, no. 7: 3.

– 1956. "Die Mission unter den Indianern." In *Jubiläumsschrift zum 25 jährigen Bestehen der Kolonie Fernheim, Chaco Paraguay*, edited by Peter Wiens and Peter P. Klassen. Winnipeg: Echo-Verlag.

Giesbrecht, Gerd G. 2000. *Ich sah der Lengua Hütten. Erfahrungen und Beobachtungen in der Missionsarbeit. Anregungen zu einem besseren Verständnis im Zusammenleben der Indianer und Deutsch-Mennoniten im Chaco von Paraguay*. Filadelfia: n.p.

Giesbrecht, Heinz Dieter. 2008. *Mennonitische Diakonie am Beispiel Paraguay. Eine diakonietheologische Untersuchung*. Löwen: Evangelisch Theologische Fakultät.

Glauser, Marcos. 2019. *Angaité's responses to deforestation. Political ecology of the livelihood and land use strategies of an indigenous community from the Paraguayan Chaco*. Vienna: LIT Verlag.

González de Oleaga, Marisa. 2008. "¿El fin de los historiadores o el fin de una hegemonía?" In *El fin de los historiadores. Pensar históricamente en el siglo XXI*, edited by Pablo Sánchez León and Jesús Izquierdo Martín, 153–78. Madrid: Siglo XXI.

– 2013. "Tocar timbres o la utopía en el museo." In *En primera persona. Testimonios desde la utopía*, edited by Marisa González de Oleaga, 301–20. Barcelona: Ned Ediciones.

– 2014. "La tribu desafiada: el pasado es de todos." In *¡Qué hacemos con el pasado? Catorce textos sobre historia y memoria*, edited by Esther Pascua Echegaray. N.p.: Ediciones Contratiempo.

González, Martín. 1556. "Carta de Martín González, clérigo, al Emperador Don Carlos, dando noticia de las expediciones hechas y de los atropellos cometidos después de la prisión del gobernador Alvar Núñez Cabeza de Vaca – Asunción, 25 de junio de 1556." In *Cartas de Indias*, 604–18 (1877). Madrid: Ministerio de Fomento (Imprenta de Manuel Hernández).

Grubb, Wilfred Barbrooke. 1911. *An Unknown People in an Unknown Land*. London: Seeley & Co.

– 1914. *A Church in the Wilds*. London: Seeley & Co.

Hack, Henk. 1960. "Akkulturation bei den Lengua im paraguayischen Chaco." *34. Amerikanistenkongress in Wien*, 644–52.

Hall, Stuart. "Introduction: Who Needs 'Identity'?" In *Questions of Cultural Identity*, edited by Stuart Hall and Paul du Gay, 1–17. London: SAGE.

Hassoun, Jacques. 1996. *Los contrabandistas de la memoria*. Buenos Aires: Ediciones de la Flor.

Hein, David. 1990. *Los Ayoreos – nuestros vecinos. Comienzos de la Misión al Norte del Chaco*. Filadelfia: n.p. [German language edition: 1990. *Die*

Ayoreos – unsere Nachbarn. Anfaenge der Mission im noerdlichen Chaco. Filadelfia: n.p.]

Hoyos, Arturo. 1932. "El proceso de la usurpación boliviana del Chaco, escrito por el capitán de sanidad del ejército de aquel país doctor Arturo Hoyos." Published in *El Orden.* Asunción: n.p.

Hunt, Richard J. 1915. "El choroti o yófuaha." *Revista del Museo de La Plata* 23.

– 1932. *The Livingstone of South America.* London: Seeley & Co.

Illich, Ivan. 1998. "Un alegato en favor de la investigación de la cultura escrita lega." In *Cultura escrita y oralidad,* edited by David R. Olson and Nancy Torrance, 47–70. Barcelona: Gedisa. [Original English-language edition: *Literacy and Orality,* edited by David R. Olson and Nancy Torrance. Cambridge: Cambridge University Press, 1991].

International Labour Organization. 1989. *Indigenous and Tribal Peoples Convention (No. 169).* https://www.ilo.org/wcmsp5/groups/public/---americas/---ro-lima/documents/publication/wcms_345065.pdf.

Izquierdo Martín, Jesús. 2008. "La memoria del historiador y los olvidos de la memoria." In *El fin de los historiadores. Pensar históricamente en el siglo XXI,* edited by Pablo Sánchez León and Jesús Izquierdo Martín, 179–208. Madrid: Siglo XXI.

Janz, Heinrich. 1996. "Cacique Molina." In *Kaputi Mennonita. Arados y fusiles en la guerra del Chaco,* edited by Peter P. Klassen, 146–7. 3rd edition. Asunción: Imprenta Modela S.A.

Joy, Juan Carlos. 1992. *Los fortines de la guerra. Toponimia chaqueña.* Asunción: Estudio Gráfico.

Kaethler, Frieda. 1996. "Los lenguas, víctimas de la guerra." In *Kaputi Mennonita. Arados y fusiles en la guerra del Chaco,* edited by Peter P. Klassen, 143–5. 3rd edition. Asunción: Imprenta Modela S.A.

Kalisch, Hannes. 2004. "El multilingüismo paraguayo. Apuntes hacia una noción integrada de 'bilingüismo'." *Acción. Revista paraguaya de reflexión y diálogo* 247: 33–6.

– 2006–15. "Construcción y aprendizaje." Articles in *Acción. Revista paraguaya de reflexión y diálogo.* www.enlhet.org/pdf/nne23-aprendizaje.pdf.

– 2006. "La profesionalidad autóctona I. Una dimensión para definir criterios de calidad." *Acción. Revista paraguaya de reflexión y diálogo* 269: 14–16.

– 2007. "La profesionalidad autóctona II. Un espacio de construcción participativo." *Acción. Revista paraguaya de reflexión y diálogo* 272: 16–19.

– 2009a. "Enlhet." In *Lexikon der Mennoniten in Paraguay,* 122–8. Asunción: Verein für Geschichte und Kultur der Mennoniten in Paraguay.

– 2009b. "Espacios de construcción. La conjugación del espacio vivencial y el espacio social." *Acción. Revista paraguaya de reflexión y diálogo* 295: 27–29.

– 2010. "Escritura y oralidad enlhet-enenlhet: sentido y significado de las publicaciones monolingües en la lengua autóctona." In *Educación, lenguas y culturas en el Mercosur: Pluralidad cultural e inclusión social en Brasil y en Paraguay*, edited by José Maria Rodrigues, 235–60. Biblioteca paraguaya de antropología, vol. 77. Asunción: CEADUC.

– 2011a. "Constelaciones históricas chaqueñas." *Acción. Revista paraguaya de reflexión y diálogo* 314: 26–33.

– 2011b. "Nengelaasekhammalhkoo: An Enlhet Perspective." In *The Palgrave International Handbook of Peace Studies: A Cultural Perspective*, edited by Wolfgang Dietrich, Josefina Echavarría Álvarez, Gustavo Esteva, Daniela Ingruber, and Norbert Koppensteiner, 387–414. London: Palgrave McMillan.

– 2012a. "'El concepto enlhet-enenlhet de apyoholhma,' 'persona con poder': Composición semántica original y connotaciones actuales." *Suplemento Antropológico* 47, no. 2: 351–69.

– 2012b. "El derecho a vivir desde las lenguas indígenas, o, Pensando el conocimiento desde las sociedades autóctonas." In *Melià ... escritos de homenaje*, edited by Ignacio Telesca and Gabriel Insaurralde, 83–100. Asunción: ISEHF.

– 2013. "Sumisión y resistencia." *Acción. Revista paraguaya de reflexión y diálogo* 336: 7–10.

– 2014a. "Espacio propio y participación." In *Tekoporã. Cuadernos Salazar 2*, edited by Lea Schvartzman, 30–3. Asunción: Centro Cultural de España "Juan de Salazar."

– 2014b. "Lecturas y contralecturas. La necesidad del espacio propio." In *Tekoporã. Cuadernos Salazar 2*, edited by Lea Schvartzman, 106–13. Asunción: Centro Cultural de España "Juan de Salazar."

– 2014c. "Construcciones de aceptación, primera parte." *Acción. Revista paraguaya de reflexión y diálogo* 344: 13–15.

– 2014d. "Construcciones de aceptación, segunda parte." *Acción. Revista paraguaya de reflexión y diálogo* 350: 20–3.

– 2015. "La construcción propia entre sumisión y resistencia." *Acción. Revista paraguaya de reflexión y diálogo* 360: 20–5.

– 2018. "Dónde estamos. La condición *colonial*." *Acción. Revista paraguaya de reflexión y diálogo* 389: 15–18. www.enlhet.org/pdf/nne23-aprendizaje.pdf.

– 2019. "Los enlhet no teníamos cosas. La transfiguración semántica como reflejo de la condición colonial." *Suplemento Antropológico* 54, no. 2: 297–320.

– 2020. "¡El papel los enflaquece! La historia de la escuela entre los enlhet." *Acción. Revista paraguaya de reflexión y diálogo* 402: 28–33.

– 2021. "'They Only Know the Public Roads': Enlhet Territoriality during the Colonization of Their Lands." In *Reimagining the Gran Chaco: Identities, Politics and the Environment in South America*, edited by Silvia Hirsch, Paola Canova, and Mercedes Biocca, 93–117. Gainsville, FL: University of Florida Press.

– Forthcoming. "¿Quieren acaso volver al pasado? Un viaje por el espinoso paisaje de una sociedad colonizada." In *De memoria*, edited by Marisa González and Hannes Kalisch. Madrid: Postmetrópolis.

Kalisch, Hannes, and Ernesto Unruh, eds. 2014. *Wie schön ist deine Stimme. Berichte der Enlhet in Paraguay zu ihrer Geschichte.* Asunción: Centro de Artes Visuales/Museo del Barro.

– 2020. *¡Qué hermosa es tu voz! Relatos de los enlhet sobre la historia de su pueblo.* Asunción, Ya'alve-Saanga: Centro de Artes Visuales/Museo del Barro, Nengvaanemkeskama Nempayvaam Enlhet, ServiLibro.

Kalisch, Hannes, and Lanto'oy' Unruh. 2019. *Koo Campo Largo enlhet apkelaoklha'a.* Map with Enlhet place names in the region of Campo Largo. Ya'alve-Saanga: Nengvaanemkeskama Nempayvaam Enlhet. https://enlhet.org/pdf/nne53_mapa_campo_largo.pdf.

– 2020. *Koo Ya'alve-Saanga enlhet apkelaoklha'a.* Map with Enlhet place names in the region of Ya'alve-Saanga. Ya'alve-Saanga: Nengvaanemkeskama Nempayvaam Enlhet. https://enlhet.org/pdf/nne56_mapa_ya'alve-saanga.pdf.

Kalisch, Hannes, and Ronaldo Unruh, prod. 2013. *El País de los Enlhet: Peetempok.* Video, 50 mins., Spanish and Enlhet. Ya'alve-Saanga: Nengvaanemkeskama Nempayvaam Enlhet. https://www.enlhet.org/audiovisual.html.

Kam'aatkok Ketsek, Kaymaap-Takhaalhet, and Sekhay'-Pva'. 2010. *¡Entalhnemkek valay apkenmopoy'!* Produced by Hannes Kalisch and Lanto'oy' Unruh. Video, 119 mins., Enlhet. Ya'alve-Saanga: Nengvaanemkeskama Nempayvaam Enlhet. https://www.enlhet.org/audiovisual.html.

Kaymaap-Maama, Kenteem, Yaamasma'ay', and Heeva'ay'. 2012. *Apva'at.* Produced by Hannes Kalisch and Lanto'oy' Unruh. Video, 102 mins., Enlhet. Ya'alve-Saanga: Nengvaanemkeskama Nempayvaam Enlhet. https://www.enlhet.org/audiovisual.html.

Kenteem. 2008. *Yevey'-Aatong.* Produced by Hannes Kalisch and Lanto'oy' Unruh. Video, 40 mins., Enlhet. Ya'alve-Saanga: Nengvaanemkeskama Nempayvaam Enlhet. https://www.enlhet.org/audiovisual.html.

Kidd, Stephen W. 1992. "Religious Change: A Case Study Amongst the Enxet of the Paraguayan Chaco." University of Durham, unpublished.

– 1999. "The Morality of the Enxet People of the Paraguayan Chaco and Their Resistance to Assimilation." In *Peoples of the Gran Chaco*, edited by Elmer S. Miller, 37–60. Westport, CT: Bergin & Garvey.

Klassen, Paulhans. 2008. *Die das Leid trugen.* Filadelfia: n.p.

Klassen, Peter P. 1980. "Begegnung von Indianern und Mennoniten in christlicher Verantwortung." In *Evangelium in indianischen Kulturen*, 52–66. Hamburg: Evangelische Pressestelle für Weltmission.

– 1983. *Immer kreisen die Geier: Ein Buch vom Chaco Boreal in Paraguay.* Filadelfia: n.p.

- 1991. *Die Mennoniten in Paraguay, Band 2. Begegnung mit Indianern und Paraguayern*. Bolanden-Weierhof: Mennonitischer Geschichtsverein.
- ed. 1996. *Kaputi Mennonita. Arados y fusiles en la guerra del Chaco*. 3rd ed. Asunción: Imprenta Modela S.A.
- 1999. *Tierra de sol, sangre y sudor: Un libro sobre el Chaco Paraguayo*. Filadelfia: n.p.
- 2001. *Die Mennoniten in Paraguay, Band 1. Reich Gottes und Reich dieser Welt*. 2nd ed. Bolanden-Weierhof: Mennonitischer Geschichtsverein.
- 2012. "Ein kleines Dorf im Chacokrieg." *Mennoblatt* 83, no. 19: 4–6.

Kleinpenning, Jan M.G. 2009. "The Mennonite Colonies in Paraguay. Origin and Development." *Ibero-Bibliographien* 5. Berlin: Ibero-Amerikanisches Institut.

Krieg, Hans. 1948. *Zwischen Anden und Atlantik. Reisen eines Biologen in Südamerika*. Munich: Carl Hanser.

Ley de Lenguas. 2010. Ley N° 4.251 de Lenguas. *Gaceta oficial de la República del Paraguay*, no. 257: 52–60. https://www.bacn.gov.py/leyes-paraguayas/2895/ley-n-4251-de-lenguas.

Loewen, Jacob A. 1964. *Wissenschaftliche Untersuchung über die Frage der Ansiedlung der Lengua- und Chulupí-Indianer im Chaco von Paraguay*. Hillsboro, KS: n.p. [Original in English: Loewen, Jacob A. 1964. *Research Report on the Question of Settling Lengua and Chulupi Indians in the Paraguayan Chaco*. Hillsboro, KS: n.p.]
- 1965. "The Way to First Class. Revolution or Ronversion?" *Practical Anthropology* 12, no. 5: 193–209.
- 1966. "From Nomadism to Sedentary Agriculture." *América Indígena* 26: 27–42.

Maangvayaam'ay'. 2015. *Maalbek*. Produced by Hannes Kalisch and Lanto'oy' Unruh. Video, 177 min, Enlhet. Ya'alve-Saanga: Nengvaanemkeskama Nempayvaam Enlhet. https://www.enlhet.org/audiovisual.html.
- 2021. *Apkelpalhkeeykam' yaamvalay enlhet*. Apkelenyemay'aklha' enlhet, no. 40 (Biblioteca de la memoria hablada, no. 40). Produced by Hannes Kalisch and Lanto'oy' Unruh. Account recorded in Na'teema-Amyep, June 2015, 7:44 mins., Enlhet. Ya'alve-Saanga: Nengvaanemkeskama Nempayvaam Enlhet. https://enlhet.org/memoria_hablada.html.

Melià, Bartomeu. 1997. *Pueblos indígenas en el Paraguay. Demografía histórica y análisis de los resultados del Censo Nacional de Población y Viviendas 1992*. Fernando de la Mora: DGEEC.

Melietkesammap. 2007. *Halhema-Teves. Apkeltennaikamaha Melietkesammap aktemakha nelvetai'a takha'*. Edited by Manolo Romero and Hannes Kalisch. *Biblioteca paraguaya de antropología*, vol. 59. Ya'alve-Saanga: Nengvaanemkeskama Nempayvaam Enlhet.

Melteiongkasemmap. 2016. *Altanema-Seiana'. Los Enenlhet, su territorio y los paraguayos. Relatos de Melteiongkasemmap sobre la historia de su pueblo*.

Produced by Hannes Kalisch and Lanto'oy' Unruh. Video, 1:15 mins., Toba-Enenlhet with Spanish subtitles. Ya'alve-Saanga: Nengvaanemkeskama Nempayvaam Enlhet. https://www.enlhet.org/audiovisual.html.

Métraux, Alfred. 1946. "Ethnography of the Chaco." In *Handbook of South American Indians*, vol. 1, *The Marginal Tribes*, edited by Julian Stewart, 197–370. Washington: Government Printing Office.

Metyeyam', Sa'kok-Nay', Seepe-Pta'heem-Pelhkapok, and Kenteem. 2011. *Éramos nosotros, los que vivieron aquí*. Produced by Hannes Kalisch and Lanto'oy' Unruh. Video, 56 mins., Enlhet with Spanish subtitles. Ya'alve-Saanga: Nengvaanemkeskama Nempayvaam Enlhet. https://www.enlhet.org/audiovisual.html.

Mumford, Lewis. 1934. *Technics and Civilization*. New York: Harcourt.

Murphy, Bernice. (2005). "Memory, History and Museums." *Museum International* 57, no. 3: 70–8.

National Constitution of Paraguay. 1992. Asunción: n.p.. https://www.oas.org/juridico/spanish/par_res3.htm.

Nengvaanemkeskama Nempayvaam Enlhet. 2018. *Los enlhet en Boquerón*. Produced by Hannes Kalisch and Lanto'oy' Unruh. Video, 6:08 mins., Spanish. Ya'alve-Saanga: Nengvaanemkeskama Nempayvaam Enlhet. https://www.enlhet.org/boqueron.

Oeser, Rudolf. 2008. *Epidemien. Das große Sterben der Indianer*. 2nd edition. Norderstedt: Books on Demand.

Organization of American States. 1969. *American Convention on Human Rights*. https://www.oas.org/dil/esp/tratados_b-32_convencion_americana_sobre_derechos_humanos.htm.

Panikkar, Raimon. 1993. "La diversidad como presupuesto para la armonía entre los pueblos." *Wiñay Marka*, no. 20: 15–20. Barcelona: n.p.

Piedras Monroy, Pedro. 2012. *La siega del olvido. Memoria y presencia de la represión*. Madrid: Siglo XXI.

Protokollheft für Lehrerkonferenzen. 1933–35. Filadelfia: Archiv der Kolonie Fernheim.

Querejazu Calvo, Roberto. 1965. *Masamaclay. Historia política, diplomática y militar de la Guerra del Chaco*. La Paz: n.p.

Quintana Villasboa, Noelia. 2016. "La Batalla de Boquerón, triunfo de la estrategia." *ABC Digital*, 29 September. https://www.abc.com.py/nacionales/la-batalla-de-boqueron-triunfo-de-la-estrategia-1523300.html.

Quiring, Walter. 1936. *Deutsche erschließen den Chaco*. Karlsruhe: Heinrich Schneider.

Ratzlaff, Gerhard. 1993. *Entre dos fuegos: Los menonitas en el conflicto limítrofe entre Paraguay y Bolivia 1932–1935*. Asunción: n.p.

– 2004. *Vater Abram: Von der Ukraine über Sibirien und China nach Paraguay und Kanada*. Asunción: n.p.

– 2015. "Mennoniten erleben den Chacokrieg: Ein Überblick." *Jahrbuch für Geschichte und Kultur der Mennoniten in Paraguay* 16: 119–51.

Ratzlaff, Heinrich. 2012. "Loma Plata – das größte Siedlungslager der kanadischen Mennoniten in der Chacowildnis." *Jahrbuch für Geschichte und Kultur der Mennoniten in Paraguay*, year 13: 59–84.

Redekop, Calvin. 1973. "Mennonite Mission in the Paraguayan Chaco." *International Review of Mission* 62: 302–17.

– 1980. *Strangers become Neighbors: Mennonite and Indigenous Relations in the Paraguayan Chaco*. Scottdale: Herald Press.

Regehr, Walter. 1979. *Die lebensräumliche Situation der Indianer im paraguayischen Chaco. Humangeographisch-ethnologische Studie zu Subsistenzgrundlage und Siedlungsform akkulturierter Chacovölker*. Basler Beiträge zur Geographie, 25. Basel: Wepf & Co.

Richard, Nicolás. 2007. "Cette guerre qui en cachait une autre. Les populations indiennes dans la guerre du Chaco." In *Les guerres du Paraguay aux XIXe et XXe siècles*, edited by Nicolás Richard, Luc Capdevila, and Capucine Boidin, 221–43. Paris: CoLibris.

– 2008. "Los baqueanos de Belaieff. Las mediaciones indígenas en la entrada militar al Alto Paraguay." In *Mala guerra: los indígenas en la Guerra del Chaco (1932–35)*, edited by Nicolás Richard, 291–332. Asunción, Paris: Museo del Barro, ServiLibro, CoLibris.

Santos-Granero, Fernando. 2004. "Escribiendo la historia en el paisaje: espacio, mitología y ritual entre la gente yanesha." In *Tierra adentro. Territorio indígena y percepción del entorno*, edited by Alexandra Surralles and Pedro García Hierro. IWGIA, Documento no. 39. Copenhagen.

Schartner, Sieghard, and Wilmar Stahl. 1986. *Wer ist mein Naechster? Indianermission im zentralen Chaco von Paraguay, 1936–1986*. Filadelfia: Luz a los Indígenas, ASCIM.

Schvartzman, Lea. 2015. "'Nuevo' rumbo para los pueblos indígenas. Al borde del abismo." In *Des-cartes: estampas de las derechas en Paraguay*, edited by Lorena Soler and Rocco Carbone, 199–214. Buenos Aires: Punto de Encuentro.

Schvartzman, Mauricio. 1983. "El 'indio' y la sociedad: los prejuicios étnicos en el Paraguay." *Suplemento Antropológico* 18, no. 1: 179–243.

Seepe-Pyoy'. 2021. *Nanaava'a*. Apkelenyemay'aklha' enlhet, no. 2 (Biblioteca de la memoria hablada, no. 2). Produced by Hannes Kalisch and Lanto'oy' Unruh. Account recorded in Paz del Chaco, January 2019, 7:49 mins., Enlhet. Ya'alve-Saanga: Nengvaanemkeskama Nempayvaam Enlhet. https://enlhet.org/memoria_hablada.html.

Siemens, Nikolai. 1943. "Zur Indianermission." *Mennoblatt* 14, no. 6: 5–6.

– 1948. "Im Chamacocogebiet." *Mennoblatt* 19, no. 1: 3–4.

– n.d. "Indianermission im Chaco von Paraguay, 1930–1947." Filadelfia: Manuscript in the archive of Colonia Fernheim.

Sooso'. 2021. *Moktay' pook valay*. Apkelenyemay'aklha' enlhet, no. 20 (Biblioteca de la memoria hablada, no. 20). Produced by Hannes Kalisch and Lanto'oy' Unruh. Account recorded in Paz del Chaco, December 2015, 7:19 mins., Enlhet. Ya'alve-Saanga: Nengvaanemkeskama Nempayvaam Enlhet. https://enlhet.org/memoria_hablada.html.

Sousa Santos, Boaventura de. 2010. *Descolonizar el saber, reinventar el poder*. Montevideo: Trilce.

– 2011. "Epistemologías del Sur." *Utopía y Praxis Latinoamericana* 16, no. 54: 17–39.

– 2014. *Epistemologies of the South: Justice Against Epistemicide*. Abingdon: Routledge.

Spivak, Gayatri. 1994. "Can the Subaltern Speak?" In *Colonial Discourse and Post-Colonial Theory. A Reader*, edited by Patrick Williams and Laura Chrisman, 66–111. New York: Columbia University Press.

Stahl, Wilmar. 1980. "Mission und Indianersiedlung." In *50 Jahre Kolonie Fernheim. Ein Beitrag in der Entwicklung Paraguays*, 131–69. Filadelfia: Kolonie Fernheim.

– 1982. *Escenario indígena chaqueño. Pasado y presente*. Filadelfia: ASCIM.

– 1993. "Antropología de acción entre indígenas chaqueños. Una evaluación." *Suplemento Antropológico* 28, no. 1/2: 25–42.

– 2007. *Culturas en Interacción: Una Antropología Vivida en el Chaco Paraguayo*. Asunción: El Lector.

Sterpin, Adriana. 1993. "La chasse aux scalps chez les Nivacle du Gran Chaco." *Journal de la Société des Américanistes* 79: 33–66.

Stoesz, Edgar. 2008. *Like a Mustard Seed: Mennonites in Paraguay*. Scottdale: Herald Press.

Stoesz, Edgar, and Muriel T. Stackley. 1999. *Garden in the Wilderness: Mennonite Communities in the Paraguayan Chaco, 1927–1997*. Winnipeg: Canadian Mennonite Bible College.

Supreme Court of Justice of Paraguay. 2003. *Digesto Normativo sobre Pueblos Indígenas en el Paraguay, 1811–2003*. Asunción: Corte Suprema de Justicia – División de Investigación, Legislación y Publicaciones.

Susnik, Branislava. 1972. "Dimensiones migratorias y pautas culturales de los pueblos del Gran Chaco y de su periferia (enfoque etnológico)." *Suplemento Antropológico* 7: 85–105.

Todorov, Tzvetan. 2000. *Los abusos de la memoria*. Barcelona: Paidós.

– 2002. "Los dilemas de la memoria." Conference paper 25 March 2002, Cátedra Latinoamericana Julio Cortázar, Universidad de Guadalajara. Trans. Dulce Ma. Zúñiga. https://www.academia.edu/5290525/Dilemas_de_la_memoria_Todorov.

– 2010. *La conquista de América: el problema del otro*. 2nd Spanish edition. Mexico: Siglo XXI.

Tola, Florencia C. 2016. "El 'giro ontológico' y la relación naturaleza/cultura. Reflexiones desde el Gran Chaco." *Apuntes de Investigación del* CECYP 27: 128–39.

Ulmke, Cristine, and Lily August. 2004. *Kleiner Pflanzenführer für den paraguay- ischen Chaco*. Herborn: Uniglobia.

UltimaHora Opinión. 2011. "La guerra del chaco dejó un legado que no está siendo honrado." *UltimaHora*, 12 June. https://www.ultimahora.com/la-guerra-del-chaco-dejo-un-legado-que-no-esta-siendo-honrado-n436735.html.

UNESCO Universal Declaration on Cultural Diversity. 2001. https://www.ohchr.org/EN/ProfessionalInterest/Pages/CulturalDiversity.aspx.

United Nations Declaration on the Rights of Indigenous Peoples. 2006. https://www.un.org/esa/socdev/unpfii/documents/DRIPS_en.pdf.

Universal Declaration of Human Rights. 1948. https://www.un.org/en/universal-declaration-human-rights/.

Unruh, Ernesto, and Hannes Kalisch. 2000. "Ya'alva Pangcalhva. Apqueleltem-naycam' apquelvaanyam' enlhet acteemaclha' apquelvetangvaecloo apque-leyvaam nanoo' nahan seclhooc apquelnay'a Ya'alve-Saanga." *Biblioteca para-guaya de antropología*, vol. 33. Ya'alve-Saanga: Nengvaanemquescama Nem-payvaam Enlhet.

– 2001. "Ya'alva Pangcalhva II. Mook mokham apqueleltemnaycam' apquelvaan-yam' enlhet acteemaclha' apquelvetangvaecloo apqueleyvaam nanoo' nahan seclhooc apquelnay'a Ya'alve-Saanga." *Biblioteca paraguaya de antropología*, vol. 38. Ya'alve-Saanga: Nengvaanemquescama Nempayvaam Enlhet.

– 2002. "Lauft weg, der Kinderzähler kommt!" *Mennoblatt* 73, no. 15: 4–5.

– 2003. "Enlhet-Enenlhet. Una familia lingüística chaqueña." *Thule, Rivista ital-iana di studi americanistici* 14–15: 207–31.

– 2008. "*Salvación – ¿rendición ? Los enlhet y la Guerra del Chaco.*" In *Mala guerra: los indígenas en la Guerra del Chaco (1932–35)*, edited by Nicolás Ri-chard, 99–123. Asunción, Paris: Museo del Barro, ServiLibro, CoLibris.

Villagra, Rodrigo. 2014. "Nanek añy'a kempokhakme o 'en aquel tiempo de los enojados'. Testimonios de los angaité sobre la Guerra del Chaco." In Rodrigo Villagra, *Meike makha valayo, no habían paraguayos: Reflexiones etnográficas en torno a los angaité del Chaco*, 91–119. Biblioteca paraguaya de antropología, vol. 98. Asunción: CEADUC. Originally published in *Mala guerra: los indí-genas en la Guerra del Chaco (1932–35)*, edited by Nicolás Richard, 67–98. Asunción, Paris: Museo del Barro, ServiLibro, CoLibris.

Viveiros de Castro, Eduardo. 1998. "Cosmological Deixis and Amerindian Per-spectivism." *The Journal of the Royal Anthropological Institute* 4, no. 3: 469–88.

Von Bremen, Volker. 1991. "Zwischen Anpassung und Aneignung: Zur Problem-atik von Wildbeuter-Gesellschaften im modernen Weltsystem am Beispiel der Ayoréode." *Münchner Amerikanistik Beiträge* 26. Munich: Anacon.

Wiens, Hans J. 1989. *Daß die Heiden Miterben seien: Die Geschichte der Indianermission im paraguayischen Chaco*. Filadelfia: Konferenz der Mennoniten Brüdergemeinden in Paraguay.

Wiens, Robert. 2015. "Friedenszeugnis der Mennoniten im Chacokrieg: Ein Vergleich zwischen Menno und Fernheim." *Jahrbuch für Geschichte und Kultur der Mennoniten in Paraguay*, 16: 153–63.

Zook, David H., Jr. 1997. *La conducción de la Guerra del Chaco*. Asunción: El Lector.

INDEX

dispossession, 4–6, 10, 140–1, 155,
226; historical process of, 126–7,
149; and reduction, 122–3
dispossessor, 141, 143, 169–70, 225–6
diversity, 163, 165, 210, 218; elimination of, 4, 213; of responses, 157
domination, 202–3, 223; of fear, 125

education, 155, 160, 187, 197, 212;
intercultural, 225
Énxet, 3–4, 13, 17, 133–4
epistemology, 207–11, 215–16
essential, 10, 162, 216, 218, 222
event: perception of, 161–6, 172, 174,
216–20; sense of, 172; unique, 169.
See also fact; reality
exclusion: attitude of, 122, 215; and
inclusion, 209, 215; of the Indigenous, 8, 127, 151, 155, 208; logic of,
200, 211; structures of, 8, 200
experience, 120, 168–9; concrete, 11,
191, 219; experienced world, 166,
169; and expression, 175–7, 179,
185, 189–90, 219, 221; and facts,
158–63, 189; historical, 125, 180,
190, 201, 206; images of, 192; signifying of, 171–2, 175

fact, 150, 158–63, 220, 224; historical,
123–4, 161; meaning of, 217; record
of, 124, 172, 216; single fact, 163,
217. *See also* event; reality
false, 166, 174, 176, 215–16. *See also*
true
forgetting, 182, 188, 192–3, 198. *See
also* amnesia
friction, 172, 188, 204
fundamentalism, 194

gift, 114–15, 119. *See also* sharing

historiography, 174, 215–21; Paraguayan, 214
history: absence of, 177, 193–4;
colonial, 10; colonization of, 179;
Enlhet, 5, 7, 11, 141, 152, 177, 194–5,
218; Indigenous, 126; multiple,
222; of Paraguay, 9, 148, 214–15;
settlers', 152. *See also* decolonization; narrative
hypothesis, 179, 218; colonizer's, 10,
140, 152, 177, 189; Enlhet, 126–7,
141–2

identification, 188, 194
identity, 151, 187–8, 192
ideologization, 175, 179, 182, 193
ideology, 194. *See also* colonial:
ideology
imbalance, 115–17, 158, 199
imitation, 180–2. *See also*
promiscuity
inclusion, 6, 14, 208–9, 221, 225; and
exclusion, 109, 215
independence, 213; Enlhet, 138, 141,
157; from colonial logic, 157, 183;
Paraguayan 156–7, 199
inequality, 8, 114, 204
initiative, 6, 185, 204; external, 10,
177–9, 183; one's own, 183, 193
integration, 155; of accounts, 194; of
diversity, 163
interaction, 170, 194, 207; in equilibrium, 200, 203; possibilities for,
126, 165–6; with the world, 209
interculturality, 200, 225, 269n47
interpretation: academic, 213, 216;
of the accounts, 185; Enlhet, 114,
123–4, 164, 171

Lengua, 3

universal: meanings, 217; order, 160; theories, 213; universality and truth, 213, 217, 218
universe, symbolic, 10, 210

vanquished. *See* victor
victim, 122–3, 147, 152, 189, 193; of smallpox, 134–7; versus aggressor, 141

victor, 122, 164, 191; imitation of the, 180–2, 194; initiative of the, 178–9; narrative of the, 177, 182, 187, 221

worlds, different, 165–9, 194, 197, 217, 222